THE MARKETS
AND THE MEDIA

THE MARKETS AND THE MEDIA

Business News and Stock Market Movements

Thomas Schuster

LEXINGTON BOOKS

A Division of
ROWMAN & LITTLEFIELD PUBLISHERS, INC.
Lanham • Boulder • New York • Toronto • Oxford

LEXINGTON BOOKS

A division of Rowman & Littlefield Publishers, Inc.
A wholly owned subsidiary of The Rowman & Littlefield Publishing Group, Inc.
4501 Forbes Boulevard, Suite 200
Lanham, MD 20706

PO Box 317
Oxford
OX2 9RU, UK

Copyright © 2006 by Lexington Books

All rights reserved. No part of this publication may be reproduced, stored in a retrieval system, or transmitted in any form or by any means, electronic, mechanical, photocopying, recording, or otherwise, without the prior permission of the publisher.

British Library Cataloguing in Publication Information Available

Library of Congress Cataloging-in-Publication Data

Schuster, Thomas, 1965–
  The markets and the media : business news and stock market movements / Thomas Schuster.
    p. cm.
  Includes bibliographical references and index.
  ISBN-13: 978-0-7391-1254-0 (hardcover : alk. paper)
  ISBN-10: 0-7391-1254-6 (hardcover : alk. paper)
  ISBN-13: 978-0-7391-1331-8 (pbk. : alk. paper)
  ISBN-10: 0-7391-1331-3 (pbk. : alk. paper)
  1. Stocks—Prices. 2. Journalism, Commercial. I. Title.
HG4636.S354 2005
332.63'222—dc22   2005023010

Printed in the United States of America

∞™ The paper used in this publication meets the minimum requirements of American National Standard for Information Sciences—Permanence of Paper for Printed Library Materials, ANSI/NISO Z39.48-1992.

CONTENTS

Acknowledgments — vii
Preface — ix

MICRO — 1

1 Stock Recommendations and Stock Prices — 3
   1. Introduction — 4
   2. The Publicity Effect: The Big Moment of the Gurus — 5
   3. No News: Stock Recommendations — 11
   4. Performance Disturbances: Reflexive Return Reduction — 16
   5. Summary — 21
   6. Coda — 22

MESO — 33

2 News Events and Price Movements — 35
   1. Introduction — 36
   2. State of the Art: "Random Walks" and "Irrational Exuberance" — 38
   3. News Effects: Rapid Return Reactions — 40
   4. Irregular Price Regularities — 44
   5. World Events: The Effects of "Big News" — 47
   6. Summary — 51

MACRO   65

3   Meta-Communication and Market Dynamics   67
      1. Introduction   68
      2. Feedback: The Media as "Learning Lab"   70
      3. News Structures: "Use Value" and "Narrative Imperative"   73
      4. Media Manias: The "CNBC Effect"   76
      5. Meta-Communication: Dynamic Interactions   79
      6. Crash: Media and Market Panics   82
      7. Summary and Conclusions   85

Afterword: Critique of the Noise System   97

Appendix: Bibliography of Business and Financial Communication   101

Index   151

ACKNOWLEDGMENTS

I have profited from the support, the comments, and the advice of numerous people: Günter Bamberg, Brad M. Barber, Hans-Bernd Brosius, Andrew Chen, Wolfgang Donsbach, Christian Fenner, Eurico Ferreira, Werner Früh, Wolfgang Gerke, Jürgen Heinrich, Jan Pieter Krahnen, Walter Krämer, Paul Krugman, Burton Malkiel, Ike Mathur, Brigitte Nacos, Christoph Neuberger, Victor Niederhoffer, Klaus Röder, Reinhart Schmidt and Volker Wolff. My thanks go to all of them.

PREFACE

Business news that incorporates a use value was once considered an important prerequisite for the democratization of the financial markets. The media, it seems, has met this demand: Investor magazines, the business press, financial television, even general news media—the sources of business and financial news are plentiful. This has led not only to important changes in the markets, but also in the relationship between the economy and society.

Academic research does not say much about this, yet: Communication research, as far as it deals with economic communication at all, focuses on the benefits of conventional consumer reporting. The effects of business news on voter behavior have also been studied. So-called "Public Relations Research" deals primarily with investor relations. However, it seems to be leaning toward the position of potential consulting clients. In short: The new economic communication that is produced by financial and investor media and that has led to increasing amounts of coverage of the capital markets is not represented in the analyses of this discipline.

Interesting approaches can be found in interdisciplinary studies that combine insights from business and journalism research. They have found that the new business reporting tends to have a positive bias, which has led to a critique of the cooperation between analysts and journalists. In cases of the media being used by economic actors for their own particular interests, a "failure of journalism" has been diagnosed. However, the possibilities for redistribution of wealth that have resulted from the institutionalization of the new economic communication are not considered by such research. Potential changes in the dynamics of the financial markets following the spread of economic communication in the public sphere are also neglected.

Recent approaches of finance research have dealt with these questions: "Behavioral Finance" has come to the conclusion that the financial markets can only be understood by considering their communication environment. During times of an expanding economic communication the medias gain importance because it can generate an increased activity of a growing number of market participants. The practice of the new business journalism to focus on investment possibilities amplifies this trend. This view is different from the position of classical financial economics, which assumes stable structures and processes in the stock market and claims that the markets were independent from factors outside the financial system.

Since the systemic environment has moved into the focus of finance research, the conditions of the intentional manipulation of market participants via mass media have received increased attention. Such studies conclude that stock market manipulations are part of the normal state of affairs, since they are rewarded with a high probability. The few existing empirical studies on this issue have shown that the mass media, indeed, plays a role in this. However, even in this more recent research, the systemic interactions between the markets and the media are not sufficiently considered since the focus is on the processes of price formation.

The mass media directs public attention towards the economy. But the consequences of the growing public attention to the financial markets have been ambivalent. The following studies will show: For the individual market participant as well as the markets as a whole, the expansion of economic communication is of only limited benefit. The relation between the news and prices is much less direct than is frequently assumed. A direct use value of business news to generate an economic profit therefore does not exist. The mediatization of the markets has, on the other hand, had negative consequences resulting in substantial costs on the individual as well as the systemic level. The critique to be deduced from this is not of a sporadic, but of a systematic kind.

MICRO

The business media plays an active role in influencing stock prices. Statistically significant excess returns at the time of the publication of stock recommendations have been documented many times. Frequently these abnormal gains begin to accumulate long *before* the publication date. In most cases they reach their highs on the day the recommendations are disseminated to the public. With few exceptions, a price reversal sets in shortly thereafter: Excess returns in recommended stocks are, at least partially, given up. Many stocks now enter a period of underperformance, earning significant negative returns. The return reversions indicate that such stock price reactions are due to price pressure from "naive" investors hoping to profit from the experts. However, most of the media lacks any real information that is not yet reflected in stock prices. In short: There is no evidence that stock recommendations published in the media offer any systematic opportunity to outperform the market. The evidence leads to the opposite conclusion: That investors who follow such advice will lose in the long run.

STOCK RECOMMENDATIONS AND STOCK PRICES

Two hundred fifty-five columns in 26 years. This is the result of William Peter Hamilton's work for the *Wall Street Journal* from 1904 until his death in December 1929, when he died of pneumonia in his house in Brooklyn. Hamilton, successor of the founding publisher Charles Henry Dow, is considered one of the fathers of modern financial journalism. Famous then for his instinct for detecting profitable investment opportunities, Hamilton is still regarded as having been an outstanding stock market forecaster and a master of pattern recognition, even long after his death. He is even said to have predicted the great crash of 1929 three days in advance.

In December 1932, three years after Hamilton's death, Alfred Cowles, a businessman from Colorado, gave a lecture in Cincinnati, Ohio. The title of his talk was "Can Stock Market Forecasters Forecast?" Cowles, who was very interested in quantitative economics, wanted to find out if it is possible to predict trends in the development of stock prices and stock indexes. The stock market crash had cast doubt on the applicability of existing forecasting models. The text of his Ohio lecture, published in 1933 in the newly-established journal *Econometrica*, became one of the classics of modern financial literature.

In his study, Cowles examined the accuracy of prognoses of different investment experts. Among his samples are market forecasts of sixteen specialized stock market services, the investment decisions of twenty fire insurance companies, and the predictions of twenty-four financial publications, as well as William Peter Hamilton's columns in the *Wall Street Journal* (WSJ). Cowles was not really impressed with the results of the stock market specialists: Correct forecasts were accidental at best. Often, the performance of the forecasts is several percent worse than the benchmark indexes.

Even Hamilton, who had built up such an excellent reputation as an expert in stock market trends, was posthumously judged to have been only partly successful: According to Cowles, the recommendations of the financial columnist achieved an annual return of 12 per cent between 1903 and 1929. A portfolio with stocks from the benchmark index would easily have beaten this result with 15.5 per cent per annum.[1] The accuracy of the forecasts of the WSJ columnist was slightly better, but nevertheless did not differ from a random distribution. Forty-five out of ninety forecasts were correct. In brief: His hit rate was exactly fifty-fifty.

1. INTRODUCTION

With the stock market boom in the 1990s, stock market coverage enjoyed a boom as well. The upswing of the financial markets was accompanied by a systematic expansion and a strategic reorientation of the business media: Investment and finance issues received broad attention, not only in special-interest media, such as investment and financial magazines, but also in general business coverage in newspapers and on television. From specialist journals to the yellow press—the stock market became a dominant topic.

But business coverage not only expanded significantly, it also shifted its focus: Stocks, warrants, mutual funds, and how to trade them profitably became a lot more significant in this new kind of business journalism.[2] Finance and investment instruments were the number one topic. News about financial products rather than general business news or developments on the labor market prevailed in business journals at the turn of the millennium. And even years after the beginning of the stock market crash, according to the results of quantitative content analyses, almost half of all articles dealt with capital investment opportunities.[3] Other topics lagged far behind.

The tone of the articles also quickly changed. With the economization of the public sphere as a consequence of the "New Economy" boom, business and stock market coverage became increasingly positive.[4] Systematic capital appreciation by means of stock market gains seemed to be within reach for everybody. At least this was the impression conveyed by the media which, with its tips for stocks and investments, painted scenarios of collective wealth in ever more glowing colors. During the dramatic climax of the stock market boom, the already low percentage of sell recommendations in the commentaries of analysts and journalists dropped to a negligible level.[5] And even during the slump, despite contrary evidence, the view of the reporters, in the long term and in its general trend, was positive.[6]

In view of the importance attached to stock recommendations by the media, the lack of knowledge about this kind of business communication is surprising: Neither its effects nor its benefits have been researched systematically. Studies of price reactions to, and the accuracy of, stock recommendations published in the mass media have gotten avid attention from empirical financial market research for more than two decades. However, the attempt to condense this dispersed knowledge about the price formation of securities into a model of mutual interaction between financial markets and business media has never been undertaken.[7] So far, no media research has been published on this topic.

In the following, the results of thirty-three case studies on the interaction of stock recommendations and stock prices will be extracted. They will then be subject to a qualitative meta-analysis.[8] As this synthesis from existing empirical material will show, a stable pattern occurs in a long-term overview of the different phases of the market cycle. The result is a surprisingly clear picture of the chances and limits of the dissemination of investment information by the mass media. The questions to be answered are: What is the effect of stock recommendations in the business media? And, who profits from them?

2. THE PUBLICITY EFFECT: THE BIG MOMENT OF THE GURUS

Statistical evaluations of the hit rate of stock recommendations give cause to fear the worst. In their study of 1.647 stock recommendations published in leading German business magazines, Kladobra and von der Lippe (2001) come to clear conclusions: Buy recommendations comprise the overwhelming majority of stock recommendations in the business media. Temporary gains occur in barely half of all cases. Recommended stocks that fall—and are thus certain to bring a loss for the investor—outnumber by far the stocks that move up. Upside target prognoses, that is, analysts' forecasts of target prices a stock should reach within a certain period of time, are almost always missed (86.2 % of the recommendations with an "upside target").

Dorfleitner and Klein (2002) examine the quality of predictions made via chart techniques, published in the German investment magazine *Börse Online* between 1995 and 2001. They confirm similarly weak results for these price forecasts via "technical analysis": Firstly, the accuracy of these forecasts is low. Success, if it occurs at all, is only accidental. Secondly, investment strategies on the basis of these forecasts are not systematically better than the market—often, it can even be an advantage to do exactly the opposite of the analysts' projections. In brief: The published forecasts do not tell anything about future price trends.

Thus, these studies provide a clear indication that the business media as a whole have neither extraordinary forecast abilities, nor are they capable of triggering the fulfillment of their own prophesies—otherwise, the hit rate would have to be much higher: A significant proportion, beyond random probabilities, of all tips would have to be fulfilled. However, this does not seem to be the case. Stock recommendations are said to attract wide audiences to the business media. But the empirical findings concerning the success of recommendations in the media lead to the following supposition: Neither journalists nor their informants can systematically and accurately predict stock prices.

This, however, does *not* mean that stock recommendations always remain without any effect. What is decisive is the time frame: In the short term, as a series of case studies which will be examined later shows, tips in the mass media can actually influence stock prices. In the print media, on television or on the internet, recommendations given by stock market commentators seem to be an incentive for investors to buy stocks. Abrupt and significant price and volume increases of the stocks commented on can be the consequence. The experts' tips generate temporary price pressure through investors who buy the advertised stocks.[9]

Tips published on television, especially, according to the results of several studies, can cause considerable stock movements on the markets. Gerke (2000) points out several cases in which stock prices reacted to stock analyses on television. Gerke carried out a study on the German program "3sat Börse," which runs weekly on 3sat, the common channel of ARD, ZDF, ORF and SRG. He found that stock recommendations by investment gurus, in particular tips on second-line securities, can cause "extreme price movements." Cumulated price changes after well-known journalists and analysts drew public attention to certain stocks on television amounted to 24 per cent on average.

Gerke mentions a case in which the television tips of an analyst made an excess return of 9 per cent possible—*before* the program was broadcast.[10]

Such extraordinary price reactions give room to the suspicion that some journalists or analysts might be tempted to manipulate information in order to bring about price changes. The knowledge about future price surges induced by the media provides an excellent opportunity for front running: The insiders buy before the recommendation is published and liquidate their positions while the general public is still in the market. Evidence of this is always visible when the prices of certain stocks increase immediately *before* they are recommended to the broad public.

Comparable occurences were already documented for an insider trading scandal in the United States in the 1980s, which involved a columnist of the *Wall Street Journal*: R. Foster Winans, co-author of the column "Heard on the Street," passed his information on to stock brokers of the investment company Kidder Peabody before they were published and later shared the illegal profits with them. After the scandal was exposed, Winans and his contact persons were sentenced for fraud. In a study of the stocks concerned, Syed, Liu and Smith (1989) later came to the conclusion that, until the publication date, the insider tips facilitated an excess return of 6.25 per cent.

Thus, the phenomenon as such is not new. Price reactions in connection with investment tips were already observed in the United States during the 1970s and 1980s. An example is the program "Wall $treet Week," which has run on the Public Broadcasting System (PBS) since 1970: Recommendations published there repeatedly led to price reactions of the relevant stocks. Pari (1987) documents statistically significant excess returns of 0.7 per cent on the first trading day after each program is aired for the years 1983 and 1984. However, these profits were very short-lived: The overperformance reversed only one day later. In the medium term, the recommended stocks performed well below the market average. After twelve months, the performance of the recommended stocks was 8.95 per cent. The market, on the other hand, had gained 13.05 per cent.[11]

Similar results concerning "Wall $treet Week" are presented in another study: Beltz and Jennings (1997) document a "not very impressive" excess return of 0.52 per cent on the day after each program was shown for the years 1990 to 1992. They demonstrate that the "publicity effect," the statistically significant price increase of the recommended stocks, has the strongest effect on the first day after the television show—and vanishes afterward. The initially positive price movement is reversed: The stocks enter a phase of underperformance. Six months after the show, the supposed glamor stocks lag far behind the market.

Such price reactions following recommendations can be statistically significant. For the private investor who relies on this public information, however, it is impossible to benefit from the small and short-term price movements. In practical investment business, excess returns of 0.5 to 1.1 per cent are easily exhausted by transactions costs, such as order and holding charges, and the bid-ask spread (the difference between the buying and the selling price). Already the attempt to benefit from these price surges will lead to a balanced result at best. But the stocks commented on often begin to develop worse than the comparative index from the second day after the recommendation was published onward. Thus, a loss is incurred.

This is an unmistakable sign of the publicity effect: If the excess returns disappear quickly, there is reason to suspect that price reactions are not due to the inherent substance of the recommendations, but to overreactions of uninformed investors provoked by media coverage. The investor who follows such advice falls behind the market: The initial price advance is of no use to him because he does not participate in it. However, he does participate in the decline in prices. Instead of the profit he hoped for, he experiences losses relative to the market, sometimes even considerable ones.

Investment tips published on the internet can also have a strong publicity effect. An example is publications of the website *Motley Fool*, a leading finance website: In a study of the behavior of internet investors, Hirschey, Richardson and Scholz (2000) found statistically significant price surges in the stocks discussed on the website. The excess return on the day after the recommendation was 3.36 to 3.72 per cent. In combination with the price movements the day *before* and the day *after* the recommendation, the result was an average abnormal gain of 6.08 to 6.87 per cent.

Temporarily, the trading volume of the stocks discussed sharply increased as well. In the period around the publication, the average was 568.12 per cent above the normal volume—a serious indication that publications of gurus can have a strong impact on private investors. The result of the study: "Stock recommendations published on the internet move prices and trading volumes."[12] The effects were probably intensified by the fact that the majority of *Motley Fool*'s tips during the study period related to internet companies—a business, as the collapse of the "New Economy" showed, which was, indeed, mainly based on "stock price fantasies."

Similar empirical evidence has been presented for business publications in the print media. Benesh and Clark (1994) find statistically significant market reactions to recommendations of the finance magazine *Barron's*. Excess returns amount to an average of 1.8 per cent on the event day; afterwards, no unusual price movements can be found. Han and Suk (1996) document price effects after the publication of analysts' recommendations in the *Barron's* column "Research Reports". The price movement is 0.54

TABLE 1. Survey: Literature on the Effects of Stock Recommendations in the Business Media

	— Buy Recommendations —			
Researcher	Publication	Period	Sample	Excess Return[a]
Yazici and Muradoglu (2002)	Moneymatik "Investor Ali"	1993–98	199	2.49
Desai, Liang and Singh (2000)	Wall Street Journal All-Star Analysts	1993–96	1,157	0.42
Ferreira and Brooks (2000)	Wall Street Journal "Insider Trading Spotlight"	1994–95	268	0.63
Hirschey, Richardson and Scholz (2000)	The Motley Fool "Rule Breaker"	1994–98	21	1.60
Ferreira and Smith (1999)	Wall Street Journal "Small Stock Focus"	1993	398	-0.36
Greene and Smart (1999)	Wall Street Journal "Dartboard"	1988–92	199[b]	3.00
Liang (1999)	Wall Street Journal "Dartboard"	1990–94	208	2.84
Allen and Awang-Damit (1998)	Wall Street Journal "Dartboard"	1990–91	90	2.60–3.28
Beltz and Jennings (1997)	PBS "Wall $treet Week"	1990–92	734	0.52
Ghani and Thomas (1997)	Wall Street Journal "Dartboard"	1990–92	66	2.99
Albert and Smaby (1996)	Wall Street Journal "Dartboard"	1988–91	140	3.2
Han and Suk (1996)	Barron's "Research Reports"	1991	521	0.54
Sant and Zaman (1996)	Business Week "Inside Wall Street"	1976–88	328	1.16
Desai and Jain (1995)	Barron's Annual Roundtable	1968–91	1,599	1.04
Mathur and Waheed (1995)	Business Week "Inside Wall Street"	1981–89	233	1.71
Trahan and Bolster (1995)	Barron's	1988	144	2.1
Benesh and Clark (1994)	Barron's	1987–88	258	1.80
Metcalf and Malkiel (1994)	Wall Street Journal "Dartboard"	1990–92	120	n.a.
Palmon, Sun and Tang (1994)	Business Week "Inside Wall Street"	1983–89	280	1.91

(continued)

TABLE I. *(continued)*

	– Buy Recommendations –			
Researcher	Publication	Period	Sample	Excess Return[a]
Röckemann (1994)	Actien-Börse Börse Online CC-Brief Effecten-Spiegel Swingtrend	1989–91	276	0.15
Wright (1994)	Wall Street Journal "Dartboard"	1988–90	76	3.73
Barber and Loeffler (1993)	Wall Street Journal "Dartboard"	1988–90	95	3.53
Huth and Maris (1992)	Wall Street Journal "Heard on the Street"	1986	111	0.62
Liu, Smith and Syed (1992)	Wall Street Journal "Heard on the Street"	1982–85	566	1.87 1.09
Beneish (1991)	Wall Street Journal "Heard on the Street"	1978–79	286	0.90
Liu, Smith and Syed (1990)	Wall Street Journal "Heard on the Street"	1982–85	566	1.54
Pound and Zeckhauser (1990)	Wall Street Journal "Heard on the Street"	1983–85	42	0.07
Wijmenga (1990)	Elseviers Magazine Beleggers Belangen de Financiele Koerier	1978–83	160 42 127	n.a.
Syed, Liu and Smith (1989)	Wall Street Journal "Heard on the Street"	1983–84	16[c]	2.97 0.97
Pari (1987)	PBS "Wall $treet Week"	1983–84	349	0.66
Dimson and Marsh (1986)	British Finance Press	1975–82	792	n.a.
Lee (1986)	Forbes Heinz Biel Column	1962–79	374	0.87[d]
Davies and Canes (1978)	Wall Street Journal "Heard on the Street"	1970–71	597	0.92

[a] abnormal gain at the publication date in per cent
[b] including nine sell recommendations
[c] including seven sell recommendations
[d] cumulative excess return from day –3 to +5

The table comprises event studies concerning the publication of stock recommendations in the business media. Articles on the tips of stock market services were not taken into consideration. In the majority of cases, the common event study method is used. Its goal is to establish abnormal returns around an event: For this purpose, deviations of the realized returns from the expected returns are measured. The excess returns are calculated by substracting the market returns. The reference model which is used to generate the expected returns plays a decisive role. Partly, there are considerable differences in the works cited concerning the reference model and the estimate period which is used.

per cent on the day of the publication; as in other cases, it disappears one day later. The unusual price increase is reversed within five trading days by a significant negative performance.[13]

Such reactions can sometimes be especially conspicuous for smaller stocks which are not so much in the spotlight.[14] In these cases, the media can contribute to short-term overreactions among investors. Trahan and Bolster (1995) show that short-term price surges can be particularly strong for smaller companies: For one hundred forty-four stocks recommended, the researchers find abnormal returns of 2.1 per cent on average. These gains are not distributed equally over the sample: The subgroup formed by the smallest companies shows the strongest reactions to recommendations. The size of a company and the publicity effect are in inverse relation. But such gains are reversed as well: Price adjustments only take a few minutes.[15] Then profits quickly erode.

Trend stocks, which have shown a good performance in the past, can also provoke a marked response—this is one reason why numerous event studies demonstrate abnormal price increases that set in as early as several days before the publication: Many recommendations relate to "hot" stocks which are already on the move and which, according to the supposed hopes of the experts who publish the tips, can be pushed a little further with a carefully devised publication. But most of these stocks usually "cool down" quickly.[16] A more detailed analysis will show: Opinions follow the market, not the other way round.

3. NO NEWS: STOCK RECOMMENDATIONS

What are the chances of drawing profitable information from published opinions? Tumarkin and Whitelaw (2001) dealt with this question for internet message boards. They analyzed 181.633 contributions to the finance website RagingBull.com. In order to test them for their impact on prices, a relationship was established between the numbers and kinds of contributions and the price movements of the stocks mentioned. The result: A high discussion intensity and generally positive opinion coincide with abnormal gains. The more positive the comments on the stocks, the better their development—*in the days before the excited chatter on the internet.*

Positive comments, according to Tumarkin and Whitelaw, are followed by more positive comments. Positive comments are followed by a sharp increase in trading volumes. Positive comments, however, are *not* followed by significant price gains. All things considered, the returns after the event day equal zero.[17] This means that no reliable price predictions can be derived from the public response in these finance forums; the opinions expressed there do not provide forecasts that could be systematically used. Opinions do not make the market, but the market determines opinions. Or to put it differently: For the market, information published on the message boards is not news.[18]

In one of the most interesting studies of the information content of finance websites, Das and Chen (2001) come to similar insights. On the basis of a statistical evaluation of 85,000 messages on the message boards of *Yahoo!*, they find that the news volume on the internet and the trading volume on the financial markets strongly correlate. They also find a relationship between mood shifts and price fluctuations, as well as a volume of news that increases with the degree of price fluctuation. However, according to Das and Chen, market participants behave reactively. The markets are ahead of the opinions. Surprising price changes in particular are hardly ever anticipated. In brief: Information published on internet forums has no predictive value.

Die Telebörse, a German financial magazine that catered to private investors, reported similar findings. Only months before its own very premature exit from the market after only two years of existence, the magazine carried a story about the limited use of analysts' recommendations published on finance portals on the internet. The majority of the predictions are wide off the mark and of no use to the investor.[19] Thus, neither opinions of private individuals nor recommendations of investment experts seem to provide the "information lead" for the private investor, for which the internet once was enthusiastically welcomed.

Usually, tips in the print media are a bad deal for their readers as well. This is demonstrated by the stocks which are discussed in the column "Inside Wall Street" in the magazine *Business Week*: Stocks that are commented on positively, according to a study by Mathur and Waheed (1995), show a significant positive price development—*in the days and weeks before such publications*. The abnormal gain begins to accumulate about two months before the publication date. It reaches its high on the day of the publication of the column with an excess return of 1.71 per cent, with sharply increased trading volumes. From the day before to the day after, the average excess return is 2.63 per cent.[20]

But the price effect after the press coverage is only short-lived, one to two days on average. Only large investors and insiders who pay low transaction costs can benefit from these price movements. In the medium term,

Mathur and Waheed say, the stocks discussed show a *negative* performance relative to their benchmark indexes. The recommendations are of use only to those, if to anyone at all, who already own the stocks before the publication. Those who buy after the publication do not have any benefit—they have acquired an underperformer. The negative return of the recommended stocks, relative to the benchmark index, amounts to an average of 5.33 per cent after six months.[21]

In a study comprising the largest sample of "Inside Wall Street" articles so far, Sant and Zaman (1996) virtually come to the same conclusion: The majority of the commentaries in this business magazine are positive (eight-to-one). Stocks thus commented on tend to get positive excess returns around the publication date. These excess returns begin to accumulate weeks in advance. On the day the column is published, they reach their high with an excess return of 1.16 per cent. The trading volumes of the stocks concerned are far above average. From the day before to the day after, the average positive excess return is 2.44 per cent. Afterwards, a trend reversal sets in.

The negative return of the recommended stocks adds up to an average of 6.80 per cent after six months.[22] All this indicates that opinions follow the market, not the other way round. The reason is that the relevant information content is exhausted before the articles are published. Analysts would hardly be interested in disseminating insider information without having benefited from it. Price movements in connection with publications are due to the publicity effect. Thus, what happens is nothing but a self-fulfilling prophecy. Sant and Zaman state: "We conclude that *Business Week* stories are of only limited use to their readers."[23]

The same applies to the *Wall Street Journal*. The leading business newspaper in the United States has received a particularly high degree of scientific attention. There is hardly any department of the newspaper that has not been evaluated for its impact on prices. Such as the column "Investment Dartboard," which is published monthly: It is a stock market game in which four financial managers compete against each other with their tips—and against a random sample of stocks that is selected by throwing darts at the stock market pages of the *WSJ*. After six months, the return of the experts' selection is compared with the return of the random sample. A whole range of studies has dealt with "Dartboard." They all yielded similar results.

Barber and Loeffler (1993) find an abnormal return of 3.53 per cent at the publication date of the recommendations of the investment experts. In particular, companies with a small number of stocks circulating on the market are pushed by strongly increased turnovers in connection with the tips.[24] However, a price reversal sets in within a few days. During this phase, the selected stocks accumulate a negative return of 2.08 per cent. Wright (1994) also finds a positive excess return, 3.73 per cent on the publication day, which is almost completely reversed by a negative return during the following trading days: The price advance is followed by a price decline.

Greene and Smart (1999) also observe extraordinary returns accompanied by extraordinary turnovers: Gains of 3.0 per cent on day zero with turnovers of 140 per cent above average. These gains are realized almost completely in the first minutes of trading, until about one hour after the dissemination of the publication.[25] Those who join in the game afterward will be among the losers: The price advance is followed by a price decline. The biggest winners among the recommended stocks now turn into the biggest losers. According to Greene and Smart, the excess returns completely disappear within one month. It is obvious that this is another case in which private investors do not have a chance to benefit from the temporary overperformance.

Similar results can be found in a study of "Dartboard" by Allen and Awang-Damit (1998): They find an excess return of about 3.0 per cent on the publication date and show that the positive trend already sets in before the publication of the tips.[26] However, the gains disappear within a few days. The authors suppose that analysts pass the tips on to their clients before they publish them. Metcalf and Malkiel (1994) as well as Ghani and Thomas (1997) draw similar conclusions. Liang (1999), who studied almost five years of the stock market game, confirms these results: The experts' selection, according to Liang, generates a remarkable price pressure, which causes a gain of 2.84 per cent on the publication date. The trading volume is 144 per cent above average.[27] Both the excess returns and the high trading volumes set in several days before the publication.

However, the price advance is not a permanent one. The short-term excess return is followed by a price reversal within a few days. If the tips had an information content, the price increase would be more permanent. But precisely this is not the case: The quick increase in returns is followed by an immediate price decline—and a continuous deterioration of prices afterwards. For the public, this return carousel is not neutral at all: Investors who follow the recommendations lose 3.8 per cent in six months on average.[28] The conclusion of all seven studies is the same: Price pressure is generated by reactions of "naive" investors. The information content of the recommendations only plays a marginal role—if any role at all. Albert and Smaby (1996) are the only ones to find no indications of a return reversal. However, they do not find any sign of significant returns either.

Not only "Dartboard," but also the column "Heard on the Street," which has been published in the *Wall Street Journal* since 1969, have been subject to various effects studies. In their pioneering study in the 1970s, Davies and Canes (1978) obtained results which were replicated several times in later research: The publication of analysts' opinions, according to the authors, measurably interacts with stock prices. The overwhelming majority of price movements are anticipated during the days *before* the publication of the information. In comparison, the price movement on the event day is relatively low. This case is not an opportunity to outperform the market either.

These findings are generally confirmed by Syed, Liu and Smith in follow-up studies of "Heard on the Street." They observe excess returns on the day of the publication and earlier, a price reversal afterwards.[29] Davies and Canes had found only weak indications of a price reversal after the price advance. They concluded that reactions to the column were not mere self-fulfilling prophecies. However, this early study already shows that information published in the column is very quickly reflected in stock prices. Despite a supposed information content, there is therefore no chance of making an excess return after transaction costs. Even the vigilant investor will not manage to transform the theoretical gains into a real appreciation in value of his deposit. In brief: De facto, the market is efficient.

Beneish (1991) replicates important aspects of Davies and Canes' study: He shows that price gains occur in the two days before the publication of the column. He finds hints that insiders, the authors of "Heard on the Street" or their contact persons in the finance industry, become active before the publication date of the recommended stocks and trigger early price reactions. After the publication, only slight price increases are observed, which means at best small theoretical excess returns for the outsiders.[30] It is the same old story: After transaction costs, nothing is left of these purely arithmetical gains.[31]

In many cases, statistical post hoc analyses do not even indicate theoretical gains: Pound and Zeckhauser (1990) demonstrate that it is impossible to obtain excess returns with the help of takeover rumors published in "Heard on the Street." The market reacts efficiently to the rumors spread in the business paper: They are correct in less than 50 per cent of all cases and thus do not have any predictive value. They are not systematically reflected in stock prices. In fact, they usually do not have any effect on the stock market at all.[32] In other words: This information is no news for the market.

Other parts of the *Wall Street Journal* do not have a relevant impact on stock prices either—at least not a positive one. Ferreira and Smith (1999), for instance, do not find any significant excess returns for the stocks discussed in the column "Small Stock Focus." This column focuses on news about smaller companies whose stocks stood out for considerable price surges on the previous day. On the day the column is published, there are no unusual positive price movements. On the following day, however, a price reversal sets in: Return rates go down. Thus, readers who react to the reports do not make any abnormal profit—since the profit occured on the day before the publication. However, they run the risk of incurring abnormal losses—since these occur from the day after the publication onwards.

Even the leading minds in the world of finance do not shine with superior performance. This is the result of Desai and Jain's (1995) study of 1.599 stock recommendations mentioned in the annual "Roundtable" by *Barron's* between 1968 and 1991: "Roundtable" is a meeting of eight to twelve "Wall Street Superstars" (according to *Barron's*) that the magazine invites on an annual basis. But the history of the recommendations of the money managers is hardly impressive. The study, which has analyzed the most comprehensive sample with reports spanning a quarter of a century, demonstrates: The annual selection of stocks obtains an excess return of 1.04 per cent on the publication day.[33] Afterwards, very little happens.

Desai and Jain find: "For the most part, excess returns equal zero for holding periods of one to three years after the publication." From this, they conclude: "An investor who reads the recommendations in Barron's and invests accordingly would not benefit from them if he follows the buy recommendations of the Roundtable." Even the supposedly brightest minds in the investment industry thus on average do not beat the market in the long term: "All in all," Desai and Jain state, "our results indicate that the so-called 'Superstar' money managers on average do not seem to have superior qualities for recommending stocks."[34]

4. PERFORMANCE DISTURBANCES: REFLEXIVE RETURN REDUCTION

The results from these event studies can be condensed into a model: In the case of stocks with a high market capitalization and an appropriate market breadth, that is to say, stocks of companies whose development is observed by many analysts, stock recommendations are rarely accompanied by substantial, if any, price reactions. The good news has already been anticipated.

Again and again, stock prices move up before the recommendations are published, which demonstrates that the tips in the media are based on the good performance of the past. In such cases, no significant price reactions occur, probably also because a possible price pressure from naive investors is counterbalanced by the reactions of informed investors.

For stocks with a low market capitalization and little market breadth, things can be different: In these cases, prices also move before the dissemination of the recommendations, if at all, which again indicates that the tips follow good performances in the past.[35] Sometimes, particularly intense price adjustments can be noticed before the publication date, which suggests that insiders are active among those close to the tipsters. However, considerable abnormal returns are documented to companies that are less in the spotlight after the publication of the recommendations. Excess returns primarily occur on the publication day, often in connection with strongly increased turnovers of the recommended stocks. But usually, the excess returns do not stick with the prices: Prices return to normal and fall until they reach their average level within a few days. Often, they fall even lower.[36]

In sum, this process of price reactions induced by the media and the subsequent price reversal constitutes a permanent stable pattern. In the press, on television or on the internet, on Wall Street or at the stock exchanges of Amsterdam, Frankfurt, London or Istanbul, in the 1970s, 1980s or 1990s—reversals of price reactions have been documented in connection with various news media, in different countries, at different times.[37] Opinions follow the market, which, for a very short time, seems to follow the opinions, but then quickly returns to its initial status. What is much more interesting than the many buy recommendations, however, is the small number of sell recommendations: They sometimes seem to lead to permanent price changes.[38]

The problem is that these price movements are only visible in retrospect; they cannot be forecast systematically. In fact, it is impossible to say with certainty whether they are direct reactions to the contents published in the media: The case studies only provide correlations which are sometimes more, but often less significant. It would be an inadmissible causal conclusion to interpret them as immediate effects of the news content. Quite frequently, price reactions are statistically significant, but to such a small degree that no clear connection can be deduced.[39] Probably the supposed price movements are frequently only artifacts.[40] In many cases, it is even impossible to predict the general tendency of future reactions. Almost identical pieces of information can trigger diametrically opposed price movements.[41] Often, it is probably nothing more than pure coincidence.[42]

For example, no unusual excess returns were found for recommendations of leading money managers published within a quarter of a century in *Barron's*. However, such excess returns were recorded for recommendations of leading money managers in the *Wall Street Journal*—for a period of only three years.[43] As soon as the numbers seem to indicate significant excess returns, they have already disappeared again.[44] But from the point of view of the private investor, this does not make any difference, even if the reactions seem to show the "right" tendency. He or she cannot even benefit economically from positive anomalies:[45] Price reactions set in too quickly, and transaction costs exceed cumulative excess returns.

Even a specific search for the economic benefits of the recommendations of finance commentators thus leads to disappointing results. Lee (1986) explains: "Some finance columns may be capable of giving useful advice, but no finance column can permanently provide useful advice."[46] No doubt, stock recommendations can turn out to have been correct.[47] Successful streaks necessarily occur by chance. What is decisive is their probability: It is certainly not a coincidence that out of all studies, the case studies with the longest sample periods come to the conclusion that it is impossible to outperform the market with the help of financial advice published in the media.[48]

Nine out of ten studies considered by us show that no publication manages to maintain successful streaks over an extended period of time (confer Table 2). Shepard (1977) examined 1.008 recommendations in seven publications over a period of six years. He writes: "thirty-six months after their publication, the recommendations of six of the seven publications had suffered relative losses between 7 and 13 per cent."[49] Dimson and Marsh (1986) sum up: "Despite substantial differences in the performance of different publications, none of them manages to achieve a statistically significant overperformance in the period of one and two years after the publication of the recommendations."[50] Studies of the performance of investment newsletters do not come to any other conclusion.[51]

The media likes to quote individual success stories and short-term anomalies in their self-advertising. Often, the impression of a systematic overperformance is generated because of preselected samples which focus on the winners. But they do not contradict our conclusion: The longer the study period and consequently the reliability of the data, in other words, the lower the probability that periodic deviations from the norm are recorded, the clearer the result: The returns of the stock recommendations are not due to the know-how of their authors, but to a random distribution.[52]

Dimson and March are thus correct in stating: "It would be inappropriate to claim that an advice column with a good success rate can be expected to repeat its investment success."[53] The explanation for this is obvious: In highly competitive markets, a profitable information lead on the basis of public sources can only be short-lived. For this successful method immediately attracts imitators. This is particularly true for the media market, where competitors are very closely watched. Promising sources of information have an especially short half-life. Their way of analysing and presenting information will soon be copied. Possible information asymmetries will thus disappear rapidly.

As the exclusiveness of media contents declines, so does their expected benefit: "Insider tips" that are generally known are useless. Any systematic information lead is lost in no time: The bigger an opportunity, the quicker this gap is taken advantage of. By taking advantage of the gap, the conditions necessary for its existence are eliminated. With the help of digital communication tools and computer-based analysis methods, opportunities to obtain abnormal gains are detected and seized more and more quickly. Comparative information leads are thus rapidly reduced.

This does not exclude the possibility that individual publications can obtain a temporary lead.[54] But the success turns into its opposite: Publications

TABLE 2. Long-term Performance of Buy Recommendations

Researcher	Publication	6 Months	1 Year	2 Years	3 Years
Desai, Liang and Singh (2000)	Wall Street Journal	1.77	4.02	6.04	n.a.
Liang (1999)	Wall Street Journal	−3.80	n.a.	n.a.	n.a.
Beltz and Jennings (1997)	PBS	−1.03	n.a.	n.a.	n.a.
Ghani and Thomas (1997)	Wall Street Journal	4.66	n.a.	n.a.	n.a.
Sant and Zaman (1996)	Business Week	−6.80	n.a.	n.a.	n.a.
Desai and Jain (1995)	Barron's	n.a.	0.21[ab]	−0.38[ab]	−0.71[ab]
Mathur and Waheed (1995)	Business Week	−5.33	n.a.	n.a.	n.a.
Trahan and Bolster (1995)	Barron's	−2.30[a]	−6.92[a]	n.a.	n.a.
Benesh and Clark (1994)	Barron's	−4.69	−1.65[a]	n.a.	n.a.
Wijmenga (1990)	Elseviers Magazine	−2.65			
	Beleggers Belangen	0.16	n.a.	n.a.	n.a.
	de Financiele Koerier	−2.67			
Pari (1987)	PBS	−4.18	−7.23	n.a.	n.a.
Dimson and Marsh (1986)	British Finance Press	n.a.	−0.4	−1.3	n.a.
Shepard (1977)	Barron's	2.92[a]	3.41		−8.00
	Forbes	1.08[a]	−1.87	n.a.	−2.65[a]
	Wall Street Journal	−0.71[a]	−3.25		−7.86

This table gives an overview of the cumulative excess returns of stock recommendations published in the media (relative to the publication date) after 6 months, 1 year, 2 years, and 3 years.
[a] statistically not significant
[b] from the day after the publication date

that offer a valuable product will attract more and more clients—and this is exactly why they lose their information lead. If a business magazine manages to temporarily outperform the market with its recommendations, this will quickly arouse the attention of the public—when the magazine advertises this achievement to attract new readers, at the latest. However, the comparative advantage is thus lost: The more a piece of information is disseminated, the lower its economic benefit. In the long term, it is almost impossible for a business publication to supply its audience with a consistent, let alone a considerable, profit.

In fact, business magazines geared to the capital market do their users a disservice mainly with their stock recommendations. Those case studies which did not only examine the events in a very short period around the publication date, but evaluated the long-term performance of recommended stocks, come to a clear conclusion (confer Table 2). Whether the period considered is six months or one year, two years, or three years: The returns either equal almost zero or are clearly negative. There are hardly any positive exceptions. The figures leave no doubt: The majority of stock recommendations in the media make a medium-term underperformance compared to a passive investment strategy highly probable.

This really is the most realistic scenario for the private investor: For the most part, the tips obtain an abnormal negative return in the medium term, even on paper. The stock prices lag far behind in comparison to the benchmark indexes. The losses in the available case studies were between –0.71 and –6.8 per cent after six months. After one year, negative returns come to up to –7.23 per cent before transaction costs. If we add these fees to come to a more realistic picture, the losses increase even further.[55] Even in cases in which the returns are close to or slightly above zero, the final balance is negative.

It is therefore fair to say that, in the long run, investors either do not benefit from the financial advice published in the media or are even adversely affected. The tips do not offer the public the opportunity to outperform the market systematically. This opportunity is only available to those insiders, analysts and journalists, and people close to them, who put the recommendations into action before their publication. The logic behind this situation is that the potential systematic gain of the insiders is derived from the potential systematic loss of the outsiders. Therefore, it would not be surprising if, in most cases, the private investor is left with a negative balance in the end. For him, the net effect equals zero at best. However, his chances are probably even worse than fifty-fifty.

content.[60] Under pressure to comment on short-term developments, journalists pretend to be competent even if they are not.

It is therefore fair to say that the business media's claim in their advertising that they provide a benefit by offering an advantage to the majority of investors does not stand up to systematic examination. The opposite is true: Each dollar an investor spends on the business media diminishes his profit and constitutes a setback relative to the market. For the sake of honesty, financial advice in the business media should bear the following warning: "Attention: Profits obtained by following our stock recommendations are purely accidental."

6. CODA

17.457 stock forecasts in sixty-seven years: This is the result of the "virtual" William Peter Hamilton, designed by three finance experts in their computer in order to save the reputation of the "real" William Peter Hamilton: As we know, Alfred Cowles, the businessman from Colorado, had come to a critical evaluation of the *Wall Street Journal* columnist's balance in his paper "Can Stock Market Forecasters Forecast?" The accuracy of Hamilton's predictions, Cowles said, did not differ much from a random distribution. A portfolio with the stocks he recommended on average would have lagged behind more than 3.0 per cent per annum with regard to the benchmark index.

Brown, Goetzmann and Kumar (1998) carried out a secondary analysis of Cowles' data and tried to revise his findings. For this purpose, they used his two hundred fifty-five editorials to train a neuronal network on his forecasting technique and constructed a "Hamilton machine" by imitating his decision-making processes. Their goal was to put the hit rate and durability of his investment strategy to a long-term test. The result: In the reinterpretation of Brown, Goetzmann and Kumar, the annual performance of the portfolio between 1902 and 1929 came to 10.73 per cent—with a lower risk in comparison with the benchmark index. Its performance was 10.75 per cent annually.

The long-term test of the "Hamilton machine" for the period from 1930 to 1997 results in the following: Under realistic market circumstances, his strategy would not generate any considerable excess returns, since an occasional lead over the benchmark index disappears if transaction costs and the delay between the publication of the recommendation and its implementation are taken into account. If one calculates the return from the

5. SUMMARY

Stock recommendations in the business media can, under certain circumstances, influence stock prices. But if price movements occur, the rise in market prices is usually short-lived. Study after study proves: Price movements after tips published in the media are followed by price reversals. As soon as public attention decreases, prices move in the opposite direction and the excess returns tend toward zero, or even below. This is always a sign that prices are not influenced by fundamental factors, but rather by publicity in the media.

It is impossible for the private investor to benefit systematically from such U-turns in stock prices: The increases in return on the publication day are practically irrelevant for him, since they are in most cases already reflected in the opening prices. There is therefore no chance to participate in them. What is decisive is the price trend from the day after onward. But the excess returns of various holding periods, from very short periods to time frames of several years, are close to zero, or even lower. As a consequence, there is no reason to believe that journalists or their informants have the ability to systematically make a superior stock selection.[56]

Alfred Cowles already pointed out in his talk at the Econometric Society in December 1932 that some tipsters have the tendency to emphasize particularly successful stock recommendations. They simply conceal less successful tips.[57] These, however, are quite numerous: Even the best forecasters, as Cowles points out concerning the performance of financial publications, are hardly ever better than chance.[58] Many of those who do not have a feel for the right choice—and they are the majority—systematically come up with wrong tips. In this regard, nothing has changed.

In fact, an underperformance in the medium term compared with the market average is the most probable scenario: Medium-term excess returns of stocks recommended in the media are exceptional. Most tips not only are not better than the market, they even systematically fall behind. After transaction costs at the latest, the investment conditions of private investors are such that they generate a loss. Those who fall for the tricks of the noise makers systematically lose their money.

Finance commentator Jane Bryant Quinn remarks on this issue: "The articles . . . make it sound like the journalist knows the right stocks or mutual funds to buy. And the fact is, we don't know."[59] Finance studies are therefore correct in suspecting that the overwhelming majority of recommendations are based on mere noise production and thus are without any information day after the recommendation onward, which is the most realistic scenario for small investors, the performance is worse than the index. All in all, the return of the method developed by this master of pattern recognition is barely distinguishable from the market return.

NOTES

1. Cowles (1933), 315.
2. Cf. Schuster (2000a) and (2001).
3. Kepplinger and Ehmig (2002 and 2001). On the basis of a study of eleven German business magazines, Kepplinger's and Ehmig's 2002 study comes to the following conclusion: "Almost half of all articles deal with financial products, that means concrete investment opportunities." Kepplinger and Ehmig (2002), 15. The number of contributions on investment topics decreased slightly after the stock market crash. However: "Contributions which are relevant for private money and investment questions have the highest status among business magazines." More than 60 per cent of the contents dealt with these topics. Kepplinger and Ehmig (2002), 56. The analyzed magazines are: *Börse Online*, *Capital*, *DMEuro*, *Euro am Sonntag*, *Finanzen*, *Focus Money*, *Geldidee*, *Impulse*, *Managermagazin*, *Wertpapier* and *Wirtschaftswoche*.
4. For the term "economization of the public sphere" cf. in more detail Schuster (2001), 33–53 and passim.
5. According to Barber, Lehavy, McNichols and Trueman (2001) the proportion of sell recommendations dropped from 3.4 (N=19.999) to 1.8 per cent (N=39.722) between 1996 and 2000.
6. Wolf (2001), 70, 74, 76, 80. In an analysis of the coverage of the German Neuer Markt-Index, Wolf demonstrates that in the phase of stock market depression, the business media still stood by their policy of disseminating stock recommendations. 60 per cent of the overall coverage were allotted to investment recommendations and stock price forecasts. This means that "investment tips occur more frequently than any other content form." And further: "The results show that . . . coverage was optimistic for the most part and the 'over-optimism' in business coverage was confirmed." Wolf (2001), 84, 112.
7. For a general introduction to empirical capital market research cf. Möller and Hüfner (2001).
8. The vast majority of the studies considered use variations of the following event study-method: In the time around the publication of the stock recommendations—the event date—"abnormal" returns are measured. This is done by calculating an "expected" return, usually with a version of the market model, which is assumed to be constant. Afterward, the actual returns of the recommended stocks around the date of the event are determined. The difference between the actual and the expected returns constitutes the abnormal return.

9. An early discussion of such media effects can be found in Ruff (1963). He writes: "The pattern of the means shows an initial impulse for the stock price due to the recommendation, a decreasing effect as time passes and finally a waning interest in the stock." Ruff (1963), 43.

10. Gerke (2000), 162 ff.

11. Pari (1987), 75.

12. Hirschey, Richardson and Scholz (2000), 62.

13. Han and Suk (1996), 31.

14. In particular, stocks recommended by stock market letters are on average much smaller than the benchmark indexes. Metrick (1999), 1748; Jaffe and Mahoney (1999), 293; Röckemann (1994), 839.

15. Cf. Antunovich and Sarkar (2001).

16. Cf. Beltz and Jennings (1997), 24 as well as Dimson and Marsh (1986), 125.

17. Tumarkin and Whitelaw (2001), 47. Antweiler and Frank (2001), who examined more than 1.5 million contributions, find correlations between the intensity of the discussions in the internet forums and trading volumes. They do not find significant excess returns either: "The message boards do not successfully forecast stock gains." Antweiler and Frank (2004), 1279. Wysocki (1999) finds an excess return on the day of the event of 0.18 per cent after a 100 per cent increase in the number of messages. The author rightly asks "whether this result implies a feasible trading strategy" and immediately answers the question himself by saying that this is probably not the case. Wysocki (1999), 20.

18. Probably, the people who run these services also know this quite well. Asked about the benefit of the information published on his website, the managing director of *Wallstreet: Online*, the biggest German finance community, answered: "No idea." Cf. Schuster (2000b).

19. Müller (2001).

20. For comparison: The cumulative positive excess return of a period of six months before the discussions amounts to 4.74 per cent. This means that the decisive stock price increase occurs before the publication. Mathur and Waheed (1995), 591. Palmon, Sun and Tang (1994) find even higher excess returns (3.25 per cent from day −1 to day +1), but no signs of a reversal.

21. Mathur and Waheed (1995), 595.

22. Sant and Zaman (1996), 625.

23. Sant and Zaman (1996), 632.

24. However, the most part of the abnormal gain, according to Barber and Loeffler, is anticipated *before* the stock market opens. The actual price increase during the trading day is 1.54 per cent on average.

25. Greene and Smart point out that the recommendations are "priced in" within one hour and that hardly any excess returns are found afterwards: "The Dartboard Column generates a temporary price pressure . . . The excess returns on the event day are most often realized within the first trading hour." Greene and Smart (1999), 1892. The turnovers of the recommended stocks, on the other hand, remain

above average for a longer period of time: Those who trade at these exaggerated prices will lose in the long run.

26. Albert and Smaby (1996) also observe unusual excess returns that set in before the publication.

27. Liang's data is almost identical to that of Greene and Smart.

28. Liang (1999), 120.

29. Syed, Liu and Smith (1989); Liu, Smith and Syed (1990); Liu, Smith and Syed (1992).

30. Huth and Maris (1992) come to similar results.

31. This statement also applies to those studies which find the highest statistically significant excess returns on the publication day and interpret them as if they contradicted the semi-strong version of the Efficient Market Hypothesis. For instance, Ferreira and Brooks (2000) with average abnormal returns at the publication date of 0.63 per cent: Economically, that means after transaction costs, these excess returns are not significant.

32. Pound and Zeckhauser (1990), 299.

33. Desai and Jain (1995), 1264.

34. Desai and Jain (1995), 1257, 1271, 1265.

35. Pieper, Schiereck and Weber write in their study of the effects of buy recommendations of an investment newsletter: "In almost all samples, the biggest proportion of the abnormal performance is achieved before and on the day of the publication. . . ." Pieper, Schiereck and Weber (1993), 500.

36. Also for companies with little stock market capitalization, a non-reaction concerning the published stock recommendations is likely to be the most realistic scenario. Explanation: The studies considered here probably include a publication bias in that studies which find significant results are more likely than studies where this is not the case.

37. For Great Britain, Dimson and Marsh (1986) state: "Any potential short-term profit from the recommendations of the tipster would be more than compensated by the usual transaction fees in England." And they continue: "The empirical conclusion is that stock recommendations published in England possibly are of no use to anyone at all." For the Netherlands, Wijmenga (1990) points out: "In so far as abnormal gains follow recommendations, they are positive for a short period of time and negative in the long run." For Turkey, Yazici and Muradoglu (2001) state: "The results of this study show that investment advice published in a magazine is not a helpful service to the average private investor, but a lucrative deal for its 'preferred investors.'"

38. Cf. Foster (1987 and 1979) as well as Desai and Jain (2004). The data of Gerke and Oerke (1998) show individual, but no systematic reactions to buy recommendations. Sell recommendations, on the other hand, lead to obvious and systematic price movements.

39. In addition, Röckemann (1994) observes that the impact of stock recommendations "is very obvious in an aggregated form, but in the results for the individual

stock market services, effects are found to be very confusing." Röckemann (1994), 821.

40. Sahner (1979) rightly points out that scientific periodicals are full of empirical studies which show errors type I: They dismiss the null hypothesis although it is correct. Too often, Sahner says, people overlook that "non-relations can adequately describe reality." Sahner (1979), 269. Krämer and Runde write: "At a significance level of 5%, one will 'discover' on average five 'effects' in 100 trials even if none is really there. This problem has long been known in applied statistics under the heading of 'data mining.'" Krämer and Runde (1996), 293.

41. Cf. Pound and Zeckhauser (1990), passim.

42. In fact, the method provides an essential contribution to the production of the results. Dimson and Marsh (1986) deal in detail with the importance of the measuring method and the benchmark index for the evaluation of the results of event studies. The longer the time period during which the performance of stock recommendations is measured, the more significant misspecifications become. Dimson and Marsh (1986), 135 and passim; cf. also Albert and Smaby (1996), 60ff. Salinger (1992) shows that an insufficient consideration of standard deviations can lead to distorted results of event studies and a false assessment of the level of significance.

43. Desai and Jain (1995); Desai, Liang and Singh (2000). As in many other cases, nothing is left of the excess returns after transaction fees.

44. Barber, Lehavy, McNichols and Trueman (2001) find statistically significant, but for the private investor economically irrelevant excess returns in the estimates of investment analysts for the years 1986 to 1996. Barber, Lehavy, McNichols and Trueman (2003) find *no* statistically significant excess returns in the estimates of investment analysts for the years 2000 and 2001. On the contrary: What occurs are economically highly relevant losses. The stocks the analysts most warmly recommended strongly underperform the market.

45. And in many cases institutional investors neither, even if they bear low transaction costs.

46. Lee (1986), 38.

47. Cf. Glascock, Henderson and Martin (1986).

48. Sant and Zaman (1996) examined a sample from 1976 to 1988. They write: "The information published in Business Week is already 'used up' and exploited by informed traders." Desai and Jain (1995) studied a sample from 1968 to 1991. They write: "Someone who invests according to the recommendations of the Roundtable published in Barron's would not benefit from this advice." Mathur and Waheed (1995) studied a sample from 1981 to 1989. They write: "Investors who buy in the long run on the basis of secondary information in general get returns that are below the market average." Lee (1986) examined a sample from 1962 to 1979. He writes: "My empirical evidence shows that investors were not able to obtain consistent excess returns, less transaction fees, by blindly following the advice of a finance column in the media."

49. Shepard (1977), 35.
50. Dimson and Marsh (1986), 131.
51. Metrick (1999) writes: "There is no evidence that stock market letters make a superior stock selection, no matter whether in the short or in the long run." Metrick (1999), 1770. Cf. also Graham and Harvey (1997 and 1996).
52. On small sample bias cf. Krämer (1995).
53. Dimson and Marsh (1986), 131.
54. Cf. Foster (1979).
55. Jaffe and Mahoney (1999) point out that the stock recommendations of investment newsletters are particularly cost intensive since they require high turnovers of stocks. This alone considerably worsens the investment performance. Jaffe and Mahoney (1999), 296.
56. Thus, it is in no way justified to postulate the dependence of stock prices from analysts' recommendations. Cf. Medien Tenor (2002).
57. Cowles (1933), 310.
58. Cowles (1933), 324.
59. "Good Investing Isn't Sexy. A Conversation With Jane Bryant Quinn." In: abcnews.com, 08/27/98.
60. Bank (2001), 277. For more details see Schuster (2001), 114–118 and passim.

REFERENCES

Albert, Robert L. and Timothy R. Smaby. 1996. "Market Response to Analyst Recommendations in the 'Dartboard' Column. The Information and Price-Pressure Effects." In: *Review of Financial Economics* Vol. 5, No. 1 (1996): 59–74.

Allen, David S. and Hamidah Awang-Damit. 1998. "The Wall Street Journal Investment Dartboard." Flagstaff: Northern Arizona University, College of Business Administration, Working Paper.

Antunovich, Peter and Asani Sarkar. 2000. "Cheap Talk? Market Impact of Internet Stock Recommendations." Unpublished Manuscript.

Antweiler, Werner and Murray Z. Frank. 2002. "Is All That Talk Just Noise? The Information Content of Internet Stock Message Boards." In: *Journal of Finance* Vol. 59, No. 3: 1259–1295.

Bank, Matthias. 2001. *Behavioral Finance und Börsenkursmanipulation*. Nürnberg: Universität Erlangen-Nürnberg, Habilitationsschrift.

Barber, Brad, Reuven Lehavy, Maureen McNichols and Brett Trueman. 2003. "Prophets and Losses. Reassessing the Returns to Analysts' Stock Recommendations." In: *Financial Analysts Journal* Vol. 59, No. 2: 88–96.

Barber, Brad, Reuven Lehavy, Maureen McNichols and Brett Trueman. 2001. "Can Investors Profit from the Prophets? Consensus Analyst Recommendations and Stock Returns." In: *Journal of Finance* Vol. 56, No. 2: 531–563.

Barber, Brad M. and Douglas Loeffler. 1993. "The 'Dartboard' Column. Second-Hand Information and Price Pressure." In: *Journal of Financial and Quantitative Analysis* Vol. 28, No. 2 (June): 273–284.

Beltz, Jess and Robert Jennings. 1997. "'Wall Street Week with Louis Rukheyser' Recommendations. Trading Activity and Performance." In: *Review of Financial Economics* Vol. 6, No. 1: 15–27.

Beneish, Messod D. 1991. "Stock Prices and the Dissemination of Analysts' Recommendations." In: *Journal of Business* Vol. 64, No. 3: 393–416.

Benesh, Gary A. and Jeffrey A. Clark. 1994. "The Value of Indirect Investment Advice. Stock Recommendations in Barron's." In: *Journal of Financial and Strategic Decisions* Vol. 7, No. 1 (Spring): 35–43.

Brown, Stephen J., William N. Goetzmann and Alok Kumar. 1998. "The Dow Theory. William Peter Hamilton's Track Record Reconsidered." In: *Journal of Finance* Vol. 53, No. 4: 1311–1333.

Cowles, Alfred. 1933. "Can Stockmarket Forecasters Forecast?" In: *Econometrica* Vol. 1: 309–324.

Das, Sanjiv R. and Mike Y. Chen. 2001. "Yahoo! for Amazon. Sentiment Parsing from Small Talk on the Web." Santa Clara: Santa Clara University, Working Paper.

Davies, P. Lloyd and Michael Canes. 1978. "Stock Prices and the Publication of Second-Hand Information." In: *Journal of Business* Vol. 51, No. 1: 43–57.

Desai, Hemang, Bing Liang and Ajai K. Singh. 2000. "Do All-Stars Shine? Evaluation of Analyst Recommendations." In: *Financial Analysts Journal* Vol. 56, No. 3 (Mai/Juni): 20–29.

Desai, Hemang and Prem C. Jain. 2004. "Long-Run Common Stock Returns Following Financial Analysis by Abraham Briloff." In: *Financial Analysts Journal* Vol. 60, No. 2: 47–56.

Desai, Hemang and Prem C. Jain. 1995. "An Analysis of the Recommendations of the 'Superstar' Money Managers at *Barron's* Annual Roundtable." In: *Journal of Finance* Vol. 50, No. 4 (September): 1257–1273.

Dimson, Elroy and Paul Marsh. 1986. "Event Study Methodologies and the Size Effect. The Case of UK Press Recommendations." In: *Journal of Financial Economics* Vol. 17, No. 1: 113–142.

Dorfleitner, Gregor and Christian Klein. 2002. "Kursprognose mit Hilfe der Technischen Analyse. Eine empirische Untersuchung." Arbeitspapiere zur Mathematischen Wirtschaftsforschung, No. 179. Augsburg: Univeristät Augsburg, Institut für Statistik und Mathematische Wirtschaftstheorie.

Ferreira, Eurico J. and LeRoy D. Brooks. 2000. "Re-released Information in the *Wall Street Journal's* 'Insider Trading Spotlight' Column." In: *Quarterly Journal of Business and Economics* Vol. 39, No. 1 (Winter): 22–34.

Ferreira, Eurico J. and Stanley D. Smith. 1999. "Stock Price Reactions to Recommendations in the *Wall Street Journal* 'Small Stock Focus' Column." In: *Quarterly Review of Economics and Finance* Vol. 39: 379–389.

Foster, George. 1987. "Rambo IX. Briloff and the Capital Market." In: *Journal of Accounting, Auditing and Finance* Vol. 2, No. 4: 409–430.
——. 1979. "Briloff and the Capital Market." In: *Journal of Accounting Research* Vol. 17, No. 1 (Spring): 262–274.
Gerke, Wolfgang. 2000. "Mißbrauch der Medien zur Aktienkursbeeinflussung." In: Lothar Rolke and Volker Wolff (Hrsg.), *Finanzkommunikation. Kurspflege durch Meinungspflege. Die neuen Spielregeln am Aktienmarkt*. Frankfurt a.M.: F.A.Z.-Institut: 151–170.
Gerke, Wolfgang and Marc Oerke. 1998. "Marktbeeinflussung durch Analystenempfehlungen. Eine empirische Studie." In: *Zeitschrift für Betriebswirtschaft* Vol. 68, Ergänzungsheft 2: 187–200.
Ghani, Waqar and Martin R. Thomas. 1997. "The Dart Board Column. Analyst Earnings Forecasts and the Informational Content of Recommendations," In: *Journal of Business and Economic Studies* Vol. 3, No. 2: 33–42.
Glascock, John L., Glenn V. Henderson and Linda J. Martin. 1986. "When E.F. Hutton Talks . . ." In: *Financial Analysts Journal* Vol. 42, No. 3 (May/June): 69–72.
Graham, John R. and Campbell R. Harvey. 1997. "Grading the Performance of Market-timing Newsletters." In: *Financial Analysts Journal* Vol. 53, No. 6: 54–66.
Graham, John R. and Campbell R. Harvey. 1996. "Market Timing Ability and Volatility Implied in Investment Newsletters' Asset Allocation Recommendations." In: *Journal of Financial Economics* Vol. 42, No. 3: 397–421.
Greene, Jason and Scott Smart. 1999. "Liquidity Provision and Noise Trading. Evidence from the 'Investment Dartboard' Column." In: *Journal of Finance* Vol. 54, No. 5: 1885–1899.
Han, Ki C. and David Y. Suk. 1996. "Stock Prices and the *Barron's* 'Research Reports' Column." In: *Journal of Financial and Strategic Decisions* Vol. 9, No. 3 (Fall): 27–32.
Hirschey, Mark, Vernon J. Richardson and Susan Scholz. 2000. "How 'Foolish' Are Internet Investors?" In: *Financial Analysts Journal* Vol. 56, No. 1 (January/February): 62–69.
Huth, William L. and Brian A. Maris. 1992. "Large and Small Firm Stock Price Response to 'Heard on the Street' Recommendations." In: *Journal of Accounting, Auditing, and Finance* Vol. 7: 27–47.
Jaffe, Jeffrey F. and James M. Mahoney. 1999. "The Performance of Investment Newsletters." In: *Journal of Financial Economics* Vol. 53, No. 2 (August): 289–307.
Kepplinger, Hans Mathias and Simone C. Ehmig. 2002. *Content Guide Wirtschaftsmagazine 2002. Eine Contentanalyse deutscher Wirtschaftsmagazine im Auftrag von Geldidee and Wertpapier*. Hamburg: Bauer Verlagsgruppe.
Kepplinger, Hans Mathias and Simone C. Ehmig. 2001. *Content Guide Wirtschaftsmagazine 2001. Eine Contentanalyse deutscher Wirtschaftsmagazine im Auftrag von Geldidee*. Hamburg: Bauer Verlagsgruppe.

Kladroba, Andreas and Peter von der Lippe. 2001. "Die Qualität von Aktienempfehlungen in Publikumszeitschriften." Essen: Diskussionsbeiträge aus dem Fachbereich Wirtschaftswissenschaften der Universität Essen, No. 117.

Krämer, Walter. 2001. "Kapitalmarkteffizienz." In: Manfred Steiner and Wolfgang Gerke (Hrsg.), *Handwörterbuch des Bank- und Finanzwesens*. Stuttgart: Schäffer-Poeschel: 1267–1274.

———. 1995. "The Probability of a 'Gross' Violation of an Efficient Markets Variance Inequality." In: *Empirical Economics* Vol. 20: 473–478.

Krämer, Walter and Ralf Runde. 1996. "Stochastic Properties of German Stock Returns." In: *Empirical Economics* Vol. 21: 281–306.

Lee, Chi-wen Jevons. 1986. "Information Content of Financial Columns." In: *Journal of Economics and Business* Vol. 38: 27–39.

Liang, Bing. 1999. "Price Pressure. Evidence from the 'Dartboard' Column." In: *Journal of Business* Vol. 72, No. 1: 119–134.

Liu, Pu, Stanley D. Smith and Azmat A. Syed. 1992. "The Impact of the Insider Trading Scandal on the Information Content of the *Wall Street Journal's* 'Heard on the Street' Column." In: *Journal of Financial Research* Vol. 15, No. 2: 181–188.

Liu, Pu, Stanley D. Smith and Azmat A. Syed. 1990. "Stock Price Reactions to *The Wall Street Journal's* Securities Recommendations." In: *Journal of Financial and Quantitative Analysis* Vol. 25, No. 3 (September): 399–410.

Mathur, Ike and Amjad Waheed. 1995. "Stock Price Reactions to Securities Recommended in *Business Week's* 'Inside Wall Street.'" In: *Financial Review* Vol. 30, No. 3 (August): 583–604.

McQueen, Grant and V. Vance Roley. 1993. "Stock Prices, News, and Business Conditions." In: *Review of Financial Studies* Vol. 6, No. 3: 683–707.

Medien Tenor. 2002. "'Entwicklungshelfer' der Kapitalmärkte. Aktienkursentwicklung in Abhängigkeit von Analystenaussagen in der Wirtschaftspresse im 1. Quartal 2002." In: *Medien Tenor Forschungsbericht* No. 120: 78f.

Metcalf, Gilbert E. and Burton G. Malkiel. 1994. "The *Wall Street Journal* Contests. The Experts, the Darts, and the Efficient Market Hypothesis." In: *Applied Financial Economics* Vol. 4, No. 5 (October): 371–374.

Metrick, Andrew. 1999. "Performance Evaluation With Transactions Data. The Stock Selection of Investment Newsletters." In: *Journal of Finance* Vol. 54, No. 5 (October) : 1743–1775.

Möller, Hans Peter and Bernd Hüfner. 2001. "Kapitalmarktforschung, empirische." In: Manfred Steiner and Wolfgang Gerke (eds.), Handwörterbuch des Bank- and Finanzwesens. Stuttgart: Schäffer-Poeschel: 1275–1293.

Müller, Volker. 2001. "Mit zweifelhaften Empfehlungen." In: *Die Telebörse*, No. 40: 80–82.

Palmon, Oded, Huey-Lian Sun and Alex P. Tang. 1994. "The Impact of Publication of Analysts' Recommendations on Returns and Trading Volume." In: *Financial Review* Vol. 29, No. 3 (August): 395–417.

Pari, Robert A. 1987. "Wall Street Week Recommendations. Yes or No?" In: *Journal of Portfolio Management* Vol. 14, No. 1: 74–76.

Pearce, Douglas K. and V. Vance Roley. 1985. "Stock Prices and Economic News." In: *Journal of Business* Vol. 58, No. 1: 49–67.

Pieper, Ute, Dirk Schiereck and Martin Weber. 1993. "Die Kaufempfehlungen des 'Effecten-Spiegel.' Eine empirische Untersuchung im Lichte der Effizienzthese des Kapitalmarktes." In: *Zeitschrift für betriebswirtschaftliche Forschung* Vol. 45: 487–509.

Pound, John and Richard J. Zeckhauser. 1990. "Clearly Heard on the Street. The Effect of Takeover Rumors on Stock Prices." In: *Journal of Business* Vol. 63, No. 3: 291–308.

Röckemann, Christian. 1994. "Anlageempfehlungen von Börseninformationsdiensten und Anlegerverhalten. Eine empirische Analyse für den deutschen Aktienmarkt." In: *Zeitschrift für betriebswirtschaftliche Forschung* Vol. 46: 819–848.

Ruff, Raymond T. 1963. "Effect of a Selection and Recommendation of a 'Stock of the Month.'" In: *Financial Analysts Journal* Vol. 19, No. 2: 41–43.

Sahner, Heinz. 1979. "Veröffentlichte empirische Sozialforschung. Eine Kumulation von Artefakten? Eine Analyse von Periodika" In: *Zeitschrift für Soziologie* Vol. 8, No. 3: 267–278.

Salinger, Michael. 1992. "Standard Errors in Event Studies." In: *Journal of Financial and Quantitative Analysis* Vol. 27, No. 1 (März): 39–52.

Sant, Rajiv and Mir A. Zaman. 1996. "Market Reaction to Business Week 'Inside Wall Street' Column. A Self-fulfilling Prophecy." In: *Journal of Banking and Finance* Vol. 20: 617–643.

Schuster, Thomas. 2001. *Die Geldfalle. Wie Medien und Banken die Anleger zu Verlierern machen.* Reinbek: Rowohlt.

———. 2000a. "Zwischen Boom und Crash." In: *Message. Internationale Fachzeitschrift für Journalismus* No. 3 (July): 10–17.

———. 2000b. "Virtuelle Finanz-Gemeinschaften. Die gefährliche Jagd nach heissen Börsentipps." In: *Süddeutsche Zeitung*, 28.01.2000: 32.

Shepard, Lawrence. 1977. "How Good is Investment Advice for Individuals?" In: *Journal of Portfolio Management* Vol. 3, No. 2 (Winter): 32–36.

Stice, Earl K. 1991. "The Market Reaction to 10-K and 10-Q Filings and to Subsequent *The Wall Street Journal* Earnings Announcements." In: *Accounting Review* Vol. 66, No. 1 (January): 42–55.

Syed, Azmat A., Pu Liu and Stanley D. Smith. "The Exploitation of Inside Information at the *Wall Street Journal*. A Test of Strong Form Efficiency." In: *Financial Review* Vol. 24, No. 4 (1989): 567–579.

Thompson, Robert B., Chris Olsen and J. Richard Dietrich. 1987. "Attributes of News About Firms. An Analysis of Firm-Specific News Reported in the *Wall Street Journal Index*." In: *Journal of Accounting Research* Vol. 25, No. 2 (Fall): 245–274.

Trahan, Emery A. and Paul J. Bolster. 1995. "The Impact of Barron's Recommendation on Stock Prices." In: *Quarterly Journal of Business and Economics* Vol. 34 (Fall): 3–15.

Tumarkin, Robert and Robert F. Whitelaw. 2001. "News or Noise? Internet Postings and Stock Prices." In: *Financial Analysts Journal* Vol. 57, No. 3 (May/June): 41–51.

Wijmenga, R.Th. 1990. "The Performance of Published Dutch Stock Recommendations." In: *Journal of Banking and Finance* Vol. 14: 559–581.

Wolf, Katja. 2001. *Finanzberichterstattung in Special-Interest-Zeitschriften. Ein Vergleich der Berichterstattung in der Hoch- and der Tiefphase der Börse.* Dresden: TU Dresden, Magisterarbeit.

Wright, David W. 1994. "Can Prices be Trusted? A Test of the Ability of Experts to Outperform or Influence the Market." In: *Journal of Accounting, Auditing and Finance* Vol. 9 (Frühjahr): 307–323.

Wysocki, Peter D. 1999. "Cheap Talk on the Web. The Determinants of Postings on Stock Message Boards." Ann Arbor: University of Michigan Business School Working Paper.

Yazici, Bilgehan und Gülnur Muradoglu. 2002. "Dissemination of Stock Recommendations and Small Investors. Who Benefits?" In: *Multinational Finance Journal* Vol. 6, No. 1: 2

MESO

Numerous empirical studies have demonstrated that asset prices react rapidly, if at all, to news published in the mass media. In many cases, the information has been discounted and prices have already moved upon primary publication through news wires, press releases, or firm announcements. Any remaining information is usually quickly priced in after dissemination through the mass media. But not always: Often enough, delayed price adjustments, and underreactions as well as overreactions, can be observed after particular news reports have been published. This points to inadequacies in the efficient markets hypothesis *as well as* in Behavioral Finance theories: Delayed reactions seem too often to be explained as "anomalies" within models of rational pricing. But they appear too erratically to be explained as "normalities," such as in newer models of systematically irrational pricing. In other words: Asset prices frequently do not react to news published in the media. Sometimes they do. The evidence leads to the following conclusion: That markets can be efficient and inefficient at the same time.

NEWS EVENTS AND PRICE MOVEMENTS

Synchronization was perfect, and after the event, commentators in the media shuddered to acknowledge it. The signs of destruction left no room for doubt about the perpetrators' intentions: The plan was to hit the core of capitalism, symbol and control center of the globalized economy, in a coolly calculated strike. The north tower had just gone up in flames when many television stations were already broadcasting live. At the moment when the Twin Towers collapsed, a good hour later, the international public had tuned in.[1] The whole world was watching as, on the sunny morning of September 11th, 2001, the World Trade Center was reduced to a pile of rubble.

The tremendous speed of the real-time conflict forced a rapid counter-reaction. The response of the world's financial markets was immediate and severe: The London Stock Exchange experiences the heaviest crash in its history, the Financial Times Stock Exchange (FTSE) 100 Index fell by 5.7 per cent. The Compagnie des Agents de Change (CAC) 40-Index in Paris lost 7.4 per cent. Also, in Frankfurt, panic selling was reported and the Deutscher Aktien Index (DAX) lost 8.5 per cent of its value—one of the largest daily price losses in its history. The Nikkei Index in Tokyo dropped below 10,000 points for the first time since 1984.[2] In return, the prices for gold and crude oil sharply increased. The dollar plunged. The shock waves of the news from New York City shook markets around the globe.

Decision makers in international financial institutions took emergency measures: The U.S. Federal Reserve Bank, the European Central Bank, the

Bank of Japan and many of their colleagues in the international prudential supervision and regulatory agencies held crisis talks. They hastened to assure the markets that they would allocate the necessary funds in order to keep international payment systems operational and avoid an imminent financial collapse. Interest rates were lowered and substantial financial aid was dispensed to protect the industries directly concerned from the worst.[3]

Markets continued to vibrate for quite some time from the psychological shock of the terrorist attacks. In fact, the financial fallout at the target of the attack, Wall Street, was relatively small in comparison: Stockbroking did not even start on September 11th and remained closed for several days, which prevented immediate shock reactions. Hardly two months later, and thus much faster than many other international stock exchanges in regions far away from the explosion, the U.S. indexes reach the level they had before the attacks.[4] But most other international indexes recovered in the medium term as well. It seems as if the serious price losses immediately after the attacks, particularly in Europe, were overreactions triggered by the shock.

Undoubtedly, it was the incredibility of the events "as such" that caused these overreactions. However, it is not physical violence alone that defined the significance of this world event, but also its psychological multiplication through simultaneous global broadcasting via the mass media. The whole world was watching, knowing that the rest of the world was watching. Accordingly, reactions were vehement. Although it is impossible to separate the event itself from its media broadcast—the two are inseparably intertwined—there is a lot to be said for the fact that the specific quality of the cataclysm is due to its deliberate realization as a media event.[5] In view of this, it is appropriate to assume an autonomous share of the media in these (over)reactions.

1. INTRODUCTION

A whole industry lives on it: Investment magazines, financial networks, business papers, and even the general daily press, convey the impression that information selected and presented by them permits conclusions about future movements of the stock markets. The media, as well as certain market observers, seems to maintain that business news circulating in public has significant, economically realizable and relevant information. Some even suppose that business news provokes systematic price movements in the financial markets. It seems the media is not just an observer, it is a mover of markets.

"Knowing what will be important" is the slogan of the German edition of the *Financial Times*. "Facts make money" explains the German investment magazine *Focus Money*. "Profit from it" promises United States finance television network Consumer News and Business Channel (CNBC). Such slogans nurture the idea of news producers as visionary forecasters or powerful movers of markets. It is in the media's commercial interest to convince the public that its news moves stock prices. The higher the potential of business coverage to forecast or influence stock prices, the higher the benefit that can be expected from intensive media consumption. This again increases the incentive to buy such media products.

Actual or supposed market manipulations also nurture the idea of the media as an influential mover of stock prices: In numerous cases, business journalists or their contacts in the industry were accused of having influenced investment behavior through well-directed publications of investment tips and exaggerated forecasts of price movements to manipulate the prices of certain market values.[6] For some time, such attempts at instrumentalizing the press and television became the content of media coverage itself.[7] Supposed attempts to manipulate by financial shows on television received particular attention.[8]

On the other hand, many investors had to realize with the breakdown of the "New Economy" that the potential of the business media to move stock prices is a lot smaller than individual cases of manipulation seem to suggest: While the media was still dreaming of a permanent stock market upswing, the financial markets crashed, shattering the hopes of many investors. But the journalists stuck to their positive message: Even in the middle of the stock market crisis, the number of buy recommendations by far exceeded the number of sell recommendations.[9] Obviously, the business media neither serves as an early warning system nor as reliable forecaster or maker of stock prices. Is the published information not relevant to stock prices after all?

Despite the self-confident statements of certain media or finance professionals, the actual quality of the interaction of markets and the media is far from being established. On the part of finance studies, the topic has received a lot of attention, mainly in connection with the question of exactly how information is processed in the financial markets. This is based on a very narrow definition of "information content" that reduces the term to news content that provokes prompt stock price movements. Media studies have mostly analyzed the effects of business news from the point of view of its supposed influence on voters' behavior, thus in a political context, if at all.[10] So far, the interaction of markets and the media has not been studied by this discipline.

In the following, the results of empirical research on the functioning of data processing in the financial markets will be extracted and examined in a qualitative meta-analysis. The goal is to understand the immediate effects of the media on financial markets. As a synthesis of the existing material will show, a long-term analysis reveals recurring patterns. There is a relationship between markets and the media, the media can have an effect on the markets. However, there is only a limited possibility of summarizing how this happens in universally applicable terms. The following questions are to be answered: Does news published in the mass media have an immediate effect on financial markets? And if so, in what way?

2. STATE OF THE ART: "RANDOM WALKS" AND "IRRATIONAL EXUBERANCE"

Does news have price effects on the financial markets or not? This question is part of a central and heated debate in economics that is far from being settled. In numerous studies, exponents of empirical capital market research have come to the conclusion that new information is reflected in stock prices quickly. This is why they call markets "efficient" and consider news to be generally ineffective.[11] Advocates of Behavioral Finance, however, document multiple cases of delayed price reactions after the arrival of new information and therefore describe the markets as "inefficient."[12] They consider the news in the media to be potentially effective.

The theoretical premises of the two approaches and their implications could hardly be more different: As Paul Samuelson (1965) explains in his classic text "Proof That Properly Anticipated Prices Fluctuate Randomly," the current price of a stock is the best estimate of its true value. If the correct future price was already known, according to Samuelson, the price would immediately move in this direction. But this, precisely, is not the case. As a consequence, price fluctuations come about. The theory says, according to Eugene Fama's (1970) classic definition of the "efficient market hypothesis," "that security prices at any time 'fully reflect' all available information."[13] A specification of this sentence shows that price formation in the financial markets follows a random walk.[14] In brief: In a market reacting efficiently to information, stock price changes cannot be predicted.[15]

The concept of efficient markets implies that the analysis and evaluation of information available to the public does not promise above-average returns. If stock prices only react to future, that is, unknown, data, publicly accessible news, as it is disseminated by the mass media, is almost irrelevant to price formation. It is anticipated by the market. Price adjustments which have not been realized prior to publication take place without any delay.[16] In a nutshell: The prices already "contain" the news. As a result, prices always represent an adequate reflection of fundamental values.[17] An analysis of media content in order to find future price patterns thus is obsolete because it would not create an additional value, for there are no future price patterns that could be derived.

Conclusions from newer, behavioral approaches are different: Behavioral Finance, which is based on findings from psychology, sociology and anthropology, has emphatically pointed out the existence of so-called "market anomalies." This is a term for price movements which seem to contradict the explanations of models of rational economic behavior.[18] Factors in the market environment, according to these observations, seem to lead to deviations of prices from their rationally justifiable levels. Stock prices divert more or less strongly from fundamental values.[19] Irrational exaggerations and price bubbles are possible consequences. In brief: Stock prices do not (always) follow a random distribution.

The considerations of Behavioral Finance imply that the reports of the news media can be relevant for stock prices. As stock prices under- or overreact to good or bad news, the mass media is of importance: because it intensifies such market reactions or perhaps even provokes them itself. Robert Shiller (1999) writes regarding this: "It appears as if stock prices overreact to some news . . . before investors come to their senses and correct the prices."[20] As far as it arouses public interest, influence public opinion and unify investor behavior, the media potentially is a central factor in understanding the dynamics of financial markets.

In sum: Finance research provides substantial evidence that media reports have an impact on stock prices. And it provides substantial evidence that media reports do *not* have an impact on stock prices.

Media research has dealt with the topic, if it deals with it at all, from a different perspective: Special priority has been given to the problem of insiders in business coverage and the resulting potential conflicts of interest.[21] The reason for these studies were cases in which journalists, who were in close contact with actors in the financial markets and thus became de facto insiders, using their non-public knowledge for personal enrichment—for example, by publishing stock recommendations for companies they had business relations with in order to make speculative gains.[22]

Criticism of these occurences is based on the assumption, which is at least implied, that the business media could have an influence on investor behavior. If the media was without influence, discussions about unethical behavior of journalists would be without practical relevance, since no negative consequences would be expected from journalists breaching regulations. These negative consequences are insinuated, however, if one urges journalists to deal responsibly with their audience and warns of manipulations.[23] The scant approaches in media research in this regard, therefore, at least implicitly assume that news has at least a punctual effect on investor behavior and can lead to market distortions through manipulative influencing of investors.

Only recently have there been attempts to systematically analyze the interaction of markets and the media in communication research. Schuster (2001c and 2000a) provides solid evidence of the fact that the role of the mass media has to be taken into account to understand the dynamics of financial markets. There is sufficient proof that cause-effect relations that can be easily isolated are the exception rather than the rule. Extraordinary price movements after stock recommendations, for example, are only an exception. However, it can by no means be deduced that the media does not have any effect and that secondary information in the mass media does not have an influence on price formation. The media can produce manifest as well as latent effects.

3. NEWS EFFECTS: RAPID RETURN REACTIONS

Piles of studies of empirical financial market research make it evident: Delayed effects of news do not represent the norm. Even on days when "big events" dominate headlines in the media, according to Cutler, Poterba and Summers (1989), the price movements that occur are rather small most of the time. On the other hand, many of the largest market movements take place on days with no significant events in the news. Generally speaking, it seems to be true that no systematic relationship can be established between the publication of business and other news in the media and consequent substantial stock price changes in the financial markets. Market prices fluctuate, but often the news is not very important.

This result has been, and is still, underpinned by exponents of the theory of efficient markets in a large number of event studies: Stock prices react quickly to new information, even before it is published by the news media. Effects of new information on stock prices in the form of systematic and delayed price reactions do not represent the rule. On the contrary: Fama, Fisher, Jensen and Roll (1969) already point out in their study on market reactions to stocks splits "that stock prices adjust very rapidly to new information."[24] Shortly after the announcement of splits, the authors state, mostly within one day only, the relevant price adjustments have been carried out.[25] Therefore, it is usually impossible to achieve an abnormal gain by reacting to such data.

Ball and Brown (1968a) look at market reactions to the publication of accounting income numbers in the *Wall Street Journal*. Their result: The major part of new information is anticipated in stock prices in the preceding months. The actual publication in the newspaper has hardly any measurable effect.[26] "The market," according to Dimson and Mussavian (2000), "appears to anticipate the information, and most of the price adjustment is complete before the event is revealed to the market. When news is released, the remaining price adjustment takes place rapidly and accurately."[27] The conclusion from this is the following: That published information does not permit forecasts of stock price changes.

A multitude of event studies provide evidence for the speed with which the market really reacts. For example, to companies' press releases: Patell and Wolfson (1984) demonstrate that price movements in connection with dividend and earnings announcements through the *Dow Jones News Service* set in prior to publication. The main boost in stock prices follows five to fifteen minutes after the publication. Sixty to ninety minutes later, price adjustments are for the most part concluded.[28] While earnings announcements at least seem to trigger significant price movements around the publication date, the reactions to dividend announcements are weak and only worth mentioning in case of dividend changes. If price movements occur at all after dividend announcements, these are carried out very quickly.

Similar results are available for the German market: Gerke, Oerke and Sentner (1997) investigate market reactions to the publication of dividend changes in business newswires and in the business paper *Handelsblatt* from 1987 to 1994. Their findings show that stock prices react to dividend increases with abnormal returns of about one per cent on the same day; after that, there are no noticeable price fluctuations.[29] The situation is different, however, for negative surprises: Dividend decreases and dividend omissions are responded to with immediate declines in prices, but this reaction does not stop until several days later. In addition, it is striking that a significant share of the price adjustment happens only when the information has been disseminated in the press (and not after the agency report).

In many cases, the processing of information happens very quickly. Röder (2000a) comes to the conclusion that a certain type of company report, so-called ad hoc announcements, are processed very smoothly for companies listed in the Deutscher Aktien Index (DAX). After the publication date, no abnormal price movements can be established. The price reaction sets in during the first fifteen minutes after publication, and the major part of it is completed within the first hour of trading.[30] Stock prices of smaller companies can show delayed price reactions to company news, even on the day after the publication. But these theoretical excess returns that can be observed with hindsight can hardly be realized in practice, since the transaction costs exceed the potential gain.

Positive firm announcements, according to the results of Woodruff and Senchack (1988) on the American market are reflected especially rapidly in stock prices. Mostly, they have already been anticipated at the time of their publication. May (1994) and Röder (2000b) present similar test results for the German stock exchange. The general maxim seems to be: "No news is good news."[31] Negative information can cause stronger price fluctuations, especially in a positive market environment, by increasing insecurity about prospects for the future.[32] But even such negative information is mostly processed without greater delays. Outsiders, who buy after the public dissemination, usually do not have time to react to them. The market (re)acts (very) quickly.

But not always. Stice (1991) proves that the publication method can have an impact on the price response: Accounting income numbers, which do not produce a measurable effect at the time of their obligatory publication, might very well do so when they are published in the *Wall Street Journal* at a later date. Possibly, this is a violation of the efficient market theory, according to which republications should not produce abnormal price fluctuations. This could hint at autonomous media effects because the newspaper articles do not contain any new information. However, the figures Stice presents on movements of prices and volumes are hardly significant economically. Moreover, they concern very small companies—whose stock prices usually react more slowly because they are not in the public eye.

Beaver (1986) already provides evidence for the fact that stock prices and trading volumes can react to the publication of accounting income numbers: He documents abnormal returns and turnovers around the publication date and concludes that the accounting income reports do have an information content. Comparable extraordinary trading activities after the publication of accounting income numbers have been shown for smaller companies: Bamber (1986), for example, reports above-average turnovers at the time of earnings announcements in the *Wall Street Journal*, particularly for stocks in narrow markets. If the returns are unexpectedly high, the stocks concerned can show increased trading volume. Both Beaver's and Bamber's results indicate that extraordinary trading activities come to an end very quickly.

Rapidity in information processing seems to be the norm in the majority of cases. Announcements of macroeconomic data provoke particularly rapid reactions on the markets—if they react at all. For example inflation numbers: Schwert (1981) shows that the stock market often reacts only weakly to the release of inflation rates.[33] Pearce and Roley (1985) also find only very weak evidence of price reactions to inflation rates. Jain (1988) replicates these results: Inflation rate, industrial production or unemployment rate—the release of these statistics, for the most part, does not lead to any remarkable change in stock prices. If corresponding effects occur, they do so very quickly, generally within one hour.[34] After that, the price effect has been exhausted.[35]

Interest and currency markets react even more quickly than the stock markets. Ederington and Lee (1995 and 1993) demonstrate that in these markets, price reactions begin to set in shortly after the publication of macroeconomic data. The main price adjustments take place within only one minute. ". . . Trading profits based on the initial reaction basically disappear within this period," the authors say.[36] Andersen, Bollerslev, Diebold and Vega (2002) reveal how surprising macroeconomic information can influence exchange rates. The rates react abruptly with negative information, provoking much stronger reactions than positive information. In general: Exchange rates respond instantly to the release of economic information.[37]

Maloney and Mulherin (2003) show in a case study on the explosion of the Challenger space shuttle in 1986 that even particularly surprising non-economic news is rapidly processed by the markets: Within thirteen minutes of the agency report about the crash of the space shuttle in the *Dow Jones News Wire*, which was published eight minutes after the explosion, the stocks of several companies involved in the production of the shuttle went down. The price of one particular stock was hit especially hard. While the stock market prices of the other companies quickly recovered, this stock continued to go down in value during the day. It turned out several weeks later that this was the company responsible for the production error that had caused the accident.[38]

4. IRREGULAR PRICE REGULARITIES

Recent studies on the aggregate level of news and price fluctuations clarify that the relationship between markets and the media does not obey to any simple rule: Mitchell and Mulherin (1994) correlated news published in the *Dow Jones News Service* and the *Wall Street Journal* between 1983 and 1990 with stock market prices and trading volumes—more than 750,000 headlines. Their results show a moderate relationship of news variables with trading volumes, but only a weak relationship with stock returns. "While we find a direct, robust relation between Dow Jones news stories and stock market activity," the authors write, "the observed relation is often as weak as that reported in prior research."[39]

Berry and Howe (1994) present similar results: Using *Reuter's News Service* as an example, their study illustrates that the news flow in the course of one trading day follows a typical pattern: The volume of news increases during the first hours of trading, reaches its peak shortly after the close, and abates afterward. Berry and Howe find a similar pattern for stock exchange transactions. The returns, however, do not show any remarkable correlation.[40] Studies carried out by McQueen and Roley (1993), however, show that the effects of macroeconomic news vary with the economic climate— and that they could possibly be stronger than assumed until now: If the economy is already booming, positive news reports seem to provoke negative price reactions, whereas they lead to (weak) positive reactions in a less favorable economic climate.

Depending on the overall market situation, identical news thus seems to provoke different price reactions. This indicates that the state of the market, as well as perceptions and psychological dispositions of market participants, plays a greater role than assumed by advocates of the efficient market hypothesis. Assymetrical price movements in response to comparable news give grounds to believe that investors overreact in some cases and underreact in others. The psychological disposition of the market seems to constitute a framework for behavior within which investors carry out their transactions. This no longer excludes the possibility that prices may divert from their fundamental values. Or, to put it differently: Reactions of the market are sometimes more, sometimes less efficient.

Under certain circumstances, stock market prices (but also prices in other markets) can overreact or underreact. Underreaction means that the average return after a publication is *higher* than the return of the benchmark indexes. In other words, the price reacts to the news with a certain delay, an error which is corrected afterwards through above average returns.

It is only gradually that the news is integrated into stock prices. Overreaction means that the average return after a publication is *lower* than the return of the benchmark index. The price prematurely reacts to the news, an error, which is corrected afterwards with lower returns. The news is integrated too strongly into stock market prices.[41]

Underreactions to the publication of accounting income numbers can be considered well documented: Positive earnings surprises can lead to excess returns and higher trading volume beyond the event day. Several event studies demonstrate that positive surprises lead to excess returns over a period of several months (so-called post-event price drift).[42] This means that in certain cases business news can be followed by successive price changes which correlate, therefore constitute a trend and are, as it seems, economically significant.[43] Cutler, Poterba and Summers (1991) prove positive autocorrelations for a timespan of up to one year for returns in various international markets, including stock, currency and real estate markets: It seems to be true for a broad range of asset classes that excess returns are slightly interrelated.[44]

Chan (2003) demonstrates that abnormal returns can occur after the publication of business news. In his research of market reactions to publications in the news media such as the *Wall Street Journal*, the *Chicago Tribune*, the *New York Times* and the *Washington Post*, it turns out that stock market prices, particularly quotations of smaller companies, can fall behind their benchmark index after the publication of bad news. "It seems to take a long time," Chan states, "for news in headlines to affect prices."[45] If positive information is published, excess returns are less pronounced, but still measurable.[46] To put it differently: (Especially negative) business news (sometimes) has a lasting effect.

Besides underreactions, overreactions have also repeatedly been observed in empirical studies: In their pioneering study on this phenomenon, De Bondt and Thaler (1985) found out that former over-performers turn into losers in the medium term, and vice versa: Undervalued stocks seem to beat previous winning stocks.[47] The authors see the reason for such turnarounds in prices in investors' overreactions. In his book *Irrational Exuberance*, Robert Shiller (2000) mentions the mass media as an important factor in the generation of overreactions: Due to their capacity to arouse attention, Shiller says, the media can create positive feedback and reinforce existent trends—and contribute to the reinforcement of speculative price movements and financial bubbles.[48]

The central result of the studies on overreactions is that stock market prices can show successive (slightly) negative autocorrelations for an event space of several months up to a few years: The initial overreaction is followed by a market price correction, the return decreases and comes closer to the average. Of course, this implies that stock market prices would have to be predictable if these price fluctuations occured systematically and could be attributed to certain behavioral dispositions of the market participants. In so far as the mass media contribute to the "overdrive" in investor behavior by focusing public attention, they have to be taken into consideration as a potential driving force behind such "irrational exuberance."[49]

Barberis, Shleifer and Vishny (1998) draw up a model of mood changes among investors which could cause such fluctuations. They find an explanation in the phenomenon, well-known to psychologists, of people attaching too much significance to information that is particularly striking.[50] Accordingly, a sequence of good or bad news,[51] which already generates increased interest in itself, could induce investors to extrapolate a trend. Overreactions to news, which are followed by a deviation of stock market prices from their fundamental values, can thus be explained. If the news are extraordinarily striking, these exaggerations even seem highly probable. Unobtrusive information, which receives little attention, would accordingly lead to underreactions.[52]

It is therefore theoretically possible that striking media events, in particular, lead to overvaluations among investors and, as a consequence, to overreactions. Barberis, Shleifer and Vishny deduce the following prognosis: "The theory predicts that, holding the weight of information constant, one-time strong news events should generate an overreaction.... For example, stock prices bounced back strongly in the few weeks after the crash of 1987. One interpretation of the crash is that investors overreacted to the news of panic selling by other investors even though there was little fundamental news about security values. Thus the crash was a high-strength, low-weight news event which, according to the theory, should have caused an overreaction."[53]

It is not at all certain that over- and underreactions are "pervasive regularities."[54] What is striking, however, is that price movements, which seemed to be abnormal from the point of view of traditional financial theory, apparently occur with a relatively high frequency.[55] It remains to be seen if they really interfere with the theory. As many authors point out, there is also room for slight anomalies in traditional efficiency concepts.[56] However, unusual interrelations of markets and the media intimate that finance theory has too long followed an oversimplistic formula, in which it philosophized about frictionless information processing. Market activities following strong stimuli coming from the media also show, though, that

5. WORLD EVENTS: THE EFFECTS OF "BIG NEWS"

The effects of major media events on the financial markets represent a litmus test for the prognoses of recent behavioral approaches—a test that they only pass in part. According to the theory, conspicuous news events would have to lead to irrational price fluctuations, due to their increased visibility and following overreactions of many investors (and not to their fundamental information content). In other words: The more visibly an event appears in the media, the stronger price reactions should be, regardless of how significant the event is "in itself." The few empirical studies on the market effects of big media events only provide mixed evidence in this regard.

Fair (2002) for example tried to establish a relationship between major price movements and relevant news for the U.S. stock market between 1982 and 1999. In order to do this, he looked for extraordinary price activities, defined as price changes of more than 0.75 per cent within five minutes, on 4,417 trading days. He found such price reactions on one hundred seventy-nine days. In the following, the archives of four news providers, the *Dow Jones News Service*, the *Associated Press Newswire*, the *New York Times* and the *Wall Street Journal*, were searched for extraordinary media events. The result: Significant events, which could be considered triggers of the market activities, were found for (only) fifty-eight of the one hundred seventy-nine days.[57] On one hundred twenty-one days with strong price fluctuations, there was no important news.

In the first place, the existence of strong price fluctuations despite the absence of corresponding media reports only implies that there must be other reasons apart from the mass media to account for abnormally strong fluctuations on certain days. What is remarkable, however, is the existence of the opposite phenomenon: There are numerous news events which do *not* provoke any unusual price movements—although they seem to be very similar to the news actually moving prices. Fair writes: "There have, for example, been hundreds of important macroeconomic announcements between 1982 and 1999, and only a small fraction have led to a large stock price change. An adequate model would need to explain why . . . particular events . . . led to large price changes, while many other seemingly similar events did not."[58]

The most important study on the financial and economic effects of "big" events underpins these findings: "Many of the largest market movements in recent years have occurred on days when there were no major news events."[59] This result of the study "What Moves Stock Prices" by Cutler, Poterba and Summers (1989) shows the limits of the importance of news (and the events behind them) in explaining the dynamics of financial markets: Even the biggest price changes frequently occur without prior news—which doubtless means that price variance which cannot be explained by fundamental economic factors cannot simply and unambiguously be deduced from external events and the following media coverage either.[60]

Nevertheless, there are numerous examples of far-reaching events in the news—economic policy measures, political events, international conflicts and war—which have substantial effects on the whole market: The Standard & Poor's (S&P) Composite Stock Index, for example, lost 4.37 per cent on the Monday after the Japanese attack on Pearl Harbor. The American declaration of war against Japan on the next day was followed by a loss of 3.23 per cent. The nuclear bomb attack on Nagasaki made a difference of 1.65 per cent. On the announcement of the deployment of Russian nuclear missiles on Cuba in October 1962, the market lost 2.67 per cent. After President Kennedy was assassinated, stocks fell by 2.81 per cent. The biggest plunge occured due to a medical event: After President Eisenhower's heart attack in the fall of 1955, the market fell by 6.62 per cent.[61]

Niederhoffer (1971) states that big but isolated news, which only flashes in the media for one day, provokes fewer price movements than a series of consecutive big news, as they occur in times of international crises. Evidently, consecutive and interrelated big news, like those during the Korean War or the Cuban Missile Crisis, lead to an aggregate effect which makes increased market activities more probable. It is, however, not clear whether this observation supports the theory of Barberis, Shleifer and Vishny that "one-time strong news events should generate an overreaction" or rather calls it into question. It is clear, on the other hand, that big news can bring about overreactions. But how many of those are due to media influence?

In cases of strong price reactions, it is fair to assume that there is a causal relationship with media coverage (and the events behind it). Nevertheless, this cannot be stated without any doubt. The fact that a piece of news is followed by price movements is not conclusive proof of a causal relationship. Pure coincidence could play a role as well. Quite frequently, the direction of the price movement is different from what would be expected with regard to the "direction" of the event: The 1.65 per cent movement after Nagasaki, for instance, was *positive*. The 0.73 per cent change on the day the attempt to liberate American hostages in Iran failed as well. In brief: Big news can cause big price movements—but it is hardly possible to say in advance which, and in what direction.

Niederhoffer (1971) finds a slight indication that events which are usually considered rather positive are more frequently followed by price increases. The other way round, price losses tend to occur more often after media coverage of negative events. However, the difference is minimal: Accordingly, news about peace negotiations are followed by price increases in 58 per cent of all cases, whereas the same happens in only 50 per cent of all cases after reports of hostile negotiations.[62] That these regularities are irregular can easily be seen from the fact that (actually negative) reports about an aggravation of international tensions lead to a price *increase* in 62.5 per cent of all cases and that "extremely bad" news generally tends to bring about price gains.

Even incidents in the same event category do not always produce the same effects. Concerning terrorism: Chen and Siems (2004) demonstrate that "terrorist attacks and military invasions have great potential to effect capital markets around the world in a short period of time."[63] But an analysis of historical examples shows that these effects are highly variable: Sometimes price effects occur, sometimes they do not. Sometimes even price increases can be found, for example, on the day of the Oklahoma City bombing or the attack on the U.S. embassy in Kenya in 1998. It is true, though, that a certain connection between the dimension of the event and the corresponding market activity seems to exist: The fluctuation after September 11th *was* strong. So were price movements after Pearl Harbor or the invasion of Kuwait.

Most of the "big" news does *not* bring about any big and prompt price movements: Only after fifteen out of the forty-nine big events which Cutler, Poterba and Summers identify from 1941 to 1987 follow an index movement of more than 1.5 per cent. Many important events are hardly noticed in stock prices: The gain during the invasion of the Bay of Pigs is only 0.47 per cent. Reacting to the Soviet invasion of Afghanistan, the S&P rose by 0.11 per cent. On the occasion of the assassination attempt on Ronald Reagan, the index only lost 0.27 per cent. The death of U.S. marines in Lebanon in 1983 was a non-event at the stock market with a plus of 0.02 per cent. The Chernobyl nuclear disaster also makes only a small difference of minus 1.06 per cent.[64] Hurricane Andrew, one of the most severe natural disasters to date in the United States was followed by an excess return on the event day of minus 0.8 per cent.[65]

Establishing the actual media effects on market activities is complicated by the structural problem of separating the effects of the events "in themselves" from the effects of the news. Isolating the two aspects can be very difficult. The announcement of a lot of macroeconomic data and their publication in the media, for example, often happen simultaneously. With increasing real-time coverage, events and reports about them will even be less distinguishable in the future. The clearest conclusions can be drawn from two types of cases: Firstly, those in which no abnormal price movements can be observed, even if they are preceded by big events or big news; secondly, those in which strong price movements follow journalistic non-events.

In cases of the first type, which occur quite frequently, it is obvious that many times neither an event nor the coverage of it has an effect. This leads to the logical conclusion that there is no conclusive and systematic relationship between big news and big price movements. From cases of the second type, which are found less frequently but are thus all the more meaningful, the existence of autonomous media effects can be deduced, even if these do not occur systematically. In real life, repeatedly occurring price movements are found following news that has one decisive feature: The news itself is the event, since there is no real event behind it. Reactions to such fictitious media coverage can sometimes turn out to be very strong.[66]

The thesis of the effectiveness of big media events and resulting market overreactions therefore needs considerable qualifications: For the majority of news, no significant price correlations can be found. If they appear, they do so unsystematically. Often, it remains unclear not only whether reactions will occur and how strong they will be, but also in which direction they will go. Cutler, Poterba and Summers (1989) sum up: "For the set of events we analyze, the average absolute market move is 1.46% in contrast to 0.56% over the entire 1941–1987 period. These findings suggest a surprisingly small effect of non-economic news, at least of the type we have identified, on share prices."[67]

These observations result in important conclusions both for financial economics and for communication research of media impacts on the financial markets: The obvious "ineffectiveness" of many big media events casts serious doubt on the theory that the conspicuousness of a piece of news alone explains behavioral overreactions. Evidently, other factors have to be taken into account, which condition the effects of news on market activities and the way they manifest themselves. A simple one-factor model, which derives the price reaction from the "strength" of the news, does not do justice to the problem. "Big" news does provoke "big" market reactions—but often, it simply doesn't.

Dismissing the cases in which media effects do occur as negligible "anomalies," however, would underrate their importance. News has direct and short-term as well as indirect and long-term market effects, a quantifiable percentage of which is due to the specific mechanisms of information transmission in the mass media. This observation contradicts the idea of ineffective media which is still popular in parts of media effect research.[68] The immediacy of real-time communication prevents longer thinking and the absorption of public reactions through interpersonal communication. Especially in the financial markets, where reaction speed is essential, this can lead to rapid mood swings.

In these cases, social networks do not lead to a relativization, objectivization or attenuation of public reactions to media coverage. On the contrary: They can even have a reinforcing effect, making mutual psychological "infection" possible and facilitating collective panic attacks. Advisers cannot serve as a stabilizing factor either: In case of surprising news events, "experts" and "opinion leaders" look for advice themselves. More often than not, they succumb to the immediate power of the events or pursue their own interests in the market.

It is thus correct to refrain from monocausal explanations which try to deduce market reactions from media influence alone. Rather, it is a specific constellation of factors which decides the probability of over- or underreactions in price formation. If such a process gets going, the media is far from just playing the role of an amplifier. Rather, it is able to contribute to a qualitative turn of market acitivites to another level of activity. Under certain circumstances, events and their presentation in the news can thus decisively shape the character of processes of price formation. In brief: Frequently, news does not lead to noticeable market reactions—but sometimes, they do precisely this.

6. SUMMARY

Price formation in the financial markets is a complex function of diverse factors whose combination and weight vary with time. The nature of this systemic process makes it impossible to definitely determine to what degree different causes have an effect on prices. Individual factors have more or less impact, depending on their specific combination and the actual state of the system. It is not only the specific mixture in which certain variables determine market activities that is unclear. So far, not even the number and the character of the factors which play a role at all have been established, let alone the intensity of the impact they have on prices.[69] Accordingly, the success rate in explaining price movements greatly varies—even with hindsight.[70]

Roll (1988) shows that only 40 per cent of the price variation of an average stock can be accounted for by general economic influences, industry specific conditions and company news releases. That means that a large percentage of average price movements *cannot* be explained by news. Other important factors which have not been identified so far must play their part as well. Many things which are relevant for price movements happen behind the screen of information available to the public—we just do not know exactly what they are. This relativizes the significance of news in the mass media: It only represents one among several factors that play a role. A multitude of empirical studies shows that news does not lead to any permanent and stable, delayed price reactions (and thus cannot systematically be turned into cash either).

The attempt to convert news published in the mass media into short-term gains is therefore of little use to investors. Market participants anticipate new information, insiders use their information lead—but most of the time, the information content is exhausted *before* the public comes into play. In many cases, there is *no* immediate relationship between media contents and price movements. Slight underreactions do repeatedly occur in different asset classes. Sporadic overreactions due to media coverage and subsequent price corrections are also demonstrable. With regard to the aggregative level, however, it is very difficult to make a generalizing statement: Sometimes news does show an immediate effect, sometimes it does not.

In case of big media events and reports about incidents of global significance, especially international crises, on the other hand, there is an increased probability of abnormal price movements. The conspicuousness of these events seems to reinforce the tendency of many investors to react too strongly to prominently placed information. Especially consecutive news broadcasts, which mutually reinforces each other's effects, can lead to corresponding overreactions in the financial markets. With the current state of knowledge, though, it is hardly possible in these cases as well to forecast accurately and ex ante when abnormal price effects will occur, how strong they will be, and in which direction they will go. If effects do occur, the relationship is sporadic and unsystematic and disappears as soon as it is discovered.

But is it always discovered at once? The possibility of long-term interrelations between markets and the media and subsequent price movements away from fundamental values is admissible or not depends on the answer to this question. Experiences with the 1987 stock market crash and the internet bubble of the "New Economy" indicate that fits of collective panic or euphoria repeatedly occur in the financial markets—and therefore in stock prices which reflect a limited market rationality. If coolly calculating actors try to derive speculative gains from trend following behavior, an essential regulative element is lost. It is conceivable that extreme price movements, in particular, persist for a certain period of time, even if those who know better do not take a different direction because the market risk is too high or because they hope for a profit.

There is no doubt that the media as generators of attention possess the potential to contribute to the "overdrive" of mass behavior: In times of a greatly increased media range, economic and noneconomic events are today broadcast everywhere and in real-time. The competitive situation on the media market intensifies the exaggeration of the contents and an increase in their emotional appeal through prominent placement and an eye-catching presentation of selected issues. The induction of an emotional public response in order to generate feedback effects constitutes a priority of today's mass media, and also of the business media. There is thus absolutely no doubt that the news flow of the mass media does not follow a random pattern. A homogenization of the market response is thereby certainly not prevented.

NOTES

1. "As An Attack Unfolds, a Struggle to Provide Vivid Images to Homes." In: *New York Times*, 09/12/2001; Schuster (2001a and 2001b).

2. Figures in: "Attack Shuts Down U.S. Markets and Causes Global Declines." In: *Wall Street Journal*, 09/12/2001.

3. Organization for Economic Co-operation and Development (OECD) (2002).

4. Chen and Siems (2002).

5. Nacos (2002) shows that the dissemination and intensification of their actions over the media is part of the calculation of terrorists. Images of spectacular violent actions fit the pattern of news factors and narrative conventions of the media, a fact which makes sure that terrorist actions receive sufficient publicity. "As long as terrorists offer visuals and sound bites, drama, threats, and human interest tales, the news media will report—and actually over-report. . . ." Nacos (2002), 4.

6. For more details see Schuster (2001c), 127–153.

7. "Börsenjournalist verurteilt." In: *Frankfurter Allgemeine Zeitung*, 08/31/2002; "Erstes Insiderurteil gegen einen Journalisten." In: *Süddeutsche Zeitung*, 08/31/2002; "Der dubiose Guru von Kulmbach." In: *Der Spiegel*, 07/02/2002; "Im Börsenbetrugsfall Opel kommt es wohl zur Anklage." In: *Süddeutsche Zeitung*, 10/26/2001; "Nun ist die Harmonie dahin. Egbert Prior und die Haffa-Brüder stehen sich vor Gericht gegenüber." In: *Süddeutsche Zeitung*, 01/17/2001; "Wirtschaftskrimineller oder Opfer der Justiz?" In: *Süddeutsche Zeitung*, 01/10/2001; Thomas Schuster, "Schwacher Charakter, volle Börse. Insider-Handel:

Der erste Finanzjournalist steht vor der Anklage." In: *Frankfurter Allgemeine Zeitung*, 11/02/2000; "Riesen-Börsen-Betrug." In: *Bild*, 10/31/2000; Thomas Schuster, "Wie man der Börse aufspielt. Ad hoc, ad hoc: Pressemeldungen narren die Wirtschaftspresse." In: *Frankfurter Allgemeine Zeitung*, 09/19/2000; "Insiderhandel: Schwer in den Griff zu kriegen." In: *Wirtschaftswoche*, 08/24/2000; "Aufregung um Börsenguru Bernd Förtsch." In: *Süddeutsche Zeitung*, 08/17/2000; "Die rechten Artikel zur rechten Zeit." In: *Süddeutsche Zeitung*, 12/17/1999.

8. "Macht und Ohnmacht der Börsenpolizei." In: *Frankfurter Allgemeine Zeitung*, 01/18/2001; "Egbert Prior wegen Kursmanipulation angeklagt." In: *Frankfurter Allgemeine Zeitung*, 01/10/2001; "Neuer Ärger um '3Sat-Börse.'" In: *Der Spiegel*, 05/29/2000; "Wohl kein Verfahren rund um Consors." In: *Süddeutsche Zeitung*, 01/17/2000; "Zocken an der Börse wird zum Volkssport." In: *Süddeutsche Zeitung*, 08/27/1999; "Neuer Verdacht." In: *Der Spiegel*, 08/16/1999; "Insider-Verdacht gegen Kunden von Consors." In: *Süddeutsche Zeitung*, 08/13/1999; "Anklage gegen 3sat-Börsenspezialisten." In: *Neue Zürcher Zeitung*, 11/21/1998; "Der Aktien-Berater Egbert Prior: Zuschauen und Reichwerden?" In: *Süddeutsche Zeitung*, 07/07/1998.

9. Kladroba and von der Lippe (2001) examined 5,985 recommendations which were published between January and June 2001 in the following magazines: *DM*, *Börse Online*, *Focus Money*, *Geldidee*, *Telebörse* and *Aktien Research*. Only every tenth stock review recommended a sale. The result in detail: 66.9% buy, 22.2% hold, 10.9% sell. Cf. Madrick (2001 and 1999).

10. Cf. exemplarily Friedrichsen (2001) and Gavin (1998).

11. For an introduction to the theory of efficient markets cf. Beechey, Gruen and Vickery (2000) and Dimson and Mussavian (2000).

12. For an introduction to the theory of behavioral finance cf. Barberis and Thaler (2002), Shiller (1999) and Thaler (1999).

13. Fama (1970), 383.

14. Fama (1970), 387 emphasizes that the random walk model is not identical to the efficient market theory, but represents a specific version of it.

15. The efficient market hypothesis is based on the view of conventional neoclassical economics, according to which economic subjects are rational, utility-maximizing agents. Decision-making processes therefore follow an expected utility function, they are based on a matter-of-fact cost-benefit analysis. Advocates of this view readily admit that not all subjects behave rationally. They say it is sufficient if this applies to a leading group which makes sure that prices are correct.

16. Even the advocates of the efficient market hypothesis do not deny that markets are never 100 per cent efficient. Fama (1970) points out that the theory that prices always reflect all available information is an extreme null hypothesis ("We do not expect it to be literally true."). He also gives different examples of—in his view not economically significant—persistence in price movements. In his view, inefficiencies are most obvious in the possibility of using advantages from insider information. Grossman und Stiglitz (1980) argue that it has to be possible for informed

market actors to compensate the costs of their information research through abnormal returns. For empirical findings on Germany cf. Möller (1985).

17. That means, as Krämer (2001), 1269 puts it: "An efficient market does not look back." Dimson and Mussavian (2000), 962 f. write: "The theory involves defining an efficient market as one in which trading on available information fails to provide an abnormal profit."

18. Behavioral finance gets its most important impetus from the prospect theory by Kahneman and Tversky (1979), from the theory of cognitive dissonance by Festinger (1957) as well as from studies on overconfidence by Fischhoff, Slovic and Lichtenstein (1977).

19. Shiller (1984 and 1981) and Summers (1986).

20. Shiller (1999).

21. Weischenberg (2001), 292 ff.

22. Cf. Gerke (2000) and Wolff (2000).

23. Weischenberg (2001), 293 writes: "A lot of German media contributed in an ethically problematic way to the creation of a myth of wealth without work through the 'new economy.' Stock exchange transactions were presented as a huge spectacle of the 'fun society,' economic risks were played down and and profit prospects euphorized. A kind of 'investor journalism' emerged as a subdivision of business coverage. What was particularly conspicuous were some journalists who did not have any problem with working parallelly in journalism and in investment counseling. By mingling journalism and business, they act irresponsibly in two ways: With regard to the media public, which is unclear about collisions of interest and with regard to private investors by making possibly negligent or even wrong promises."

24. Fama, Fisher, Jensen and Roll (1969), 20.

25. Fama, Fisher, Jensen and Roll (1969), 18.

26. Ball and Brown (1968a), 176 write: "The annual income report does not rate highly as a timely medium, since most of its content (about 85 to 90 per cent) is captured by more prompt media which perhaps include interim reports."

27. Dimson and Mussavian (2000), 962.

28. Patell and Wolfson (1984), 224.

29. Gerke, Oerke and Seatner use daily data, not ticker data, which is why they cannot give any information on the exact adjustment speed of the stock prices.

30. Röder (2000b), 16.

31. May (1994), 345.

32. Conrad, Cornell and Landsman (2002).

33. Schwert (1981) writes: "For the days after the announcement, the market seems to react slowly to the announcement of unexpected inflation, but the magnitude of the reaction is so small that there is probably no opportunity for a profitable trading strategy." Schwert (1981), 28.

34. Jain (1988), 228.

35. The studies quoted at this point refer to the primary publications of the relevant authorities, the Federal Reserve Bank, the Bureau of Labor Statistics etc., not

to the secondary publications in the mass media. Since the introduction of finance television and above all the Internet with its real-time information, primary and secondary publication are increasingly taking place simultaneously.

36. Ederington and Lee (1993), 1189.

37. Almeida, Goodhart and Payne (1998) and Goodhart, Hall, Henry and Pesaran (1993) arrive at similar results. Balduzzi, Elton and Green (2001) present comparable findings for the bond market: Price adjustment due to macroeconomic information occurs within one minute after the publication of the data.

38. Blose, Bornkamp, Brier, Brown and Frederick (1996) come to very similar results. According to their figures on all National Aeronautics & Space Administration (NASA) contractors, the stocks of those whose turnovers were most dependent on the shuttle production reacted significantly. Most seriously concerned was the price of Morton Thokiol, the manufacturer of the defective sealing rings.

39. Mitchell and Mulherin (1994), 949.

40. In a study of the effects of cover stories published in newspapers, Chan, Chui und Kwok (2001) find similar results as Berry and Howe and Mitchell and Mulherin: They find a moderate relationship between news and trading volumes, with barely detectable effects on returns. Interestingly, Chan et al. find that economic news stimulates trading volume, whereas political news tends to go along with a reduction in the volume of trade. The authors attribute this to the poorer quality of political news with regard to price forecasts which can be deduced from them.

41. For a good starting point for literature on the predictability of stock prices on the basis of short-term autocorrelations cf. French and Roll (1986) and Lo and MacKinlay (1988).

42. For an overview of the research results cf. Bernard (1992).

43. Cf. Pritamani and Singal (2001).

44. Cutler, Poterba and Summers (1991), 536 write: "The estimated monthly autocorrelations are not only statistically but also substantively significant, often implying negative expected returns." Fama (1991), 1602 points out that it should not be surprising in view of the large number of empirical event studies if some of them come across anomalies such as the post-announcement drift. In his view, it is important to keep in mind that event studies provide the clearest evidence in favor of market efficiency (not least because they are least troubled by methodological problems like the joint-hypothesis problem). However, it is difficult to thereby refute the point made by Cutler et al. that the price patterns they document represent statistic regularities in a variety of markets. Then again, they make the following restriction: "While these findings appear in many markets, they are not universal." Cutler, Poterba and Summers (1991), 535.

45. Chan (2003), 255.

46. Daniel and Titman (2003) find no evidence of such an underreaction.

47. Conrad and Kaul (1993) provide evidence for the fact that De Bondt and Thaler's results were generated through methodological errors.

48. Shiller (2000), 71–95.
49. On overreactions cf. also Liu (2000) and Dharan and Ikenberry (1995).
50. Cf. Griffin and Tversky (1992) and Shoemaker (1996).
51. In their model, Barberis, Shleifer and Vishny use a generalized concept of news, which does not distinguish between primary information (for example press conferences) and secondary information (for example newspaper articles).
52. For an alternative model which seeks to explain over- and underreactions with the help of the concepts of *overconfidence* and *biased self-attribution* cf. Daniel, Hirshleifer and Subrahmanyam (1998).
53. Barberis, Shleifer and Vishny (1998), 28f.
54. As Barberis, Shleifer and Vishny (1998) put it.
55. Behavioral Finance literature has researched a number of other unusual systematic price effects, but those are not of immediate interest in our context of examining the relationship between markets and the media. They include: the small firm effect, the value effect, and numerous "seasonal effects," such as the Monday effect, the turn-of-the-month effect or the January effect. For an introduction cf. Shleifer (2000) and Lo and MacKinlay (1999).
56. Cf. Exemplarily Dimson and Mussavian (2000), 963: "To make sense, the concept of market efficiency has to admit the possibility of minor market inefficiencies." Cf. note 16.
57. Fairs findings show that the majority of the news which is followed by a price movement is directly or indirectly related to questions of monetary policy. With five out of fifty-eight events, the Iraq conflict also has a strong influence.
58. Fair (2002), 719.
59. Cutler, Poterba and Summers (1989), 4f. Similarly Shiller (2000), 78f.
60. Cutler, Poterba and Summers (1989), 4f. Similarly Shiller (2000), 78f.
61. Cutler, Poterba and Summers (1989), 8.
62. Niederhoffer (1971), 211.
63. Chen and Siems (2004), 349.
64. Cutler, Poterba and Summers (1989), 8.
65. Chen and Siems (2002b), 6.
66. For detailed information see chapter 3.
67. Cutler, Poterba and Summers (1989), 8f.
68. Cf. Schenk (2003), Burkart (2002), 215–219; Jäckel (1999), 64–85, 99–131.
69. Cf. Brown (1999) and Roll (1988).
70. Andersen, Bollerslev, Diebold and Vega (2002), 4 write: "How is news about fundamentals incorporated into asset prices? The topic confronted by this question—characterization of the price discovery process—is of basic importance to all of financial economics. Unfortunately, it is also one of the least well understood issues." Roll (1988), 541 writes: "The immaturity of our science is illustrated by the conspicuous lack of predictive content about some of its most intensely interesting phenomena, particularly *changes* in asset prices."

REFERENCES

Almeida, Alvaro, Charles Goodhart und Richard Payne. 1998. "The Effects of Macroeconomic 'News' on High Frequency Exchange Rate Behavior." In: *Journal of Financial and Quantitative Analysis* Vol. 33, No. 3: 383–408.

Almeida, Alvaro, Charles Goodhart and Richard Payne. 1998. "The Effects of Macroeconomic 'News' on High Frequency Exchange Rate Behavior." In: *Journal of Financial and Quantitative Analysis* Vol. 33, No. 3: 383–408.

Andersen, Torben G., Tim Bollerslev, Francis X. Diebold and Clara Vega. 2002. "Micro Effects of Macro Announcements. Real-Time Price Discovery in Foreign Exchange?" NBER Working Paper W8959.

Arnott, Richard, Bruce Greenwald and Joseph E. Stiglitz. 1993. "Information and Economic Efficiency." Cambridge: National Bureau of Economic Research, Working Paper No. 4533.

Balduzzi, Pierluigi, Edwin J. Elton and T. Clifton Green. 2001. "Economic News and Bond Prices. Evidence From the U.S. Treasury Market." In: *Journal of Financial and Quantitative Analysis* Vol. 36, No. 4: 523–543.

Ball, Ray and Philip Brown. 1968. "An Empirical Evaluation of Accounting Income Numbers." In: *Journal of Accounting Research* Vol. 6, No. 2: 159–178.

Bamber, Linda Smith. 1986. "The Information Content of Annual Earnings Releases. A Trading Approach." In: *Journal of Accounting Research* Vol. 24, No. 1: 40–56.

Barberis, Nicholas and Richard Thaler. 2002. "A Survey of Behavioral Finance." NBER Working Paper W9222.

Barberis, Nicholas, Andrei Shleifer and Robert Vishny. 1998. "A Model of Investor Sentiment." In: *Journal of Financial Economics* Vol. 49, No. 3: 307–343.

Beaver, William H. 1968. "The Information Content of Annual Earnings Announcements." In: *Journal of Accounting Research* Vol. 6 (Supplement): 67–92.

Beechey, Meredith, David Gruen and James Vickery. 2000. "The Efficient Market Hypothesis. A Survey." Reserve Bank of Australia, Research Discussion Paper 2000–01.

Bernard, Victor L. 1992. "Stock Price Reactions to Earnings Announcements." In: Richard H. Thaler (Ed.), *Advances in Behavioral Finance*. New York: Russell Sage Foundation: 303–340.

Berry, Thomas D. and Keith M. Howe. 1994. "Public Information Arrival." In: *Journal of Finance* Vol. 49, No. 4: 1331–1346.

Blose, Laurence E., Robin Bornkamp, Marci Brier, Kendis Brown and Jerry Frederick. 1996. "Catastrophic Events, Contagion, and Stock Market Efficiency. The Case of The Space Shuttle Challenger." In: *Review of Financial Economics* Vol. 5, No. 2: 117–129.

Brown, William O. 1999. "Inside Information and Public News. R2 and Beyond." Claremont: Claremont Colleges Working Paper 1999–26.

Burkhart, Roland. 2002. *Kommunikationswissenschaft. Grundlagen und Problemfelder.* Wien: Böhlau.

Chan, Wesley S. 2003. "Stock Price Reactions to News and No-News. Drift and Reversal After Headlines." In: *Journal of Financial Economics* Vol. 70: 223–260.

Chan, Yue-cheong, Andy C.W. Chui and Chuck C.Y. Kwok. 2001. "The Impact of Salient Political and Economic News on the Trading Activity." In: *Pacific Basin Finance Journal* Vol. 9, No. 3: 195–217.

Chen, Andrew H. and Thomas F. Siems. 2004. "The Effects of Terrorism on Global Capital Markets." In: *European Journal of Political Economy* Vol. 20, No. 2: 349–366.

Chen, Andrew H. and Thomas F. Siems. 2002b. "An Empirical Analysis of the Capital Markets' Response to Cataclysmic Events." Dallas: Southern Methodist University, Cox School of Business, Working Paper.

Conrad, Jennifer, Bradford Cornell and Wayne R. Landsman. 2002. "When is Bad News Really Bad News?" In: *The Journal of Finance* Vol. 57, No. 6: 2507–2532.

Conrad, Jennifer and Gautam Kaul. 1993. "Long-Term Market Overreaction or Biases in Computed Returns?" In: *Journal of Finance* Vol. 48, No. 1: 39–64.

Cutler, David M., James M. Poterba and Lawrence H. Summers. 1991. "Speculative Dynamics." In: *The Review of Economic Studies* Vol. 58: 529–546.

Cutler, David M., James M. Poterba and Lawrence H. Summers. 1989. "What Moves Stock Prices?" In: *Journal of Portfolio Management* Vol. 15, No. 3: 4–12.

Daniel, Kent, David Hirshleifer and Avanidhar Subrahmanyam. 1998. "Investor Psychology and Security Market Under- and Overreactions." In: *The Journal of Finance* Vol. 53, No. 6: 1839–1885.

Daniel, Kent and Sheridan Titman. 2003. "Market Reactions to Tangible and Intangible Information." Austin: University of Texas, College of Business Administration, Working Paper.

DeBondt, Werner F.M. and Richard H. Thaler. 1985. "Does the Stock Market Overreact?" In: *Journal of Finance* Vol. 40, No. 3: 793–808.

Dharan, Bala and David Ikenberry. 1995. "The Long-run Negative Drift of Post-Listing Stock Returns." In: *Journal of Finance* Vol. 50, No. 5: 1547–1574.

Dimson, Elroy and Massoud Mussavian. 2000. "Market Efficiency." In: Shri Bhagwan Dahiya (Hrsg.), *The Current State of Business Disciplines.* Rohtak: Spellbound: 959–970.

Ederington, Louis H. and Jae Ha Lee. 1993. "How Markets Process Information. News Releases and Volatility." In: *Journal of Finance* Vol. 48, No. 4: 1161–1191.

Ederington, Louis H. and Jae Ha Lee. 1995. "The Short-Run Dynamics of the Price Adjustment to New Information." In: *Journal of Financial and Quantitative Analysis* Vol. 30, No. 1: 117–134.

Fair, Ray C. 2002. "Events that Shook the Market." In: *Journal of Business* Vol. 75, No. 4: 713–732.

Fama, Eugene F. 1991. "Efficient Capital Markets: II." In: *Journal of Finance* Vol. 46, No. 5 (December): 1575–1617.
———. 1970. "Efficient Capital Markets. A Review of Theory and Empirical Work." In: *Journal of Finance* Vol. 25, No. 2: 383–417.
Fama, Eugene F., Lawrence Fisher, Michael C. Jensen and Richard Roll. 1969. "The Adjustment of Stock Prices to New Information." In: *International Economic Review* Vol. 10, No. 1: 1–21.
Festinger, Leon. 1957. *A Theory of Cognitive Dissonance.* Stanford: Stanford University Press.
Fischhoff, Baruch, Paul Slovic and Sarah Lichtenstein. 1977. "Knowing With Uncertainty. The Appropriateness of Extreme Confidence." In: *Journal of Experimental Psychology. Human Perception and Performance.* Vol. 3, No. 4: 552–564.
French, Kenneth R. and Richard Roll. 1986. "Stock Return Variances. The Arrival of Information and the Reaction of Traders." In: *Journal of Financial Economics* Vol. 17, No. 1: 5–26.
Friedrichsen, Mike. 2001. *Sind Wirtschaftsthemen wahlentscheidend? Eine theoretische und empirische Analyse zum Spannungsfeld Wirtschaft, Politik und Medien.* Stuttgart: Fachhochschule, Stuttgarter Beiträge zur Medienwirtschaft.
Gavin, Neil T. (Ed.). 1998. *The Economy, Media and Public Knowledge.* London: Leicester University Press.
Gerke, Wolfgang. 2000. "Mißbrauch der Medien zur Aktienkursbeeinflussung." In: Lothar Rolke and Volker Wolff (Eds.), *Finanzkommunikation. Kurspflege durch Meinungspflege. Die neuen Spielregeln am Aktienmarkt.* Frankfurt a.M.: F.A.Z.-Institut: 151–170.
Gerke, Wolfgang, Marc Oerke and Arnd Sentner. 1997. "Der Informationsgehalt von Dividendenänderungen auf dem deutschen Aktienmarkt." In: *Die Betriebswirtschaft* Vol. 57, No. 6: 810–822.
Goodhart, Charles A.E., Steven G. Hall, S.G. Brian HeNoy and Bahram Pesaran. 1993. "News Effects in a High-Frequency Model of the Sterling-Dollar Exchange Rate." In: *Journal of Applied Econometrics* Vol. 8, No. 1: 1–13.
Griffin, D. and A. Tversky. 1992. "The Weighing of Evidence and the Determinants of Confidence." In: *Cognitive Psychology* Vol. 24: 411–435.
Grossman, Sanford J. and Joseph E. Stiglitz. 1980. "On the Impossibility of Informationally Efficient Markets." In: *American Economic Review* Vol. 70, No. 3: 393–408.
Jäckel, Michael. 1999. *Medienwirkungen. Ein Studienbuch zur Einführung.* Wiesbaden: Westdeutscher Verlag.
Jain, Prem C. 1988. "Response of Hourly Stock Prices and Trading Volume to Economic News." In: *Journal of Business* Vol. 61, No. 2: 219–231.
Kahneman, Daniel and Amos Tversky. 1979. "Prospect Theory. An Analysis of Decision Under Risk." In: *Econometrica* Vol. 47, No. 2: 263–291.

Krämer, Walter. 2001. "Kapitalmarkteffizienz." In: *Handwörterbuch des Bank- und Finanzwesens*. 3rd edition. Stuttgart: Schäffer-Poeschel: 1267–1274.

Lamb, Reinhold P. 1995. "An Exposure-Based Analysis of Property-Liability Insurer Stock Values Around Hurricane Andrew." In: *Journal of Risk and Insurance* Vol. 62, No. 1: 11–123.

Liu, Quiao. 2000. "How Good is Good News? Technology Depth, Book-to-Market Ratios, and Innovative Events." Los Angeles: University of California, Department of Economics, Working Paper.

Lo, Andrew W. and A. Craig MacKinlay. 1999. *A Non-Random Walk Down Wall Street*. Princeton: Princeton University Press.

Lo, Andrew W. and A. Craig MacKinlay. 1988. "Stock Market Prices Do Not Follow Random Walks. Evidence From a Simple Specification Test." In: *Review of Financial Studies* Vol. 1, No. 1: 41–66.

Madrick, Jeff. 2001. "The Business Media and the New Economy." Research Paper R-24. Cambridge: The Joan Shorenstein Center on the Press, Politics and Public Policy, John F. Kennedy School of Government, Harvard University.

———. 1999. "Press Coverage of America's Changing Financial Institutions." Money, Markets and the News, Monograph No. 2. Cambridge: The Joan Shorenstein Center on the Press, Politics and Public Policy, John F. Kennedy School of Government, Harvard University.

Maloney, Michael T. and J. Harold Mulherin. 2003. "The Complexity of Price Discovery in an Efficient Market. The Stock Market Reaction to the Challenger Crash." In: *Journal of Corporate Finance* Vol. 9, No. 4: 453–479.

May, Axel. 1994. *Pressemeldungen und Aktienindizes*. Kiel: Vauk.

McQueen, Grant and V. Vance Roley. 1993. "Stock Prices, News, and Business Conditions." In: *Review of Financial Studies* Vol. 6, No. 3: 683–707.

Mitchell, Mark L. and J. Harold Mulherin. 1994. "The Impact of Public Information on the Stock Market." In: *Journal of Finance* Vol. 49, No. 3: 923–950.

Möller, Hans Peter. 1985. "Die Informationseffizienz des deutschen Aktienmarktes. Eine Zusammenfassung und Analyse empirischer Untersuchungen." In: *Zeitschrift für betriebswirtschaftliche Forschung* Vol. 37, No. 6: 500–518.

Nacos, Brigitte L. 2002. *Mass-Mediated Terrorism. The Central Role of the Media in Terrorism and Counterterrorism*. New York: Rowman & Littlefield.

Niederhoffer, Victor. 1971. "The Analysis of World Events and Stock Prices." In: *Journal of Business* Vol. 44, No. 2: 193–219.

OECD. 2002. "Economic Consequences of Terrorism." Paris: OECD, Economics Department Working Papers No. 334.

Patell, James M. and Mark A. Wolfson. 1984. "The Intraday Speed of Adjustment of Stock Prices to Earnings and Dividend Announcements." In: *Journal of Financial Economics* Vol. 13: 223–252.

Pearce, Douglas K. and V. Vance Roley. 1985. "Stock Prices and Economic News." In: *Journal of Business* Vol. 58, No. 1: 49–67.

Pritamani, Mahesh and Vijay Singal. 2001. "Return Predictability Following Large Price Changes and Information Releases." In: *Journal of Banking and Finance* Vol. 25: 631–656.

Röder, Klaus. 2000a. "Die Informationswirkung von Ad hoc-Meldungen." In: *Zeitschrift für Betriebswirtschaft* Vol. 70, No. 5: 567–593.

———. 2000b. "Intraday Kurswirkungen bei Ad hoc-Meldungen." Münster: Westfälische Wilhelms-Universität Münster, Arbeitspapiere der betrieblichen Finanzwirtschaft.

Roll, Richard. 1988. "R2." In: *Journal of Finance* Vol. 43, No. 2: 541–566.

Samuelson, Paul. 1965. "Proof That Properly Anticipated Prices Fluctuate Randomly." In: *Industrial Management Review* Vol. 6: 41–49.

Schenk, Michael. 2003. "Media Effects Research 2002. State of the Art." In: Angela Schorr, William Campbell and Michael Schenk (Eds.), *Communication Research and Media Science in Europe*. Berlin: Mouton de Gruyter: 201–214.

Schuster, Thomas. 2001a. "Phantom des Terrors. Die Gewalt im Zeitalter ihrer medialen Potenzierbarkeit." In: *Frankfurter Allgemeine Zeitung*, 18.9.2001.

———. 2001b. "Mediale Mobilmachung. Nach den Selbstmord-Anschlägen verkündeten die Medien in seltener Einigkeit: ‚Es ist Krieg!'" In: *Message. Internationale Fachzeitschrift für Journalismus* No. 4 (October): 20–25.

———. 2001c. *Die Geldfalle. Wie Medien und Banken die Anleger zu Verlierern machen*. Reinbek: Rowohlt.

———. 2000a. "Zwischen Boom und Crash." In: *Message. Internationale Fachzeitschrift für Journalismus* No. 3 (July): 10–17.

———. 2000b. "Schwacher Charakter, volle Börse. Insider-Handel: Der erste Finanzjournalist steht vor der Anklage." In: *Frankfurter Allgemeine Zeitung*, 2.11.2000.

———. 2000c. "Wie man der Börse aufspielt. Ad hoc, ad hoc: Pressemeldungen narren die Wirtschaftspresse." In: *Frankfurter Allgemeine Zeitung*, 19.9.2000.

Schwert, G. William. 1981. "The Adjustment of Stock Prices to Information About Inflation." In: *Journal of Finance* Vol. 36, No. 1: 15–29.

Shiller, Robert J. 2000. *Irrational Exuberance*. Princeton: Princeton University Press.

———. 1999. "Human Behavior and the Efficiency of the Financial System." In: John B. Taylor and Michael Woodford (Hrsg.), *Handbook of Macroeconomics*. Vol. 1. Amsterdam: North Holland: 1305–1340.

———. 1984. "Stock Prices and Social Dynamics." In: *Brookings Papers on Economic Activity* Vol. 2: 457–498.

———. 1981. "Do Stock Prices Move Too Much to be Justified by Subsequent Changes in Dividends?" In: *American Economic Review* Vol. 71, No. 3: 421–436.

Shleifer, Andre. 2000. *Inefficient Markets. An Introduction to Behavioral Finance*. New York: Oxford University Press.

Shoemaker, P. J. 1996. "Hardwired for News. Using Biological and Cultural Evolution to Explain the Surveillance Function." In: *Journal of Communication* Vol. 46, No. 3: 32–47.

Stice, Earl K. 1991. "The Market Reaction to 10-K and 10-Q Filings and to Subsequent The Wall Street Journal Earnings Announcements." In: *The Accounting Review* Vol. 66, No. 1: 42–55.

Summers, Lawrence H. 1986. "Does the Stock Market Rationally Reflect Fundamental Values?" In: *Journal of Finance* Vol. 41, No. 3: 591–601.

Thaler, Richard H. 1999. "The End of Behavioral Finance." In: *Financial Analysts Journal* Vol. 55, No. 6: 12–17.

Weischenberg, Siegfried. 2001. *Nachrichten-Journalismus. Anleitungen und Qualitäts-Standards für die Medienpraxis*. Wiesbaden: Westdeutscher Verlag.

Wolff, Volker. 2000. "Garanten des Vertrauens? Die besondere Verantwortung von Finanzjournalisten." In: Lothar Rolke and Volker Wolff (Eds.), *Finanzkommunikation. Kurspflege durch Meinungspflege. Die neuen Spielregeln am Aktienmarkt*. Frankfurt a.M.: F.A.Z.-Institut: 96–106.

Woodruff, Catherine S. and A.J. Senchack. 1988. "Intradaily Price-Volume Adjustments of New York Stock Exchange (NYSE) Stocks to Unexpected Earnings." In: *Journal of Finance* Vol. 43, No. 2: 467–491

Woodruff, Catherine S. und A.J. Senchack. 1988. "Intradaily Price-Volume Adjustments of New York Stock Exchange (NYSE) Stocks to Unexpected Earnings." In: *Journal of Finance* Vol. 43, No. 2: 467–491.

MACRO

A widely held belief in financial economics suggests that stock prices always adequately reflect all available information. Price movements away from fundamentals are assumed to occur infrequently, if at all. "False" prices are supposed to be corrected by the counteractions of "rational" investors reestablishing equilibrium. However, empirical evidence of widespread irrationality among investors, as well as theoretical insights into the properties of complex systems, suggests that this view is too static. In fact, it can be shown that under certain conditions dynamic disequilibria have a considerable probability of being "locked in." The mass media plays no mean role in this: By conditioning trend-following behavior and fostering coordination among large numbers of investors, the media can help bring about such destabilizing moves. Media attention can induce positive feedback by increasing the level of excess noise in the market while decreasing the number of perceived behavioral options. Meta-communication thus generated is a prime source of instability in financial markets.

3

META-COMMUNICATION AND MARKET DYNAMICS

A sensation seems to be in the making. "Within a year, if all goes well, the first cancer patient will be injected with two new drugs that can eradicate any type of cancer, with no obvious side effects and no drug resistance—in mice."[1] This breathtaking news is reported by the *New York Times* on the front page of its Sunday issue. Renowned cancer experts, among them a Nobel Prize laureate, are said to be "electrified" by the results. Whereas existing drugs were only able to slow down growth, the new substances are said to lead to the complete eradication of tumors. The company that holds the licence for the active substances is mentioned as well: Entremed. The stock price of the small biotechnology company reacted immediately. It increased by 600 per cent.

The news is spectacular and exciting. But it is not new. The *New York Times* itself had reported about the new therapy for tumors in animals in an article half a year earlier.[2] The first text already contained all ingredients of the sensational cover story: the ground-breaking research results; enthusiastic comments from experts; and the name of the licensee: Entremed. Cable News Network (CNN) and *CNBC* also cover the story. These reports are based on research results published in *Nature* magazine—the original source about the successful elimination of malignant melanomas in mice.[3] In brief: The information which is presented in the spectacular *Times* cover story half a year later is, strictly speaking, old hat.

All the more surprising is the sudden and immense increase of the Entremed stock: 600 per cent. The *New York Times* was obviously surprised about the effect of its own coverage and nervously backed out.[4] Financial economists were amazed by the stock price reaction to the non-event as well.[5] For, economically speaking, the cover story was news without an information content: The facts had long been known to the market. According to the efficient market hypothesis, which says that all available information is always completely reflected in prices, the *re*publication of the story should not have provoked any significant price reactions. Journalistic reruns should remain ineffective.

But what happened in this case was exactly the opposite. The Entremed stock reacted twice: To the publication of the original news. And, much more violently, to the prominently placed rerun of the research report on the *Times* cover. One of the biggest price gains ever, 600 percent. But it was not just that: The stocks of a number of other biotechnology companies were infected by the euphoria and experience strong price increases as well—although nothing new was published about them at the time.[6] The stocks of a whole branch of industry rose, it seemed, because some newspaper journalists had repackaged already known research results a second time.

1. INTRODUCTION

Conventional financial market research assumes that price movements away from fundamental values are rather rare and that, if they occur, they are often quickly corrected. Stock prices thus would always adequately reflect all available information. According to this model, the mass media does not play a substantial role in price formation. Rather, it is important as a transmission channel in which news is passed on to market participants as quickly as possible. In fact, this approach sees the mass media as a factor that contributes to the *increase* of market efficiency: By providing information relevant for stock prices more and more quickly for a continuously broadening audience, it accelerates the process of finding the "correct price."

In order for this to happen, there is one prerequisite: Information that the media offers about the real economic situation has to be as accurate as possible. This means that the contribution of the mass media to market efficiency decisively depends on the question of whether they can paint, naively speaking, an "undistorted" picture of economic activity. If they cannot, it is very well conceivable that media impact leads to unusual effects which are in no way related to fundamental values. However, the findings of communication research that show that the media may play a lot of different roles are legion, but definitely not this one: the role of providers of reality "as it is." Thus, as long as the media is ignored as an autonomous factor which conditions market reactions, a decisive piece of a very complex puzzle is left out.

The media structures contents by selecting and evaluating; the weighting of information in the media, however, never corresponds to the distribution of information in reality. The media produce explanations by establishing logical links and causal relations; these interpretations, though, are only more or less adequate to reality. The media enriches information by adding new elements, such as "emotion" or "suspense"; through this process, however, the character of the information is altered. The media can even create its own events where nothing would happen otherwise—or it can encourage others to do so. In short: The media selects, interprets, emotionalizes and creates facts.

As a generator of attention, the media is prone to condition selective awareness: The media not only reduces reality by lowering information density. It focuses reality by accumulating information where "actually" none exists. The goal behind this is to win public attention, to control it and to keep it as long as possible. Ideally (from the point of view of the media), feedback loops are generated in which selected news events increase attention, which serves as a proof for the importance of the news, the visibility of which is then increased even further. These mechanisms can be found not only in the entertainment sector, they can also be encountered in the information media, the general news media, and in the business media.

One thing is certain, and that is that the media are far from being the neutral transmitter of news, as suggested in the abstract world of efficient markets. The news stream of the mass media definitely does not follow a random pattern. This does not necessarily and systematically lead to nonrandom prices: As empirical evidence of the effects of news on stock prices demonstrates, price reactions triggered by media reports are nothing unusual, but most of the time they do not occur systematically. In principle, however, there is the possibility that the media, due to their function of generating selective awareness and selective behavior, induce and reinforce specific market reactions which develop into dynamic interactions afterward.

In the following, the results of psychological studies, of empirical media research, and of empirical financial economics, as well as recent theoretical work on complex systems, are consulted in order to gain an insight into the dynamics of markets under growing media presence. The underlying idea is that financial markets are dynamic systems whose behavior can change in interaction with environmental conditions and due to internal mechanisms, and which thus do not permanently show the same stable processes. The assumption is that the interpenetration of markets and the media has brought about major changes. The following questions are to be settled: Do dynamic interactions between markets and the media exist? And if so, what are they?

2. FEEDBACK: THE MEDIA AS "LEARNING LAB"

One precondition for the emergence of systematic price movements is the establishment of feedback between stock prices and investors: Investment decisions in this case are not orientated to fundamentals, but to price developments in the past. If the media functioned as a link supporting such processes, considerable dynamic interactions would be conceivable. Shiller (2002) argues that it is possibly feedback processes that underlie many of the daily price fluctuations which are so difficult to explain. In the short, medium or long term, on a smaller as well as on a larger scale, according to Shiller, feedback does not seem to be unusual in speculative markets.

Does the media have the potential to generate such a feedback? The results of media effects research clearly indicate it. Nobody disputes that the media marks out the limits of discourse and influences patterns of perception by setting the public agenda. The news, especially television news, defines the thematic grounds on which the majority of the audience moves.[7] Media accounts thus have an immediate influence on the relative attention which individual topics gain in the public awareness. By emphasizing certain contents and suppressing others, the media does not only have an impact on what preoccupies people's minds, but also on *how* they judge these things.[8] The manner in which news presents the world influences the perceptions of the audience.

Such consequences of the consumption of media constructions of reality can be measured in spot checks. Cumulatively, they condense into patterns of perception which are strongly conditioned by media representations: Regular media consumption can have the effect of cultivating attitudes and opinions which come closer and closer to the media version of reality.[9] These perceptions, on the other hand, can constitute the basis for future patterns of behavior. Conditioning the perceptions of large numbers of individuals could thus cumulatively generate a kind of homogenous mass behavior.[10] The overrepresentation of certain media contents increases the probability of behavioral dispositions condensing into certain patterns. In a word: The mass media is a motor of social feedback, potentially a very strong one.

There are more and more theoretical, experimental and empirical findings indicating feedback induced by the media in the financial markets: Merton (1987) demands that the "evolution of institutions and information technologies" be taken into account in order to adequately describe the long-term dynamics of the financial markets.[11] An investor could only buy a stock if he knew it. But the attention of investors is not distributed equally across the market. The media therefore plays a key role: "A newspaper or other mass media story about the firm or its industry," Merton says, "that reaches a large number of investors who are not currently shareholders, could induce some of this number to incur the set-up costs and follow the firm."[12] In brief: The media draws potential investors into the market.

Merton makes the attempt to explain the changes in market dynamics within the framework of conventional models of rational investor behavior. For this purpose, however, he starts from the—hardly realistic—assumption that media accounts of companies and industries are always caused by changes in fundamental factors. He is wise to point out that the expansion of the influence of mass media specifically supports models of *irrational* investor behavior. "In such models," according to Merton, "media coverage, public relations and other forms of investment marketing could play an important causal role in creating and sustaining speculative bubbles and fads among investors."[13]

Psychological studies examined how such speculative dynamics can be generated. Experiments carried out by Andreassen and Kraus (1988) indicate that test persons in simulated stock markets tend to extrapolate trends from past price changes if they believe to have noticed them.[14] Andreassen (1990) provides evidence for the fact that business news does have a corresponding influence on investor behavior in real markets: More importance is attached to current information in comparison to more dated information. The specific way of presenting news, for example emphasizing it through techniques of dramatizing or emotionalizing, seems to activate decision-making rules which bring about a preference for this information.[15]

More recent empirical findings by Barber and Odean (2002) complement these psychological results. They show that stock selection on the part of investors takes place in a structured way: Stocks which generate special attention, due to high turnovers, strong price fluctuations or media coverage, are given priority. The decision-making problem, to choose a single stock from an immense number of existing company values, is solved by simple heuristics: Investors buy stocks which stand out. Barber and Odean come to the conclusion: "Just as publicity may help firms to sell their goods to the public, it may also help them to sell their stock."[16] In short: There is hardly any doubt that the media structures the decision-making process of many market participants.[17]

But structure in which way? Andreassen points out that the news media in general tend to provide explanations which are in accord with the reported events: ". . . The media must focus on prominent recent changes. To then explain why these changes have occurred, the media must search for information consistent with these changes, and selectively present favorable information about the company after positive price movements and unfavorable information after negative price movements. Such reports would be expected to increase the salience of the price change information by increasing the extent to which investors believe that the price changes are meaningful, important, and systematically different from zero."[18]

A typical stock market report looks like this: Stock X increased because . . . Index Y crashed due to . . . Prices Z continue to rise after . . . Most of these explanations are post-hoc rationalizations. Correlations which do not really exist are established. Reasons are constructed which can be interchanged arbitrarily. The explanations, as it seems, are quite obvious, even if they are far-fetched. An artificial logic is created, based on a simplistic understanding of the markets, which implies: that there are simple explanations for most price movements; that price movements follow rules which then lead to systematic patterns; and of course: that the news disseminated by the media decisively contribute to the emergence of price movements.

Andreassen (1987) demonstrates which effects explanations for stock market movements usually provided by the media have on investors' behavior: In the light of the explanations in media coverage, current price changes do not appear as temporary random products, but rather as the results of trends. The media thus shifts investors' attention and motivates them to extrapolate the price movement and to follow the trend. In absence of such a media stimulus, according to Andreassen, this reaction fails to materialize. This permits the assumption that with larger parts of the public getting into the reach of the business media, the number of feedback traders, that means of investors who follow a homogenizing impulse, continues to increase.[19]

The random character of price movements and their complexity is no adequate subject for news. They are "explained away" in the media until a picture of the markets emerges which systematically deviates from real market processes. The media thus structures the decision-making horizon of the market participants following them: by focusing the audience's attention through selectivity and publicity; and by underlying random processes with a logic that gives the impression of trends (but which in fact follows the rules of journalistic strategies of presentation). It is highly probable that this kind of coverage reinforces the latent tendency of investors to see trends where there are none. And to behave accordingly.

Shiller (2000) considers that the relationship of markets and the media is a very complex one: "News stories rarely have a simple, predictable effect on the market."[20] In many ways, Shiller says, media effects are even overestimated. But the media can set the basis for certain market movements and provide their triggers. According to Shiller, "cascade effects" can be generated by attention, which generates even more attention: The news presents price changes and reinforces their "actual" weight by cumulating attention. This again leads to increased attention and potentially stronger price movements—a feedback mechanism which can provoke extreme price movements.

The bottom line is that growing media influence seems to create the conditions for an increasingly strong herd instinct among market participants. Hirshleifer and Teoh (2003) point out that under certain circumstances, a homogenization of the decisions of many investors is observable. By watching the behavior of other investors and imitating it afterward, chain reactions can be set off among market participants. According to the authors, imitating role models present in the media plays a role as well. The infection with emotions such as panic or euphoria is also a common phenomenon in practice. As a huge "learning lab," the mass media is predestined to encourage such accumulations of behavior.

3. NEWS STRUCTURES: "USE VALUE" AND "NARRATIVE IMPERATIVE"

The media follows the laws of competitive publicity—including the business media: Use value and sound information are announced. In reality, however, the tools of the attention industry are being applied: What is offered is suspense and action, stars and starlets, hopes and dreams, fantasies of redemption. And promises: Simple recipes for accumulating great wealth are booming. Behind the surface structure of the announced information, there are deep structures which evoke affective reactions among the audience. In times of fierce competition, the media is eager to increase customer loyalty by establishing an emotional feedback in order to gain competitive advantages.[21]

Mullainathan and Shleifer (2002) develop a model that indicates the kind of media deep structures these could be. It turns out that under the conditions of a competitive system, an ideological orientation of the media not only is not a problem, but it is even desirable: If the positions of various media compete, these differing perspectives result in a broader picture. What is different, however, is the effect of what the authors call "spin": the deliberate attempt to make news as conspicuous as possible in order to catch the audience's attention. The goal of the media to outdo each other, the authors say, has the effect that the stories reinforce each other—and thus continuously narrows the perspective. The keener the competition between the media, the more pronounced the homogenization and exaggeration of the contents.[22]

The competition between the media—and this includes the business media—turns into a fight for public attention. Or, as the media theorist Georg Franck remarks: "It is like being in a beer tent. If everybody speaks loudly, you have to shout in order to make yourself heard."[23] Growing competition induces the press to produce massive headlines to sell more copies. A rather strident tone prevails on television, sometimes verging on hysteria. This overstimulation tends to reinforce itself, and permanent mutual excitement becomes the predominant principle of communication. The stimulation of the public replaces the simulation of reality as a guiding principle of much of the media.[24]

The consequences can be felt in the choice of contents, as well as in the style of their presentation: The new business media concentrates on bringing out the "action" of the financial markets. Regardless of whether investors buy or sell, permanent price fluctuations are the focus of attention. The markets are presented as a game of chance or a ride on the rollercoaster. Charts show price movements of the past, which are interpreted as trends. Stock recommendations and stock price forecasts are intended to help interpret the future and to make profitable investment decisions. "News to use" is the motto of this novel kind of business coverage. The relevance of the news is derived from the implied utility.[25]

The aesthetics of presentation follow the logic of the competition for attention as well: The make-up of many business magazines is consciously designed to trigger an emotional reaction. Even news television increasingly tends to follow the path of emotionalizing. Presenting affectively charged material, bringing out the human interest components, highlighting the personality aspect—the rivalry between the media favors a climate in which the exaggeration of contents and the calculation of effects are pursued systematically. As a result, there is a permanent balancing act between the promise of trustworthiness and the temptation of effect.[26]

What differentiates the business media from one another is the presentation and the design—sensationalism, storytelling, superlatives—rather than their ideological profile. Both liberal and conservative media operate within the same discursive limits: a market ideology that considers the liberalization of the financial system as inevitable and desirable, and the involvement of larger and larger shares of the population in the stock market as a sign of progress.[27] The central questions of the business media is when to invest and how much, if at all. A relativization of this macro-story from an ideological perspective does not take place.

It is not only because of an economic boom that the tone of many business media is characterized by permanent optimism. There are economic reasons for this as well: The business media depends on a positive market environment. The success of publications oriented towards the capital market, in particular, strongly correlates with market sentiments. In rising markets, circulation and ratings rise; in falling markets, they fall.[28] Therefore positive scenarios of the future are desirable. Pessimistic prognoses are not seen fit to achieve this goal. This is obvious when looking at the ratio of buy and sell recommendations: Very rarely, articles recommend selling investment securities. The large majority of stock evaluations are buy recommendations.[29]

"There was enormous pressure to report positively about what was going on at the stock market," a journalist of a financial magazine admitted during the stock market boom.[30] And even during the downturn, the coverage highlighted the positive aspects.[31] An explanation could be: The more that people feel attracted by the markets, the higher the profits of financial service providers. As a consequence, their budgets for advertisements in the business media grow. One central aspect, however, is thus neglected: The risks of the stock markets are ignored. In many media reports, authors overlook that the chances to obtain the expected yield are bought by taking serious risks.[32] This certainly does not contribute to an increased risk awareness among investors.

James Surowiecki (2001), author for the *New Yorker* magazine, describes the changes in market dynamics in times of omnipresent business coverage: "A market is best at setting prices when the people in it make their decisions on their own. Its collective wisdom arises out of the cumulative effect of millions of independent decisions. You don't get that wisdom in a world dominated by CNBC-style coverage. In that world, every decision becomes dependent. And, in certain circumstances . . . you end up with a mob instead of a market."³³

Similarly, Bernstein (2001) is critical of the expected benefit of the swelling stream of information: "Some television stations now post reporters on trading floors at exchanges, and they report investment information measured in minutes. Such reporting is very similar to the poor reporters who must give hurricane reports from the waterfront. . . . In both cases, the reporters tend to report eye-catching but probably worthless information. Yes, there are high winds and strong surf during a hurricane. Yes, stock trading becomes more frantic when unexpected news is announced."³⁴ Moreover, Bernstein points out that a lot of economic news events are pseudo-events. Much of the seemingly surprising positive company news, for example, was carefully engineered beforehand.

Robert Shiller's (2000) observations on the media coverage during the stock market boom point in the same direction: "Many news stories in fact seem to have been written under a deadline to produce something—*anything*—to go along with the numbers from the market. . . . Sometimes the article is so completely devoid of genuine thought about the reasons for the bull market and the context for considering its outlook that it is hard to believe that the writer was other than cynical in his or her approach."³⁵ There are thus many signs indicating that the news structures of business coverage are not very beneficial to rational, critical, sensible, differentiated and diversified investor behavior.

4. MEDIA MANIAS: THE "CNBC EFFECT"

The structure of news contents would be of limited interest if it was not transferred to the behavior of investors. But the opposite is true: The media does have the potential to provoke market moves. As the following example illustrates: On Friday, June 30, 2000, the stocks of MACC Private Equities, a small investment company, suddenly rose by 80 per cent. The trading volume of the stock came to 300 per cent of the usual level. Apparently, what was behind all this was a mistake of the TV channel CNBC: Shortly before, CNBC had brought a positive report about Applied Micro Circuits, a semiconductor manufacturer, with an insertion of its ticker symbol—which is AMCC. However, what appeared on the screen was MACC. The employees of the finance channel had transposed two letters of the ticker symbol.³⁶

Nowhere else are autonomous media effects more obvious that in case of fictitious news which does not have any real economic content at all. For example, in case of manipulations of information in order to influence and deceive market participants: Price swings after the deliberate publication of false information show that news per se can be followed by substantial price movements, which are not immediately corrected by the market. In such cases of "invented" information, it turns out that investor reactions occur in the financial markets which represent a mere function of media publicity. A price reaction to the substance of the news is not possible, for there is no such substance.

A well-known example is the case of Emulex: The stock of the California maker of network products was under strong selling pressure after a fake report with a negative content had circulated on the internet: It claimed that the Chief Executive Officer (CEO) had resigned and that the company would soon publish a profit revision. The stock price fell by more than 50 per cent in only a few minutes, a decrease in the market capitalization of about two billion dollars. In other words: The fake piece of news, which had been disseminated with the intention to manipulate, had a strong effect on the stock price of the company concerned—although (or perhaps even because) it was fundamentally fictitious. The law enforcement authorities were convinced of the impact of the false report: When the author was identified, he was sentenced to a long term of imprisonment.[37]

In another case, a swindler managed to make stock prices of a company soar by publishing a false report. The stocks of Pairgain Technologies had steadily lost in market value before one day, the price suddenly rocketed. For a short period of time, the stock rose from $8.50 to more than eleven dollars, a temporary increase in value of more than 30 per cent.[38] In the market, rumors had circulated that Pairgain was to be taken over for double its actual market value. Soon afterward, it turned out that the story was completely fictitious and had been disseminated through an internet message board. In this case, the courts were convinced of the effect of the false information as well. After his arrest, the perpetrator was sentenced to pay a substantial fine.[39]

Media effects cannot always be isolated in such an accurate way. For example, the average price movements following stock recommendations, which can also be considered media non-events, are often much less pronounced than in the case of the described manipulation of information. Nevertheless, the publicity effect proves that market participants are prompted by the recommendations of stock market commentators to buy stocks. Temporary significant price increases and an often strong increase in trading volume of the stocks commented on are the result. The tips disseminated by the media generate a temporary price pressure because certain investors reach for the recommended stocks. Since most of these price reactions are not sustained, it is fair to assume that it is not the information content of the news that plays the decisive role, but rather autonomous media effects.

With the expansion of the media system, particularly the spread of television providers specializing in business topics, such media effects should have reached a new dimension. Busse and Green (2002) state that news about analysts' reports broadcast on CNBC can evoke significant price reactions. Obviously, television viewers carry out transactions on the basis of these reports: The trading volume of the stocks mentioned on television doubles in the first minutes after the program. Significant trading gains also seem possible—if people act very rapidly: The effect subsides after fifteen seconds. Investors who hesitate longer have to expect a loss, because a partial price reversal sets in, which is an indicator of an overreaction.

While Busse and Green's sample seems to show a mixture of the information and the publicity effect, Meschke (2002) hardly finds any traces of a genuine information content in the interviews with company managers, broadcast regularly on CNBC: The interviews with the CEOs are non-events, since no news is published that would not have been known to the market before. But these non-events do not remain without consequences: The attention generated in the television programs results in a short-term increase in prices and a sharply increased trading activity of the stocks concerned. Meschke finds average excess returns of 1.65 per cent on the event day with trading volumes being 1.69 per cent above the norm.

But the price gains do not last long. The price increase is followed by a loss: Within ten days after the interviews, prices go down by 2.78 per cent on average, that is, below the level of the event day. Meschke draws the following conclusion: "The presence of the CEOs on CNBC generates a temporary pressure to buy through enthusiastic investors."[40] To put it differently: Rationally deliberating agents of the efficient markets model are not at work here, but rather so-called noise traders: Investors who react to information which does not exist. This means that under certain circumstances, substantial reactions of large numbers of market participants seem to appear which cannot be explained by the content of new information.

Following an old saying by McLuhan, the medium actually seems to be the message in the case of these reactions. These occurences are very meaningful for understanding the dynamics of markets and the media since they are a matter of price movements which are causally related to the mass media—and therefore demonstrate an autonomous role of the media. However, it would be an oversimplification to be satisfied with the attempt to isolate such manifest short-term media effects: Firstly, these effects mostly occur sporadically, which makes it difficult to deduce any general statements about "laws" without overcharging them with auxiliary hypotheses.[41] Secondly, the complex systemic interactions between markets and the media would not even be considered when concentrating on isolated effects.

5. META-COMMUNICATION: DYNAMIC INTERACTIONS

Are overreactions to media reports solely the result of rash reactions of naive traders who are under a misapprehension and follow vacuous information? Or is there a change in market dynamics? The evidence suggests the latter. Dynamic price trends are elicited by different types of investors who interact with one another: growing numbers of noise traders, whose attention is drawn to the markets by the media, and who act on the basis of "used" news; and growing numbers of momentum traders who act reflectively and try to make a profit from the price movements generated by the noise traders. This would explain the observation of Black (1986) that rational and irrational traders are often difficult to distinguish.[42]

Shleifer and Summers (1990) argue that the demand pattern of investors who follow pseudo-information, such as stock recommendations, is hardly rational.[43] They say that noise traders are often subject to homogenous group behavior, which could have the effect that they gain a significant influence on the aggregate level. Despite their "actually" incorrect behavior, they could be successful temporarily as a group. This, on the other hand, brings imitators onto the scene and further increases their influence in the market.[44] The price movements thus provoked, the authors say, are not always corrected by rational investors (arbitrageurs): either because price fluctuations elicited by irrational traders increase the risk too much and prevent counteraction; or because it pays off to swim with the tide and to intensify price dynamics.[45]

If rational investors follow the latter strategy, it is temporarily impossible to distinguish between noise traders and "information holders" because they behave identically. In fact, it is conceivable that a kind of "professionalization" takes place even among noise traders, in the sense that they learn with time that they do not possess any real information and focus exclusively on anticipating the reactions of the bulk of their colleagues. The "rational" momentum traders do not behave differently anyway. The prerequisites for a reflexive behavior of investors, which ignores fundamentals and is oriented toward the behavior of others, is considerably reinforced by the feedback mechanism of the media.[46] From this point of view, the media has, above all, one function: It is a device which facilitates strategically calculated coordination.

This kind of self-reflexiveness can have various reasons: the tendency, supported by the media, to extrapolate trends; the gradual realization on the part of the noise traders that the information available to them has already been used at the time of the publication; and the increasing self-reference of the journalists: Self-referentiality has become firmly established in the media as a strategic ritual. Similar to the stock market gurus, who warn of other gurus, the media increasingly comments on current developments with reference to, or even warnings of, the coverage of other media. The participation of the journalists in the generation of many events is often explicitly pointed out.

Choosing themselves as theme for the media has the primary function of immunizing themselves against criticism of their view of reality. This choice makes it possible to simulate a distance from the things they report about. Among internet commentators in particular, this kind of pseudo-enlightenment has become very popular: The greatest "noise critics" are also the greatest "noise makers."[47] One cannot rule out the possibility that this builds up a critical attitude towards the news among the audience. Without doubt, the media-induced artificial character of the coverage comes to the fore—a possible precondition of a self-reflexive behavior on the part of the market participants, to be referred to herein as meta-communication in this context.

Morris and Shin (2001) also suppose that the growing influence of the media results in a strategically calculated behavior of the market participants, which takes media effects into account—with potentially dangerous consequences: "The very fact that the news reaches a large audience also tells the recipient that many others have also just learned this piece of news."[48] According to the authors, this could lead to an anticipating kind of behavior which is not geared to economic factors, but to the expected reactions of other investors. By trying to beat their competitors, investors provoke the anticipated reactions—and reinforce them. This can then lead to considerable overreactions.

Under such circumstances, it is not necessarily irrational from the point of view of individual market participants to chase after excessive prices: If one assumes that rising prices produce positive news, and that these tend to favor rising prices in return, it is not unreasonable to predict a continuation of such a trend. The whole world is watching and knows that the whole world is watching. What results from this logic is a noticeable homogenization of investor behavior. The noise disseminated by the media leads to repeated overreactions among investors, which can increase the noise in return and thus evoke further overreactions. One consequence could be the formation of price bubbles and finally crashes. All in all, the partly rational behavior of individual investors generates an irrational collective result.[49]

From the point of view of game theory, this process can be characterized as the Prisoner's Dilemma. Joshi, Parker and Bedau (1998) show that technical strategies (that is, trend following methods) have a competitive advantage over fundamental strategies: Technical strategies dominate, no matter which method or strategy of analysis the other market participants pursue. From an individual perspective, it would therefore be rational to integrate a technical component, which possibly has the effect that in subsequent "rounds of the game," technical strategies are preferred in the selection.[50] As soon as the majority of market participants relies on technical strategies, however, the result for every single actor deteriorates. As soon as it is pursued by the group, the individually rational behavior collectively produces a suboptimal result.[51]

The explanation for this seemingly paradoxical finding is the following: The more traders extrapolate trends, the more frequently positive feedback and self-fulfilling prophecies occur. If more and more actors follow a trend, noise and price bubbles are the consequence. Volatility increases, which makes it increasingly difficult to give accurate forecasts. On average, the result for all market participants gets worse. This process therefore shows the structure of an iterated n-person game with one dominant strategy, that produces a collectively dissatisfying result: the typical structure of the Prisoner's Dilemma.[52]

A recent theroretical approach points in the same direction: noise in the process of price formation; attempts of investors to derive a benefit from it; the dominance of trend following strategies; generation of positive feedback; and a suboptimal result for all: These are typical features of financial systems as they have recently been modeled through analogies from physics and mathematical biology.[53] Such complex adaptive systems are characterized by the fact that they do not automatically head for an equilibrium, but temporarily become more imbalanced. Slight changes accumulate into complex interactions which can cause systemic imbalances—which results in the boom-crash cycles that are so typical in the financial markets.[54]

In these models, particular attention is given to the role of the perceptions of market participants: The perceptions of market participants depend on the perceptions they expect from other market participants, who, on the other hand, take into account the perceptions of still other market participants: a self-referential and indeterminate, and above all, as Arthur (1995) points out: an instable process.[55] The investors' expectations depend on the supposed expectations of other investors, and their expectations again depend on expectations they assume other investors to have.[56] In the Rorschach image of chaotic price information, a slight hint of a pattern is enough to set off a self-reinforcing trend. Such hints are permanently provided by the professional pattern seekers from the mass media.

6. CRASH: MEDIA AND MARKET PANICS

The development and bursting of the internet bubble provides the most impressive example so far for speculative excesses going along with the medialization of the markets. Stock price variance, trading turnovers, market capitalization or permanent media presence: In practically every important category, internet companies established new records. At the end of the 1990s, they represented up to 20 per cent of the volume of stocks traded each day—at a time when the sector as a whole incurred losses.[57] At one point in time, even the renaming of companies which then somehow sounded like internet companies evoked enormous price movements. Ofek and Richardson (2002) are therefore justified in speaking of "bizarre behavior of internet prices." The investors definitely were too optimistic in their expectations for the future.

Between 1998 and 2000, the internet sector generated a return of more than 1,000 per cent[58]—a spectacular price increase that not only seemed to be fundamentally unsecured after the collapse of the stocks: A number of market observers already described the prices as unjustified during the euphoric boom period.[59] But why did an early price adjustment by sceptical actors not take place? Ofek and Richardson (2001) provide evidence indicating that the pessimists (who later turned out to be the realists) were "run over" by the optimists. According to the authors, private investors, among them many novices in the stock market, believed the internet "hype" and marched in the same direction in huge numbers.

Without any doubt, several factors play an important role: a novel kind of technology, whose potential could not be clearly estimated; exaggerated forecasts coming from many analysts, not least motivated by interconnections between investment banks and their clients; limited possibilities to sell securities short, the reason why pessimistic price assessments could not assert themselves; and generally exaggerated expectations concerning long-term stock returns. But the media—finance newspapers, investor magazines and particularly news channels such as CNBC and n-tv—served as a multiplier: They spread the "virus"—the internet story—globally, according to the overall sound of the coverage, in a positive or even euphoric tone. The good news spread rapidly—until it was taken up by the whole media system.[60]

The idea of the cyber-economy made for a strong storyline and drew plenty of attention. And it brought the media breathtaking accruals in advertising. As an empirically weak but suggestive macro-story, the fiction of the digital knowledge economy provided a projection screen for many effective micro-stories: from the emancipation of the individual due to mobile technology, to wealth for all in the stock exchange, or the revolution of economic activity via the internet. Small wonder that many investors yielded to the temptation: Obviously, the internet story was highly "infective" when it came across an appropriately preconditioned "carrier." The media hype was the sine qua non of the boom and subsequent crash of the "New Economy."

This does not imply that the price decline was a phenomenon of irrational novices jumping like lemmings over the cliff of the stock market. Schuster (2001) gives several examples proving that not only uninformed small investors followed the trend of the growth stocks.[61] To mention only one particular case: According to press reports, George Soros did not become strongly involved in technology securities until 1999, shortly before the end of the boom, and therefore suffered heavy losses after the crash. Examples like this refute the popular opinion that the internet euphoria was solely the result of the aberrant behavior of irrational private investors. The exaggerations were also brought about by big investors hoping to benefit from price increases—who stirred the euphoria even more.[62]

Ofek and Richardson (2002) pass a similar judgment: ". . . There is no doubt that very sophisticated investors, and highly regarded managers of companies, invested considerable capital in the internet sector. These investments alone suggest that a story based on an influx of irrational retail investors is probably too simplistic."[63] Most signs suggest that the internet bubble was a textbook case of speculative mania: a dynamic process in which unusual price movements arouse investors' attention and positive feedback leads to self-reinforcement. The media multiplied the stories which provided reasons for the enormous price fluctuations and animated investors to follow the trend.

In his classic account of the history of market panics, economic historian Charles Kindleberger (1978) presents a model of such financial crises. Speculative excesses, Kindleberger says, take place following a remarkably stable pattern: At first an event changes economic perspectives. Novel profit opportunities appear and are used by market participants. The chance turns into a boom: New investments lead to increases in income, which stimulate further investment. The boom leads to excess: Irrational motives dominate the behavior of a growing number of investors, and asset prices continue to go up.[64]

Until the market enters a manic phase: Now, euphoria and the desire to speculate become the guiding principles of investment decisions. The mass pursuit of returns results in a mass flight from reality. "A larger and larger group of people," according to Kindleberger, "seeks to become rich without a real understanding of the processes involved."[65] But at a certain point, some insiders opt out and take their profits. Tentatively at first, then more and more clearly, doubts arise as to the longevity of the profit scheme. When the realization sets in that the market has exaggerated, a wave of retreat sets in. Disillusionment turns into aversion; aversion results in panic.[66]

Shiller (2000) supposes that the mass media has played a role in the generation of financial manias since their invention: "The history of speculative bubbles begins roughly with the advent of newspapers. One can assume that, although the record of these early newspapers is mostly lost, they regularly reported on the first bubble of any consequence, the Dutch tulip mania of the 1630s. Although the news media . . . present themselves as detached observers of market events, they are themselves an integral part of these events. Significant market events generally occur only if there is similar thinking among large groups of people, and the news media is an essential vehicle for the spread of ideas."[67] And that is not all: The media also disseminates emotions—and reinforces them.[68]

It thus lays the groundwork for the appearance of speculative manias and market panics. It arouses investors' interest and stirs up their enthusiasm for the stock exchange. In boom times, it brings breathless stories about the upswing, which are followed by in no way less breathless stories about the coming economic crisis. The pressure to sell the same material hour after hour leads to sensationalism and exaggerations, particularly in financial television. And to the overrating of individual topics: In the media spotlight, only a few occurences are highlighted as news events. The effect is an amazing standardization of media contents. Public attention is narrowed as a consequence. A homogenous kind of mass behavior thus becomes highly probable.

Two factors play an important role in the origin of financial euphoria, both of them reinforced by the media: overrating future gains, and the "envy effect." Countless stock recommendations and stock price forecasts, the self-confident air of finance commentators and the optimistic tone of the coverage easily convey the impression that profits can be programmed. Most of the time, past gains are projected into the future, a fact that encourages trend following behavior. Frequently, profit prospects are assumed which are at the upper limit of a realistic scale of expectations. Often, they go much further.

The envy factor is also increased by the media: Reports about easy money foster emulation. Kindleberger comments: "There is nothing so disturbing to one's well-being and judgment as to see a friend get rich."[69] In times of periodic stock market booms, it seems that the whole neighborhood is rolling in money. Hardly anybody talks about the losers at the markets. The supposed profits of others are an incentive to try one's luck—and to follow the stimulus of the masses. Both factors, the overrating of future profits and the envy effect, increase the probability of irrational behavior. This public pressure has become tremendously heavier with the expansion of the business media.

7. SUMMARY AND CONCLUSIONS

The expansion of the business media has caused a change in the dynamics of investor behavior. The density as well as the frequency of news has increased significantly. Global information channels have aroused the attention of many people, who become active in the markets in ever-growing numbers. A lot of these novices receive their "basic training" in investment issues via the media, even via such an improbable candidate as television. ". . . Television news," Iyengar and Kinder (1987) write, "is in fact an educator virtually without peer."[70] The representations of the markets in the media not only influence what people think about, but also how they do this.

The influence of the news media increases the probability that trend following behavior sets in among investors: It attracts attention to short-term price changes and provides explanations which afterward evokes an impression of logic—logic that meets the demand of the media for conclusive stories. Random or chaotic price movements are "explained away" systematically. Under the impression of such stylized stories, investors tend to update developments of the past and to extrapolate trends. The strong selectivity of the media, increasing with growing competitive pressure, supports a homogenization of the contents. This provides the basis for the tendency that the behavior of increasing numbers of investors condenses into few alternatives.

The media can thus generate positive feedback in the market: it focuses attention on current price changes and reinforces the latent tendency of investors to project them into the future—and provoke overreactions in doing so. This is how price fluctuations can reinforce themselves: The media focuses public attention on some particularly striking price movements, which are then further increased by the reactions of the public. Only small numbers of naive noise traders are necessary for such a feedback process to occur: In anticipation of media-induced feedback, the incentive is high enough even for informed investors to implement a trend-following strategy—and in this way contribute to the realization of the price movements that have been forecast.

The selective awareness of investors and the selective awareness of the media reinforce each other and favor mutual overreactions. Good news leads to increased optimism and serves as an incentive to buy more. Good prices, in return, lead to good news, which tends to favor good prices. Price increases are followed by buy recommendations, and vice versa. The positive market trend and the positive media trend mutually reinforce each other, and the prevailing optimism results in expectations for the future painted in the most glowing colors. The emergence of stock market euphoria is thereby encouraged. This process is dynamic, it is self-referential, and above all: it is inherently unstable.

These dynamic interactions necessarily reach a point of culmination, when the market trend and the opinion trend decouple: The media continues to pursue it strategy of optimism, but the prices deviate from their highs. Initially, this divergence is often very small: The market lives on contradictory signals that fit various patterns of interpretation and can often be read in a positive as well as in a negative way. The market emits increasingly ambiguous signals which the media, however, tends to interpret in an unambiguous way. If the contradiction becomes too obvious, a change of tone occurs: The constant optimism is followed by skepticism and then, step by step, turns into negativism.

Bad news only reinforces the upcoming pessimism and is used as an opportunity for more and more sales. Bad prices then cause bad news in return, which tends to favor bad prices. The negative market trend and the negative media trend mutually reinforce each other, and the prevailing pessimism results in overly gloomy expectations for the future. The resulting chain reactions foster the generation of panic under certain circumstances. Until market trends and media trends are decoupled again—and the cycle of panic and euphoria starts all over again.

The picture that emerges is thus very complex: Market participants stand in a reflexive relationship, since their decisions are mutually interdependent. The expected reactions of others are taken into account, and their anticipation can result in a self-reinforcement of these reactions. Dynamic disequilibria are a real possibility if perceptions and price movements mutually reinforce each other. The effect can be a change in the fundamental values, which has repercussions on perceptions and prices. The media acts as a catalyst of these dynamic processes because it contributes to the structuring and coordination of decision-making processes and thereby accelerate and intensify feedback effects. They thus constitute a possibly destabilizing element, since they support the continuation and reinforcement of states of disequilibrium, or maybe even trigger them.

NOTES

1. "Hope in the Lab. A Special Report. A Cautious Awe Greets Drugs That Eradicate Tumors in Mice." In: *New York Times*, 05/03/1998.
2. "Tests on Mice Block a Defense by Cancer." In: *The New York Times*, 11/27/1997.
3. Boehm, Folkman, Browder and O'Reilly (1997); Kerbel (1997).
4. "In Excitement Over Cancer Drugs, A Caution Over Premature Hopes." In: *The New York Times*, 05/05/1998; "Investing It. Focus on Biotechnology. A Cautionary Tale." In: *New York Times*, 05/10/1998; "Investing It. Focus on Biotechnology. Feeling a Bit Like a Laboratory Mouse?" In: *The New York Times*, 05/10/1998.
5. Huberman and Regev (2001).
6. Huberman and Regev (2001), 392.
7. Iyengar and Kinder (1987), 21, 26, 33.
8. Iyengar and Kinder coined the term *priming* for this phenomenon. With this concept they refer to the media influencing the criteria which are invoked to judge political candidates. Iyengar and Kinder (1987), 63–112.
9. Exemplarily Gerbner (1998) and Gerbner, Gross, Morgan and Signorielli (1994).
10. Cf. Schuster (2004), 57–71.
11. Merton (1987), 486. Merton rightly points out that conventional models of price formation assume that public information is disseminated completely and immediately and then implemented by investors without any delay. Merton judges that this constitutes a very "simple information structure," which often does not depict news events in a sufficiently realistic way.
12. Merton (1987), 500.
13. Merton (1987), 503f.

14. Andreassen and Kraus (1988) quoted in Shiller (2002).

15. Andreassen (1990), 154.

16. Barber and Odean (2002), 24. Barber and Odean see differences in the behavior of private and institutional investors: "Our argument . . . does not apply with equal force to institutional investors." Their assumption is that private investors are more susceptible to conspicious signals. Barber and Odean (2002), 2.

17. The studies carried out by Andreassen as well as those by Barber and Odean therefore support the result of cognitive psychology, indicating that subjects preferably rely on information which is particularly easy to retrieve due to repetition or proximity in time. Fischhoff, Slovic and Lichtenstein (1980), 127 write: "People solve problems, including the determination of their own values, with what comes to mind. The more detailed, exacting, and creative their inferential process, the more likely they are to think of all they know about the problem. The briefer that process becomes, the more they will be controlled by the relative accessibility of various considerations."

18. Andreassen (1990), 165; similarly Pearce and Roley (1985), 49.

19. Cf. Bloomfield and Hales (2002).

20. Shiller (2000), 71.

21. In the US, the expansion of the business media already started during the 1970s. For almost three decades, the extent of business coverage has constantly increased, both in the general news media and in the area of special publications. The stock market boom setting in after 1982 supported this trend. Between 1988 and 1998, the number of business magazines in the US alone increased from 358 to 694. In Europe, the expansion of business coverage set in only later, but reached comparable levels during the 1990s. In the highly competitive communication market of the 90s, finance and business media became one of the fastest growing sectors. For a detailed account see Schuster (2001), 35–53 and Parker (1997).

22. The group mentality of journalists reinforces the tendency to homogeneity. The choice of topics and the way they are treated follow professional routines and the impulses of the group—rather than any "objective" necessities.

23. Franck (1998), 170.

24. Iyengar and Kinder (1987) point out that the liveliness of the presentations *per se* does not evoke stronger media effects. The main effect comes from the fact that public attention is structured by the selection of contents and their prioritizing. Iyengar and Kinder (1987), 34–42.

25. "German business magazines have long been going through a phase of emphasizing use value," the specialist journal *journalist* already stated some time ago. "Tips und Tricks." In: *Journalist*, 3/1997. "Our viewers aren't actually viewers," a former Senior Vice President of CNBC explains. "They're users. Other networks ask, 'What's of interest?' We ask, 'What's actionable about a piece of information?'" Quoted in "The Revolution Will Be Televised (on CNBC)." In: *Fast Company*, June 2000.

26. For details see Schuster (2001), 81–95.

27. Cf. Schuster (2001) passim as well as Madrick (2001 and 1999) and Parker (1999).

28. Czarnitzki and Stadtmann (2000).

29. This has got two reasons: Firstly, positive assessments also prevail among journalists' sources, the analysts. Secondly, the media believe that they can arouse the interest of larger target groups for their product with the help of purchase reports. Their justification is the arithmetics of public demand: A sell recommendation only addresses a minority of viewers and readers, the owners of the stock that is evaluated. A buy recommendation, on the other hand, addresses the majority of the audience, everyone who does not own the stock.

30. "Anlegermagazine leiden unter Auflagenschwund." In: *Süddeutsche*, 01/26/2001. For details concerning the positive bias of investment and financial media see Schuster (2001), 95–102.

31. Wolf (2001), 70, 74, 76, 80. Wolf demonstrates in an analysis of coverage of the German Nemax Index that the financial media unvariedly pursued their policy of disseminating stock recommendations during the phase of the stock market downturn. 60 per cent of overall coverage was allotted to investment tips and price forecasts. "The results prove that . . . coverage was predominantly optimistic and that 'positivism' in financial coverage was confirmed." Wolf (2001), 84, 112.

32. In investment practice, the question at which risk a certain return is bought plays a crucial role. For many finance media, this has been a question of minor importance during the stock market boom, and continues to be one. For example in popular hitlists of stocks and funds: By fixating on the performance, attention is focused on investment return. How the return is generated remains a secondary issue.

33. Surowiecki (2001).

34. Bernstein (2001), XIV.

35. Shiller (2000), 74

36. Meschke (2002), 2; Bernstein (2001), 18.

37. Cf. Bank (2001); Benning (2000); "Guilty Plea is Set in Internet Hoax Case Involving Emulex." In: *New York Times*, 12/29/2000; "On Hair-Trigger Wall Street, A Stock Plunges on Fake News." In: *New York Times*, 08/26/2000.

38. "Fake News Account On Web Site Sends Stock Price Soaring." In: *New York Times*, 04/08/1999; "Fake Story Shows Net Perils." In: Cnnfn.com, 04/08/1999. For a detailed account see Schuster (2001), 192–194.

39. "Pairgain Worker Sentenced in Fraud Case." In: *The New York Times*, 08/31/1999; "PairGain Web Hoax: Hoke Grounded." In: Zdnet.com, 08/30/1999; "Arrest Made in PairGain Stock Scam." In: Zdnet.com, 04/15/1999.

40. Meschke (2002), 4. Meschke points out that during the study period from 1999 to 2001, CEOs of technology companies quoted in the Nasdaq index very frequently appeared as guests on CNBC. The journalists obviously preferred the stock market segment which scored the highest price gains at the time.

41. Depending on the study period and the selection of the sample, this would only lead to the "waves" well known in media effect research: Alternating periods

in which experts tend to agree on the existence of "strong" and then again of "weak" media effects.

42. Black (1986), 532 writes: "There will always be a lot of ambiguity about who is an information trader and who is a noise trader." Cf. De Long, Shleifer, Summers and Waldmann (1989).

43. Shleifer and Summers (1990), 23. For details see Cutler, Poterba and Summers (1991 and 1990); De Long, Scleifer, Summers and Waldmann (1991, 1990 and 1989).

44. For a long time, economic theory started from the assumption that irrational investors quickly disappear from the market because they systematically lose capital to rational opponents. Exemplarily Friedman (1953). De Long, Scleifer, Summers and Waldmann (1991), on the other hand, point out that noise traders possibly obtain higher returns than rational investors under certain circumstances, since they take higher risks and realize profits for this (unconsciously taken) risk. This is why they might even dominate the market.

45. It is thus incorrect, as Black (1986), 532 states, that "as the amount of noise trading increases, it will become more profitable for people to trade on information." Black starts from the fact that with increasing noise, rational investors make increasingly aggressive attempts to move prices into the direction of the fundamental values. He points out himself, though, that the information lead "does not guarantee a profit." On the one hand, the risk becomes higher with increasing noise and increasing size of the speculative positions. On the other hand, information traders cannot be sure either if they perhaps only react to noise as well. Black does not consider the possibility that information holders also consciously and deliberately react to noise.

46. Farmer (2002) points out that not only trend following strategies, but also fundamental strategies may induce positive autocorrelations and excessive volatility.

47. Exemplarily: Richard McCaffery, "The Market's Missing Ingredient." In: www.fool.com, 08/10/2001.

48. Morris and Shin (2001), 2.

49. Morris and Shin (2001), 5 write: "The heightened sensitivities of the market could magnify any noise in the public information to such a large extent that public information ends up by causing more harm than good."

50. Brian Arthur (1995), 24 writes: "Trend expectations in sufficient density in the population of expectations are mutually reinforcing."

51. For an introduction into the Prisoner's Dilemma cf. Axelrod (1984) as well as Rapoport and Chammah (1965). For an overview of evolutionary game theory cf. Lindgren (1997) and Friedman (1991).

52. Moreover, the principle applies (regardless of the payoff-structure of different strategies towards each other) that the expected profit of a strategy is diminished with growing numbers of users.

53. An excess of "anomalies" in the context of the efficient market theory incited various researchers to make attempts to come closer to the actual financial markets in their models. They rightly state that conventional finance theory relies too much

on simplistic and unrealistic assumptions—primarily the axiom of "rational agents" and a concept of equilibrium derived from Newtonian physics. The core of studies on complex adaptive systems consists in adapting biological theories and their principles of selection in order to deduce rules of economic selection. The objective is to improve the representation of dynamic interactions in markets which appear as exceptions to the rule in models of efficient markets. For an introduction cf. Mauboussin (2002); Farmer and Lo (1999); Arthur et al. (1997); Holland (1995); Blume and Easley (1992); Anderson, Arrow and Pines (1988).

54. Mauboussin (2002), 13, considers the four following characteristics to be typical for these systems: aggregation, adaptive decision rules, non-linearity and feedback.

55. Also cf. Arthur (1997 and 1988).

56. In his theory of reflexivity, George Soros focused on interactions of perceptions and *prices*. Soros (1998, 1994, 1987) repeatedly points out that economic factors and views of market participants are mutually dependent. "Reflexivity," according to Soros, "is, in effect, a two-way feedback mechanism in which reality helps shape the participants' thinking and the participants' thinking helps shape reality. . . ." Soros (1994). Consequently, this is an indeterminate process which does not automatically head for a state of equilibrium. Price perceptions of market participants are not mere reflections of real economic values; they can provoke changes in these values, which then result in dynamic disequilibria. According to Soros, this is the main difference of his theory and the model of efficient markets, since real economic values are assumed as given in the latter, which means that they are not influenced by the perceptions of market participants.

57. Ofek and Richardson (2002), passim.

58. Figure in Ofek and Richardson (2001).

59. Cf. Exemplarily Thaler (1999), 13.

60. For details see Madrick (2001), passim as well as Schuster (2001), 19–53.

61. Schuster (2001), 67 f.

62. Cf. "'Macro' Investors Era May Be Over: Soros Out of the Game." In: *National Post*, 06/27/2000. Soros is of the opinion that it can be a successful speculative strategy to imitate noise traders and not to build up a counterposition until shortly before the trend reversal. Cf. Soros (1987) as well as Shleifer and Summers (1990), 28.

63. Barber and Odean (2002) provide evidence showing that private investors are particularly strongly influenced by conspicuous news in their investment decisions. Institutional investors are less susceptible in this regard. This leads to the conclusion that systematic price movements are more often provoked by the former. Ofek and Richardson (2001) argue accordingly for the case of the internet bubble. The economist Paul Krugman, on the other hand, is of the opinion that the herd instinct is more pronounced among professional fund managers than among private investors. Personal communication, 01/19/2001 and Krugman (1997).

64. Also cf. Galbraith (1954). For the counterposition, which seriously questions the existence of price bubbles cf. Garber (2001 and 1989). For the current discussion about speculative mania in the financial markets, its effects on the real economy and possible political counter-measures cf. Hunter, Kaufman and Pomerleano (2003).

65. Kindleberger (1978), 16.

66. Galbraith (1954) describes the bursting of a bubble as follows: At first, the bubble is defended by those who profit from it, critics are ignored or discredited. Then, the programmed collapse takes its course: Business outlooks and price forecasts are systematically missed. Many promises turn out to be lies. Many people lose their money, financial devastation is the consequence. But the shock is only short-lived, the markets have no memory. The reasons for the crash are not discussed, the disaster quickly sinks into oblivion. And speculation starts all over again.

67. Shiller (2000), 71.

68. The biologist Richard Dawkins (1976) developed a concept of self-replicating ideas which he calls "memes" in his book *The Selfish Gene*. According to Dawkins, "memes" lead a life of their own, they spread like a virus and sometimes cause mass infections. Memes are passed on from one person to the next through imitation. This theory of thought infections, which are also and particularly spread by the media, gave cause to the assumption that memetic infections play a role in the financial markets. This theory is somewhat tautological and should probably only be considered as a graphic metaphor. As such, however, it is quite interesting heuristically, since it focusses attention on processes of mass dissemination of irrational ideas and ways of behavior, such as mass hysteria and panic. Cf. Dawkins (1999 and 1976); Frank (1999); Lynch (1996).

69. Kindleberger (1978), 15.

70. Iyengar and Kinder (1987), 2.

REFERENCES

Admati, Anat R. and Paul Pfleiderer. 1988. "A Theory of Intraday Trading Patterns: Volume and Price Variability." In: *Review of Financial Studies*, Vol. 1, No. 1: 3–40.

Anderson, Philip W., Kenneth J. Arrow and David Pines (Eds.). 1988. *The Economy as an Evolving Complex System*. Reading: Addison-Wesley.

Andreassen, Paul B. 1990. "Judgmental Extrapolation and Market Overreaction. On the Use and Disuse of News." In: *Journal of Behavioral Decision Making* Vol. 3: 153–174.

———. 1987. "On the Social Psychology of the Stock Market. Aggregate Attributional Effects and the Regressiveness of Prediction." In: *Journal of Personality and Social Psychology* Vol. 53, No. 3: 490–496.

Andreassen, Paul B. and Stephen Kraus. 1988. "Judgmental Prediction by Extrapolation." Cambridge: Harvard University, Department of Psychology, Ms. unpublished.

Arthur, W. Brian. 1997. "Beyond Rational Expectations. Indeterminacy in Economic and Financial Markets." In: John N. Drobak and John V.C. Nye (Eds.), *Frontiers of the New Institutional Economics*. New York: Academic Press: 291–304.

———. 1995. "Complexity in Economic and Financial Markets." In: *Complexity* Vol.1, No. 1: 20–25.

———. 1988. "Self-Reinforcing Mechanisms in Economics." In: Philip W. Anderson, Kenneth J. Arrow and David Pines (Eds.), *The Economy as an Evolving Complex System*. Reading: Addison-Wesley: 9–31.

Arthur, W. Brian, John H. Holland, Blake LeBaron, Richard Palmer and Paul Tayler. 1997. "Asset Pricing Under Endogenous Expectations in an Artificial Stock Market." In: W. Brian Arthur, Steven N. Durlauf and David A. Lane (Eds.), *The Economy as an Evolving Complex System II*. Reading: Addison-Wesley: 15–44.

Axelrod, Robert. 1984. *The Evolution of Cooperation*. New York: Basic Books.

Barber, Brad M. and Terrance Odean. 2002. "All That Glitters. The Effect of Attention and News on the Buying Behavior of Individual and Institutional Investors." Davis: University of California, Graduate School of Management, Working Paper.

Benning, Jim. 2000. "The Lesson of Emulex." In: *Online Journalism Review*, 8.9.

Bernstein, Richard. 2001. *Navigate the Noise. Investing in the New Age of Media and Hype*. New York: Wiley.

Black, Fischer. 1986. "Noise." In: *Journal of Finance* Vol. 41, No. 3: 529–543.

Bloomfield, Robert and Jeffrey Hales. 2002. "Predicting the Next Step of a Random Walk. Experimental Evidence of Regime-Shifting Beliefs." In: *Journal of Financial Economics* Vol. 65, No. 3: 397–414.

Blume, Lawrence and David Easley. 1992. "Evolution and Market Behavior." In: Journal of Economic Theory Vol. 58, No. 1: 9–40.

Boehm, Thomas, Judah Folkman, Timothy Browder and Michael S. O'Reilly. 1997. "Antiangiogenic Therapy of Experimental Cancer Does Not Induce Acquired Drug Resistance." In: *Nature* Vol. 390, No. 6658: 404–407.

Busse, Jeffrey A. and T. Clifton Green. 2002. "Market Efficiency in Real-Time." In: *Journal of Financial Economics* Vol. 65, No. 3: 415–437.

Camerer, Colin F. and George Loewenstein (Eds.). 2003. *Behavioral Economics. Past, Present, Future*. Princeton: Princeton University Press.

Cutler, David M., James M. Poterba and Lawrence H. Summers. 1991. "Speculative Dynamics." In: *The Review of Economic Studies* Vol. 58: 529–546.

Cutler, David M., James M. Poterba and Lawrence H. Summers. 1990. "Speculative Dynamics and the Role of Feedback Traders." In: *American Economic Review* Vol. 80, No. 2: 63–68.

Czarnitzki, Dirk and Georg Stadtmann. 2000. "The Behaviour of Noise Traders. Empirical Evidence on Purchases of Business Magazines." Zentrum für Europäische Wirtschaftsforschung (ZEW).

Dawkins, Richard. 1999. "The Selfish Meme." In: *Time*, 19.4.

———. 1976. *The Selfish Gene*. Oxford: Oxford University Press.

De Long, J. Bradford, Andrei Shleifer, Lawrence H. Summers and Robert J. Waldmann. 1991. "The Survival of Noise Traders in Financial Markets." In: *Journal of Business* Vol. 64, No. 1: 1–19.

De Long, J. Bradford, Andrei Shleifer, Lawrence H. Summers and Robert J. Waldmann. 1990. "Noise Trader Risk in Financial Markets." In: *Journal of Political Economy* Vol. 98, No. 4: 703–38.

De Long, J. Bradford, Andrei Shleifer, Lawrence H. Summers and Robert J. Waldmann. 1989. "The Size and Incidence of the Losses from Noise Trading." In: *The Journal of Finance* Vol. 44, No. 3: 681–695.

Farmer, J. Doyne. 2002. "Market Force, Ecology, and Evolution." In: *Industrial and Corporate Change* Vol. 11, No. 5: 895–953.

Farmer, J. Doyne and Andrew W. Lo. 1999. "Frontiers of Finance. Evolution and Efficient Markets." In: *Proceedings of the National Academy of Sciences* Vol. 96: 9991–9992.

Fischhoff, Baruch, Paul Slovic and S. Lichtenstein. 1980. "Knowing What You Want. Measuring Labile Values." In: Thomas S. Wallsten (Ed.), *Cognitive Processes in Choice and Decision Behavior*. Hillsdale: Erlbaum Associates: 117–141.

Frank, Joshua. 1999. "Applying Memetics to Financial Markets. Do Markets Evolve Towards Efficiency?" In: *Journal of Memetics* Vol. 3, No. 2: 87–99.

Friedman, Daniel. 1991. "Evolutionary Games in Economics." In: *Econometrica* Vol. 59, No. 3: 637–666.

Friedman, Milton. 1953. *Essays in Positive Economics*. Chicago: University of Chicago Press.

Gadarowski, Christopher. 2002. "Financial Press Coverage and Expected Stock Returns." Ithaca: Cornell University, School of Hotel Administration, Financial Management Department, Working Paper.

Galbraith, John Kenneth. 1954. *The Great Crash 1929*. Boston: Houghton Mifflin.

Garber, Peter M. 2001. "Famous First Bubbles. The Fundamentals of Early Manias." In: *Journal of Political Economy* Vol. 109, No. 5: 1150–1179.

———. 1989. "Tulipmania." In: *Journal of Political Economy* Vol. 97, No. 3: 535–560.

Gerbner, George. 1998. "Cultivation Analysis. An Overview." In: *Mass Communication and Society* Vol. 1, No. 3/4: 175–194.

Gerbner, George, Larry Gross, Michael Morgan and Nancy Signorielli. 1994. "Growing Up With Television. The Cultivation Perspective." In: Jennings Bryant and Dolf Zillmann (Ed.), *Media Effects. Advances in Theory and Research*. Hillsdale: Lawrence Erlbaum: 17–41.

Haggerty, Mike and Wallace Rasmussen. 1994. *The Headline vs. the Bottom Line. Mutual Distrust Between Business and the News Media.* Nashville: Freedom Forum First Amendment Center.

Hirshleifer, David and Siew Hong Teoh. 2003. "Herd Behavior and Cascading in Capital Markets. A Review and Synthesis." In: *European Financial Management* Vol. 9: 25–66.

Holland, John H. 1995. *Hidden Order. How Adaptation Builds Complexity.* Reading: Addison-Wesley.

Huberman, Gur and Tomer Regev. 2001. "Contagious Speculation and a Cure for Cancer. A Nonevent that Made Stock Prices Soar." In: *Journal of Finance* Vol. 56, No. 1: 387–396.

Hunter, William C., George G. Kaufman and Michael Pomerleano. 2003. *Asset Price Bubbles. Implicatons for Monetary, Regulatory, and International Policies.* Cambridge: Massachusetts Institute of Technology (MIT) Press.

Iyengar, Shanto and Donald R. Kinder. 1987. *News That Matters.* Chicago: The University of Chicago Press.

Joshi, Shareen, Jeffrey Parker and Mark A. Bedau. 1998. "Technical Trading Creates a Prisoner's Dilemma. Results from an Agent-Based Model." Santa Fe: Santa Fe Institute, Working Paper.

Kerbel, Robert S. 1997. "A Cancer Therapy Resistant to Resistance." In: *Nature* Vol. 390, No. 6658: 335–336.

Kindleberger, Charles P. 1978. *Manias, Panics, and Crashes. A History of Financial Crises.* New York: Wiley, 2000.

Krugman, Paul. 1997. "Seven Habits of Highly Defective Investors." In: *Fortune*, 29.12.

Lindgren. 1997. "Evolutionary Dynamics in Game-Theoretic Models." In: W. Brian Arthur, Steven N. Durlauf and David A. Lane (Eds.), *The Economy as an Evolving Complex System II.* Reading: Addison-Wesley: 337–367.

Lynch, Aaron. 1996. *Thought Contagion. How Belief Spreads Through Society.* New York: Basic Books.

Madrick, Jeff. 2001. "The Business Media and the New Economy." Research Paper R-24. Cambridge: The Joan Shorenstein Center on the Press, Politics and Public Policy, John F. Kennedy School of Government, Harvard University.

Mauboussin, Michael J. 2002. "Revisiting Market Efficiency. The Stock Market as a Complex Adaptive System." In: *Journal of Applied Corporate Finance* Vol. 14, No. 4: 47–55.

Merton, Robert C. 1987. "A Simple Model of Capital Market Equilibrium with Incomplete Information." In: *Journal of Finance* Vol. 42, No. 3: 483–510.

Meschke, J. Felix. 2002. "CEO Interviews on CNBC." Tempe: Arizona State University, Working Paper.

Morris, Stephen and Hyun Song Shin. 2001. "The CNBC Effect. Welfare Effects of Public Information." New Haven: Yale University, Cowles Foundation for Research in Economics, Discussion Paper No. 1312.

Mullainathan, Sendhil and Andrei Shleifer. 2002. "Media Bias." Cambridge: Harvard University, Institute for Economic Research, Working Paper No. 1981.

Ofek, Eli and Matthew Richardson. 2002. "The Valuation and Market Rationality of Internet Stock Prices." In: *Oxford Review of Economic Policy* Vol. 18, No. 3: 265–287.

Ofek, Eli and Matthew Richardson. 2001. "DotCom Mania. The Rise and Fall of Internet Stock Prices." National Bureau Economic Research (NBER) Working Paper W8630.

Parker, Richard. 1997. "The Public, the Press, and Economic News." In: *Harvard International Journal of Press Politics* Vol. 2, No. 2: 127–131.

Pearce, Douglas K. and V. Vance Roley. 1985. "Stock Prices and Economic News." In: *Journal of Business*, Vol. 58, No. 1: 49–67.

Rapoport, Anatol and Albert M. Chammah. 1965. *Prisoner's Dilemma*. Ann Arbor: The University of Michigan Press.

Samuelson, Paul A. 1998. "Summing Up on Business Cycles. Opening Address." In: Jeffrey C. Fuhrer and Scott Schuh (Eds.), *Beyond Shocks. What Causes Business Cycles*. Boston: Federal Reserve Bank of Boston: 33–36.

Schuster, Thomas. 2004. *Staat und Medien. Über die elektronische Konditionierung der Wirklichkeit*. 2., erweiterte Auflage. Wiesbaden: VS Verlag.

———. 2001. *Die Geldfalle. Wie Medien und Banken die Anleger zu Verlierern machen*. Reinbek: Rowohlt.

Shiller, Robert J. 2002. "From Efficient Market Theory to Behavioral Finance." New Haven: Yale University, Cowles Foundation Discussion Paper No. 1385.

———. 2000. *Irrational Exuberance*. Princeton: Princeton University Press.

Shleifer, Andrei and Lawrence H. Summers. 1990. "The Noise Trader Approach to Finance." In: *Journal of Economic Perspectives*, Vol. 4, No. 2: 19–33.

Soros, George. 1998. *The Crisis of Global Capitalism. Open Society Endangered*. New York: Public Affairs.

———. 1994. "The Theory of Reflexivity." Speech Delivered April 26, 1994 to the Massachusetts Institute of Technology (MIT) Department of Economics World Economy Laboratory Conference Washington, D.C.

———. 1987. *The Alchemy of Finance. Reading the Mind of the Market*. New York: Simon and Schuster.

Surowiecki, James. 2001. "The Financial Page. Manic Monday (And Other Popular Delusions)." In: *New Yorker* 03/26.

Thaler, Richard H. 1999. "The End of Behavioral Finance." In: *Financial Analysts Journal* Vol. 55, No. 6: 12–17.

Wright, David W. 1994. "Can Prices be Trusted? A Test of the Ability of Experts to Outperform or Influence the Market." In: *Journal of Accounting, Auditing and Finance* Vol. 9: 307–323.

AFTERWORD: CRITIQUE OF THE NOISE SYSTEM

News that is disseminated by the business press and by financial television usually does not represent "information" in the sense that it could be utilized. It appears as data with a certain content, but in fact, it is for the most part nothing but noise—empty information particles, which are already contained in stock market prices. Investors who follow such pseudo-information can be considered as noise traders. Their investment decisions are based on data that do not have any actual meaning.

Much ado about nothing? Not at all, since the dependence on empty information particles makes investors more susceptible to mood swings. They follow the vagaries of the market, rumors and, with particularly severe consequences, past performance. They chase after trends because they fallaciously believe that future price developments follow the past. And they make markets more susceptible to fluctuations by evoking nervous overreactions and reinforcing them.

Since the 1990s in particular, the volume of news in the media that is related to the capital market has strongly increased. The army of noise traders has seen a millionfold increase in members. Actions of a growing number of private, and professional investors are subject to increasing mood swings. Especially in times of stock market boom: Rising prices increase the reach of the business media—and thereby also the noise in the market.

Financial economists argue that noise is actually the precondition for the existence of liquid markets: Stock market transactions are only carried out if the opponents hold different opinions about the future prospects of the relevant investments. These differences of opinion necessarily originate from qualitatively different information—and thus from the existence of noise. A certain "noise level" is therefore indispensable for trading activities to take place.[1]

Only if there is sufficient noise in the market do information holders have an incentive to act. Otherwise, they would have to compete with equally informed market participants, which would significantly reduce the amount of business. In order to avoid this and in order to have sufficient numbers of less well-informed opponents, it is in their interest to install trading platforms, to create financial instruments, to advertise them and to produce noise to cause demand.

From this point of view, it is in the interest of information holders if there are numerous business media, that disseminate pseudo-information with little content, which convey a "sense of market," although they are basically worthless. If they did not already exist, these market participants would have to invent the media, to make the idea of the markets popular and to gain new investors. It may be an odd coincidence: This is exactly what is observable in practice.[2]

But noise has got more effects: It makes it more difficult to arrive at a clear picture of the market situation. A wall of worthless information obscures the view of the actual economic circumstances: Noise makes market signals ambiguous, an adequate evaluation of investments becomes increasingly difficult—even for "informed" market participants. Noise thus does not only fulfill its "natural" function of generating liquidity in the markets: It makes prices less efficient.

This provides an opportunity for informed investors to take advantage of the mistakes that naive noise traders make under the impression of contaminated news: They are able to anticipate overreactions, which occur due to positive feedback processes—and thereby reinforce them. And they can build up counter-positions, in order to lead prices back to their correct level and separate noise traders from their money in the process.

However, this is not a zero-sum game. Inefficient prices imply an increased susceptibility to fluctuations, an additional systematic market risk. The unpredictability of prices increases if investors' behavior is conditioned by noise. Systematic market risks, however, concern *all* market participants, they cannot be eliminated through counter-measures. The related costs are borne by *all* market participants as well.

Noise destabilizes. Pseudo-signals obstruct the view of the real economic situation and contribute to the generation of self-reinforcing price dynamics. And they react in an unpredictable way on the economic situation. Part of these pseudo-signals are forecasts of finance gurus, most of the information disseminated by brokerage houses and banks as well as the non-events of the news media.

With the expansion of the noise system, destabilizing forces have increased. The markets are far from reaching a permanent state of equilibrium. The probability of dynamic self-runners increases with growing levels of noise. More than ever, the statement applies that markets may be efficient on the micro level, whereas they can be inefficient on the macro-level.[3] And that they possibly are increasingly inefficient.

There is, of course, the possibility to benefit from more pronounced market fluctuations: Noise traders can obtain higher profits, in ignorance of the risk they are exposed to. Information traders can try to take advantage of the mistakes of the noise traders. Profit and loss are not always accurately distributed between rational and irrational investors. Often, it is hardly possible or even impossible to distinguish between the two.

Potentially, however, the benefit for all is reduced, while the risk increases disproportionately—*for everybody*. Although the exact level might be difficult to estimate quantatively: From a certain point, the costs of the noise outweigh its benefits, until everyone loses in the end. Noise turns out to be counterproductive on a macroeconomic level, since it leads to a waste of capital.

Excessive noise disturbs the adequate use of resources and undermines trust in the markets. Rational investors are deterred, because they consider the risks to be too high. The others only learn afterward: When investors have to realize that they suffered damage because their picture of the markets corresponded to an artificial scenery of noise, collective disillusionment is a probable consequence.

Only few actors benefit: Those who profit from an increase in trading volume and higher turnovers of information; and those who successfully bet against uninformed investors, who follow pseudo-information. Many become poorer; only a few get the chance to systematically enrich themselves.

NOTES

1. Black (1986).
2. Schuster (2001).
3. Samuelson (1998).

REFERENCES

Black, Fischer. 1986. "Noise." In: *Journal of Finance* Vol. 41, No. 3: 529–543.

Samuelson, Paul A. 1998. "Summing Up on Business Cycles. Opening Address." In: Jeffrey C. Fuhrer and Scott Schuh (Eds.), *Beyond Shocks. What Causes Business Cycles*. Boston: Federal Reserve Bank of Boston: 33–36.

Schuster, Thomas. 2001. "Der Preis war eigentlich gar nicht der Rede wert. Das blieb dem gescheiterten Käufer RTL erspart: Wie bei n-tv die Börsenberichte jahrelang von Banken und Industrie finanziert wurden." In: *Frankfurter Allgemeine Zeitung*, 10/06.

APPENDIX: BIBLIOGRAPHY OF BUSINESS AND FINANCIAL COMMUNICATION

"Abruptes Ende eines Höhenflugs." In: *Werben und Verkaufen* No. 46 (2001): 116–118.

Adoni, Hanna and Akiba A. Cohen. "Television News and the Social Construction of Economic Reality." In: *Journal of Communication* Vol. 28, No. 4 (1978): 61–70.

Afheldt, Heik. "Am Fachleser orientieren. Aufgaben und Ziele eines Wirtschaftsmagazins." In: Gero Kalt (ed.), *Wirtschaft in den Medien*. Frankfurt a.M.: IMK, 1990: 181–187.

Albert, Robert L. and Timothy R. Smaby. "Market Response to Analyst Recommendations in the 'Dartboard' Column. The Information and Price-Pressure Effects." In: *Review of Financial Economics* Vol. 5, No. 1 (1996): 59–74.

Albrecht, Christoph. "Zukunftsperspektiven und Spezialisierungsfelder. Wirtschaft in der Alternativpresse." In: Stephan Ruß-Mohl and Heinz D. Stuckmann (eds.), *Wirtschaftsjournalismus. Ein Handbuch für Ausbildung und Praxis*. München: List, 1991: 227–230.

Allen, David S. and Hamidah Awang-Damit. "The Wall Street Journal Investment Dartboard." Northern Arizona University, College of Business Administration, Working Paper, 1998.

Alles über die Zeitung. Frankfurter Allgemeine, Zeitung für Deutschland. Frankfurt a.M.: Frankfurter Allgemeine Zeitung, 1992.

Althen, Adolf. "Berührungsängste, Sachzwänge, Einsdreißig. Chancen und Grenzen öffentlich-rechtlicher Wirtschaftsjournalisten." In: Gero Kalt (ed.), *Wirtschaft in den Medien*. Frankfurt a.M.: IMK, 1990: 107–115.

Altmeppen, Klaus-Dieter (ed.). *Ökonomie der Medien und des Mediensystems*. Opladen: Westdeutscher Verlag, 1996.

"Analysten im Wandel. Vergleich der Berichterstattung über Analysten-Aussagen 2000 und 2001." In: *Medien Tenor* Vol. 9, No. 116 (2002): 47.

"Analysts' Role is Now More Like Journalism." In: *Investor Relations Business*, 10/1/2000.

Anderson, Christopher. *Blaming the Government. Citizens and the Economy in Five European Democracies*. London: M. E. Sharpe, 1995.

"Anchors Away From L.A. College Roots." In: *Variety*, 04/26/1999.

Andrew, John. *How to Understand the Financial Press*. London: Kogan Page, 1993.

Anhold, Hein. *Wirtschaftsnachrichten erklärt und entschlüsselt*. Frankfurt a.M.: Fischer, 1989.

"Anklage gegen 3sat-Börsenspezialisten." In: *Neue Zürcher Zeitung*, 11/21/1998.

"Anlegermagazine leiden unter Auflagenschwund." In: *Süddeutsche Zeitung*, 1/26/2001.

Antrecht, Rolf. *Special Wirtschaftsmedien*. Hamburg: New-Business, 2000.

Antunovich, Peter and Asani Sarkar. "Cheap Talk? Market Impact of Internet Stock Recommendations." Ms. unveröffentlicht, 2000.

Antweiler, Werner and Murray Z. Frank. 2002. "Is All That Talk Just Noise? The Information Content of Internet Stock Message Boards." In: *Journal of Finance* Vol. 59, No. 3: 1259–1295.

Apostolou, Nicholas G. *Keys to Understanding the Financial News*. Hauppauge: Barron's, 1994.

Aronoff, Craig E. (ed.). *Business and the Media*. Santa Monica: Goodyear, 1979.

Arrese, Ángel. *Economic and Financial Press. From the Beginnings of the First Oil Crisis*. Pamplona: Ediciones Universidad de Navarra, 2001.

"At CNBC, a Bigger 'Business.'" In: *Variety*, 7/10/2000.

"Aufgabe einer Wirtschaftszeitung." In: *Handelsblatt*, 5/16/1951.

"Aufregung um Börsenguru Bernd Förtsch." In: *Süddeutsche Zeitung*, 8/17/2000.

Ayerst, David. *Guardian. Biography of a Newspaper*. London: Collins, 1971.

Babe, Robert E. (ed.). *Information and Communication in Economics*. Boston: Kluwer, 1994.

Babe, Robert E. *Communication and the Transformation of Economics. Essays in Information, Public Policy, and Political Economy*. Boulder: Westview, 1995.

Bachmann, Dorit. "Medienspezifische Präsentation. Boulevardzeitung." In: Stephan Ruß-Mohl and Heinz D. Stuckmann (eds.), *Wirtschaftsjournalismus. Ein Handbuch für Ausbildung und Praxis*. München: List, 1991: 138–142.

Baentsch, Wolfram. "Medienspezifische Präsentation. Wirtschaftsmagazin." In: Stephan Ruß-Mohl and Heinz D. Stuckmann (eds.), *Wirtschaftsjournalismus. Ein Handbuch für Ausbildung und Praxis*. München: List, 1991: 150–152.

Baerns, Barbara. "Öffentlichkeitsarbeit als Determinante journalistischer Informationsleistung. Thesen zur realistischeren Beschreibung von Medieninhalten." In: *Publizistik* Vol. 24, No. 3 (1979): 310–316.

Baerns, Barbara. "Orientierungshilfen. Wirtschaftsjournalismus in der früheren DDR." In: Stephan Ruß-Mohl and Heinz D. Stuckmann (eds.), *Wirtschaftsjournalismus. Ein Handbuch für Ausbildung und Praxis. München: List, 1991: 260–264.

Baerns, Barbara. "Redaktionelle Werbung im Wettbewerb von Tageszeitungen. Probleme und Befunde einer Untersuchung zur Trennung von redaktionellem Text und Anzeigen." In: H.-D. Fischer and Barbara Baerns (eds.), *Wettbewerbswidrige Praktiken auf dem Pressemarkt*. Baden-Baden: Nomos, 1979: 99–123.

Baerns, Barbara. "Möglichkeiten journalistischer Informationsbeschaffung in der Privatwirtschaft." In: Klaus Schredelseker and Norbert Koubek (eds.), *Information, Mitbestimmung und Unternehmenspolitik*. Frankfurt a.M.: Haag + Herchen, 1984: 183–206.

Baerns, Barbara. *Öffentlichkeitsarbeit oder Journalismus? Zum Einfluß im Mediensystem*. Köln: Verlag Wissenschaft und Politik, 1991.

Baerns, Barbara: "PR, Journalismus, Medien. Die Forschung macht verborgene Beziehungen sichtbar." In: Gero Kalt (ed.), *Öffentlichkeitsarbeit und Werbung*. Frankfurt a.M.: IMK, 1993: 53–62.

Baird, Russell and A. T. Turnball. *Industrial and Business Journalism*. Philadelphia: Chilton, 1961.

Baltl, Hermann. "Zur Wirtschaftsjournalistik." In: *Wirtschaftspolitische Blätter* 6, 1975.

Barber, Brad M. and Douglas Loeffler, "The 'Dartboard' Column. Second-Hand Information and Price Pressure." In: *Journal of Financial and Quantitative Analysis* Vol. 28, No. 2 (1993): 273–284.

Barber, Brad M. and Terrance Odean. "All that Glitters. The Effect of Attention and News on the Buying Behavior of Individual and Institutional Investors." Davis: University of California, Graduate School of Management, Working Paper, 2002.

Barbier, Hans D. "Wirtschaftsjournalismus auf dem Prüfstand, aus der Sicht des Journalismus." In: Siegfried Klaue (ed.), *Marktwirtschaft in der Medienberichterstattung*. Düsseldorf: Econ, 1991: 29–34.

Barker, Robert. "How Timely Are the Tube's Tips?" In: *Business Week*, 11/29/1999.

Barreto, Souza and Nadja Cleyde. *Zwischen den Zeilen lesen. Eine Inhaltsanalyse der entwicklungspolitischen Berichterstattung des Handelsblatts, der Frankfurter Allgemeinen Zeitung und der Frankfurter Rundschau*. Saarbrücken, 1987.

Bartels, Larry. "Messages Received. The Political Impact of Media Exposure." In: *American Political Science Review* Vol. 87 (1993): 267–285.

Bartiromo, Maria and Catherine Fredman. *Use the News. How to Separate the Noise from the Investment Nuggets and Make Money in Any Economy*. New York: HarperCollins, 2001.

Becker, Holger. *Die Wirtschaft in der deutschsprachigen Presse. Sprachliche Untersuchungen zur Wirtschaftsberichterstattung in der "Frankfurter Allgemeinen Zeitung," der "Neuen Zürcher Zeitung," der "Presse" und im "Neuen Deutschland."* Frankfurt a. M.: Lang, 1995.

Becker, Kent G., Joseph E. Finnerty and Joseph Friedman. "Economic News and Equity Market Linkages Between the U.S. and U.K." In: *Journal of Banking and Finance* Vol.19, No.7 (1995): 1191–1210.

Becker, Kent G., Joseph E. Finnerty and Kenneth J. Kopecky. "Economic News and Intraday Volatility in International Bond Markets." In: *Financial Analysts Journal* Vol.49, No.3 (1993): 81–86.

Behrens, Günter. "Eine Programmsparte im Schatten. Wirtschaftsmagazine im Fernsehen." In: Helmut Kreuzer and Karl Prümm (eds.), *Fernsehsendungen und ihre Formen*. Paderborn: Igel, 1979: 328–347.

Beike, Rolf and Johannes Schlütz. *Finanznachrichten lesen, verstehen, nutzen. Ein Wegweiser durch Kursnotierungen und Marktberichte*. Stuttgart: Schäffer-Poeschel, 1996.

Bell, Daniel et al. *Writing for Fortune. Nineteen Authors Remember Life on the Staff of a Remarkable Magazine*. New York: Time, 1980.

Bell, David. "The Business Information Industry in 2001. A View from the Financial Times Group." In: *European Business Information Conference* (1995): 19–40.

Beloch, Horst. "Fremdkörper für den Durchschnittsleser. Defizite bei den Tageszeitungen." In: Gero Kalt (ed.), *Wirtschaft in den Medien*. Frankfurt a.M.: IMK, 1990: 189–194.

Beloch, Horst. "Wirtschaftsjournalismus. Verständlichkeit, Bringschuld der Redaktionen." In: *Medien-Kritik* No. 10 (1990): 11–12.

Beltz, Jess and Robert Jennings. "'Wall Street Week with Louis Rukeyser' Recommendations. Trading Activity and Performance." In: *Review of Financial Economics* Vol. 6, No. 1 (1997): 15–27.

Benabou, Roland and Guy Laroque. "Using Privileged Information to Manipulate Markets. Insiders, Gurus, and Credibility." In: *Quarterly Journal of Economics* Vol. 107 (1992): 921–958.

Bender, Klaus. "Wirtschaft in der Morgenleiste. Programmpläne der neuen WDR-Regionalfenster." In: *Medienspiegel* Vol. 8, No. 20 (1984): 2–3.

Beneish, Messod D. "Stock Prices and the Dissemination of Analysts' Recommendations." In: *Journal of Business* Vol. 64, No. 3 (1991): 393–416.

Benesh, Gary A. and Jeffrey A. Clark. "The Value of Indirect Investment Advice. Stock Recommendations in Barron's." In: *Journal of Financial and Strategic Decisions* Vol. 7, No. 1 (1994): 35–43.

Berentson, Jane (ed.). *Dressing for Dinner in the Naked City and Other Tales from the Wall Street Journal's "Middle Column."* New York: Hyperion, 1994.

Bergler, Sabine and Sonja Knoll. "Coreference Patterns in the Wall Street Journal." In: *Language and Computers* Vol. 16 (1996): 85–95.

Berke, Jürgen. "Pläne für mehr Berichte aus dem Arbeitsleben in Nordrhein-Westfalen." In: *WDR print* No. 124 (1986): 3.

Bernard Rubin and Associates. *Big Business and the Mass Media*. Lexington: Lexington Books, 1977.

Bernstein, Richard. *Navigate the Noise. Investing in the New Age of Media and Hype*. New York: Wiley, 2001.
"Besser als ihr Ruf." In: *Werben und Verkaufen* No. 46 (2001): 138.
Bethell, Tom. *Television Evening News Covers Inflation, 1978–79. An Analysis*. Washington, D.C.: Media Institute, 1980.
Bibliographie der Wirtschaftspresse. Dokumentation ausgewählter Zeitschriftenaufsätze aus den Beständen der Bibliothek des HWWA-Instituts für Wirtschaftsforschung. Hamburg, 1949.
"Big Business im Blätterwald." In: *Horizont*, 1/20/2000.
Blood, Deborah J. and Peter C. B. Phillips. "Recession Headline News, Consumer Sentiment, the State of the Economy and Presidential Popularity. A Time Series Analysis 1989–1993." In: *International Journal of Public Opinion* Vol. 7, No. 1 (1995): 2–22.
Bode, Hermann. *Die Anfänge wirtschaftlicher Berichterstattung in der Presse. Eine volkswirtschaftliche Studie als Beitrag zur Geschichte des Zeitungswesens*. Heidelberg: Dissertation, 1908.
Böhmer, Reinhold. "Schreiben und Redigieren." In: Stephan Ruß-Mohl and Heinz D. Stuckmann (eds.), *Wirtschaftsjournalismus. Ein Handbuch für Ausbildung und Praxis*. München: List, 1991: 111–126.
Bojunga, Harold. "Internationale Wirtschaftsberichterstattung." In: Stephan Ruß-Mohl and Heinz D. Stuckmann (eds.), *Wirtschaftsjournalismus. Ein Handbuch für Ausbildung und Praxis*. München: List, 1991: 111–125.
Bojunga, Harold. "Zukunftsperspektiven und Spezialisierungsfelder. Internationale Wirtschaftsberichterstattung." In: Stephan Ruß-Mohl and Heinz D. Stuckmann (eds.), *Wirtschaftsjournalismus. Ein Handbuch für Ausbildung und Praxis*. München: List, 1991: 218–22.
"Börsen-Journalismus. Neue Regeln für die Insider." In: Bernd-Jürgen Martini (ed.), *Journalisten-Jahrbuch 1989*. München: Ölschläger, 1988: 45.
Börsen-Zeitung (ed.). *Wirtschaftsjournalismus heute. Festschrift zum 60. Geburtstag von Bernd Baehring Chefredakteur der Börsen-Zeitung*. Frankfurt a.M.: Börsen-Zeitung.
Bös, Josef. "Einige Gedanken über die Wirtschaftspresse." In: Franz Hieronymus Riedl (ed.), *Humanitas Ethnica. Festschrift für Theodor Veiter*. Stuttgart: Braumüller, 1967.
Boschbach, Gerd Wolfgang and Hans-Walther Rother. "Gefragt. Der aktuelle politische Hintergrund. Wirtschaftsthemen in den politischen Montagsmagazinen der ARD." In: *Medienspiegel* Vol. 2, No. 7 (1978): 2–5.
Böse, Georg. *Wirtschaft und Presse. Ein historisch-soziologischer Versuch über die Wechselwirkungen zwischen der Wirtschaft und der Presse*. Heidelberg: Dissertation, 1931.
Bott, Hermann. "Arbeitsmittel und Recherchewege. Fallstudie: Neue Heimat." In: Stephan Ruß-Mohl and Heinz D. Stuckmann (eds.), *Wirtschaftsjournalismus. Ein Handbuch für Ausbildung und Praxis*. München: List, 1991: 93–99.

Boynton, G. R. and Christophe Deissenberg. "Models of the Economy Implicit in Public Discourse." In: *Policy Sciences* Vol. 20 (1987): 129–151.

Brady, Ray. "What Does Financial Reporting Look Like Today? Give 'em the Scores and Show a Few Highlights of the Game." In: *Nieman Reports* Vol. 55, No. 2 (2001): 83–83.

Brawand, Leo. *Die Spiegel-Story. Wie alles anfing*. Düsseldorf: Econ, 1995.

Brech, John. "Über den Wandel der wirtschaftlichen Berichterstattung." In: *Wirtschaftsdienst Hamburg* Heft 10 (1958): 558–560.

Breining, Thomas. "Zukunftsperspektiven und Spezialisierungsfelder. Wirtschaftsthemen im Lokalen." In: Stephan Ruß-Mohl and Heinz D. Stuckmann (eds.), *Wirtschaftsjournalismus. Ein Handbuch für Ausbildung und Praxis*. München: List, 1991: 224–226.

Breit, Ernst. "Einseitiges über Halbwahrheiten. Kritikpunkte aus Sicht der Gewerkschaften." In: Gero Kalt (ed.), *Wirtschaft in den Medien*. Frankfurt a.M.: IMK, 1990: 21–26.

Brett, Michael. *How to Read the Financial Pages*. London: Random House, 2000.

Brettschneider, Frank. "Economic Affairs, Media Coverage, and the Public's Perception of the Economy in Germany." In: Angela Schorr, Bill Campbell and Michael Schenk (eds.), *Communication Research in Europe and Abroad. Challenges of the First Decade*. Berlin: DeGruyter, 2002.

Brettschneider, Frank. "Reality Bytes. Wie die Medienberichterstattung die Wahrnehmung der Wirtschaftslage beeinflußt." In: Jürgen W. Falter, Oscar W. Gabriel and Hans Rattinger (eds.), *Wirklich ein Volk? Die politischen Orientierungen von Ost- und Westdeutschen im Vergleich*. Opladen: Leske + Budrich, 2000: 539–569.

Brettschneider, Frank. "Up and Down. Wirtschaft in den Fernsehnachrichten und in der Wahrnehmung der Bevölkerung." In: *Medien Tenor Forschungsbericht* No. 101 (2000): 18–22.

Bridges, Janet A. and Lamar W. Bridges. "Changes in News Use on the Front Pages of the American Daily Newspaper, 1986–1993." In: *Journalism and Mass Communication Quarterly* Vol. 74, No. 4 (1997): 826–838.

Broichhausen, Klaus. "Informationen pfundweise. Wirtschaftskorrespondenten der Bundeshauptstadt." In: Gero Kalt (ed.), *Wirtschaft in den Medien*. Frankfurt a.M.: IMK, 1990: 315–322.

Brown, Janelle. "New Ethics for the New Economy?" In: Salon.com, 8/6/1999.

Brown, Stephen J., William N. Goetzmann and Alok Kumar. "The Dow Theory. William Peter Hamilton's Track Record Reconsidered." In: *The Journal of Finance* Vol. 53, No. 4 (1998): 1311–1333.

Brückner, Thomas. *Zur Kritik des Wirtschaftsteils von Tageszeitungen. Eine inhaltsanalytische Betrachtung der Rolle von Technik und Arbeit in der Berichterstattung zur ökonomischen Entwicklung*. Dortmund, 1983.

"Buffett Issues His Annual Report. Pariahs this Year Include News Media, Wall St. and Chief Executives." In: *The New York Times*, 3/12/2001.

Bundeszentrale für politische Bildung (ed.). *Wirtschaft. Ein Arbeitsbuch für Journalisten*. Bonn: Bundeszentrale für politische Bildung, 1996.

Burkhard, Michael. "Auf der Insel der Wirtschaftsseeligen. Wie informiert WM, das Wirtschaftsmagazin in SAT 1?" In: *Funkreport* 15 (1985): 2–3.

Busch, Friedhelm. "Zukunftsperspektiven und Spezialisierungsfelder. Geld, Banken, Börsen." In: Stephan Ruß-Mohl and Heinz D. Stuckmann (eds.), *Wirtschaftsjournalismus. Ein Handbuch für Ausbildung und Praxis*. München: List, 1991: 200–202.

Business Journalism in the New Information Economy. Freedom Forum, Media Studies Center, 1999.

"Business Reporting is Hot! Hot! Hot!" In: www.salon.com, 9/20/2000.

"Business Reporting: Behind the Curve." In: *Columbia Journalism Review*, November/Dezember 2000: 18–21.

Busse, Jeffrey A. and T. Clifton Green. "Market Efficiency in Real-Time." Atlanta: Emory University, Goizueta Business School, Working Paper, 2001.

Byland, Terry. *Understanding Finance with the Financial Times*. London: Harrap, 1988.

Calian, Carnegie Samuel. *The Gospel According to the Wall Street Journal*. Atlanta: John Knox, 1975.

Case Studies on Presentation of Business on Television. London, 1973.

Chan, Wesley S. "Stock Price Reaction to News and No-News. Drift and Reversal After Headlines." Cambridge: MIT Sloan School of Management, Working Paper, 2002.

Chmielewicz, Klaus S. "Berichterstattung über die Betriebswirtschaftslehre in der Tages- und Wochenpresse." In: *Die Betriebswirtschaft* 3 (1980): 445–448.

Christians, F. Wilhelm. "Zur Kritik des Wirtschaftsjournalismus. Der Bankier." In: Stephan Ruß-Mohl and Heinz D. Stuckmann (eds.), *Wirtschaftsjournalismus. Ein Handbuch für Ausbildung und Praxis*. München: List, 1991: 46–48.

Clinton, Patrick. *Guide to Writing for the Business Press*. Lincolnwood: NTC, 1997.

"CNBC Suffers Slings and Arrows of Market's Slide." In: *New York Times*, 3/26/2001.

"CNBC. All's Well, Almost." In: *Mediaweek* No. 17 (1997): 6ff.

"CNBC. Ausbau zur weltweiten Macht im Wirtschafts-TV." In: *Der Spiegel*, 6/22/1998.

"CNN's Ratings Decline as Rivals Lure Away Its Viewers. Time Warner Unit Struggles Against Inroads by CNBC and Fox News." In: *Wall Street Journal Abstracts*, 3/31/2000.

Cole, Arthur H. *The Historical Development of Economic and Business Literature*. Boston: Kress Library of Business and Economics, Publication No. 12., 1957.

Colón, Aly. "Ethics in Business Journalism." In: Terri Thompson (ed.), *Writing About Business*. New York: Columbia University Press, 2001: 255–262.

"Confessions of a Former Mutual Funds Reporter." In: *Fortune*, 4/26/1999.

Conniff, Kimberly. "Money Press. Guardians of the Dow." In: *Brill's Content*, February 2000: 109–111, 127.
Corner, John. "Television News and Economic Exposition." In: Neil T. Gavin (ed.), *The Economy, Media and Public Knowledge*. London: Leicester University Press, 1998: 53–70.
Cowles, Alfred. "Can Stockmarket Forecasters Forecast?" In: *Econometrica* Vol. 1 (1933): 309–324.
Cruz, Humberto. "Financial Pornography Preys on Unwary Investors." In: *Sun-Sentinel*, 10/7/1996
Cunningham, Don. "The Business of Business News." In: *International Broadcast Engineer* No. 280 (September 1996): 50–52.
Czarnitzki, Dirk and Georg Stadtmann. "The Behavior of Noise Traders. Empirical Evidence on Purchases of Business Magazines." Zentrum für Europäische Wirtschaftsforschung, ZEW Discussion Paper No. 00–65, December 2000.
"Dabeisein ist alles. Erfolg von Finanz- und Börsenzeitungen." In: *Der Wirtschaftsredakteur* Vol. 35, No. 10 (2000): 6–7.
Dahrendorf, Ralf. "Unsere Presse. Zwölfte Folge: Schöne Wirtschaft." In: *Merkur* Vol. 43, No. 8 (1989): 728–732.
"Das Ende der heimlichen Herrscher. Analystenzitate in der Wirtschaftspresse Februar bis November 2000." In: *Medien Tenor Forschungsbericht* No. 102 (2000): 32–33.
"Das Montagsfieber." In: *Der Spiegel*, 2/28/2000.
Das, Sanjiv R. and Mike Y. Chen. "Yahoo! for Amazon. Sentiment Parsing from Small Talk on the Web." Santa Clara: Santa Clara University, Working Paper, 2001.
Dauenhauer, Erich. "Die Kaufmännischen Zeitschriften Deutschlands im 18. Jahrhundert." In: *Publizistik* Vol. 10, No. 4 (1965): 471–476.
Davies, P. Lloyd and Michael Canes. "Stock Prices and the Publication of Second-Hand Information." In: *Journal of Business* Vol. 51, No. 1 (1978): 43–57.
Davis, Aeron. "Public Relations, Business News and the Reproduction of Corporate Elite Power." In: *Journalism* Vol. 1, No. 3 (2000): 282–304.
Davis, Evan. "Economic News and the Dynamics of Understanding. A Response." Neil T. Gavin (ed.), *The Economy, Media and Public Knowledge*. London: Leicester University Press, 1998: 156–159.
Dawkins, William and Colin Inman. *Inside the FT. An Insight Into the Art of FT Journalism*. London: Financial Times, 1998.
de Weck, Roger. "Die Gier der Medien." In: *Die Zeit*, 12/29/1999.
Dealy, Francis X., Jr. *The Power and the Money. Inside the Wall Street Journal*. Secaucus: Carol, 1993.
Deetjen, Gottfried. *Industriellenprofile in Massenmedien. Ein neuer Ansatz zur Aussagenanalyse*. Studien zur Massenkommunikation 8. Hamburg: Hans-Bredow-Institut, 1977.

"Der Aktien-Berater Egbert Prior: Zuschauen und Reichwerden?" In: *Süddeutsche Zeitung*, 7/7/1998.

"Der Aufstieg des TV-Unternehmers Michael Bloomberg." In: *Der Spiegel*, 7/20/1998.

"Der Mensch hinter der Nachricht. Was Wirtschaftsjournalisten heute können müssen." In: *Der Wirtschaftsredakteur* Vol. 36, No. 13 (2001): 4–5.

Desai, Hemang, Bing Liang and Ajai K. Singh. "Do All-Stars Shine? Evaluation of Analyst Recommendations." In: *Financial Analysts Journal* Vol. 56, No. 3 (2000): 20–29.

Desai, Hemang and Prem C. Jain. "An Analysis of the Recommendations of the 'Superstar' Money Managers at *Barron's* Annual Roundtable." In: *Journal of Finance* Vol. 50, No. 4 (1995): 1257–1273.

Desai, Hemang and Prem C. Jain. "Long-Run Common Stock Returns Following Financial Analysis by Abraham Briloff." Washington: Georgetown University, Working Paper, 2000.

Deutscher Industrie- und Handelstag (ed.). *Thema: Wirtschaft. Wirtschaftspublizistik im Wandel*. Bonn, 1977.

Die Frankfurter Allgemeine Zeitung. Verkürzte Ausgabe der grossen FAZ-Dokumentation. Frankfurt a.M.: Frankfurter Allgemeine Zeitung, 1995.

"Die Sieger kommen aus der zweiten Reihe. Medien-Image der DAX 30-Unternehmen in tonangebenden Zeitungen und TV-Nachrichten im Jahr 2000." In: *Medien Tenor Forschungsbericht* No. 105 (2001): 24–28.

"Die Versuchung des schnellen Geldes. Insider-Regeln für Journalisten." In: *Süddeutsche Zeitung*, 4/20/2000.

Dimson, Elroy and Paul Marsh. "Event Study Methodologies and the Size Effect. The Case of UK Press Recommendations." In: *Journal of Financial Economics* Vol. 17, No. 1 (1986): 113–142.

Dohrendorf, Rüdiger. *Zum publizistischen Profil der "Frankfurter Allgemeinen Zeitung." Computergestützte Inhaltsanalyse von Kommentaren der FAZ*. Frankfurt a.M.: Lang, 1990.

Doeblin, Jürgen. "'Wir wollen nicht nur Umsatzzahlen hören.' Was halten und erwarten Wirtschaftsjournalisten von Öffentlichkeitsarbeitern?" In: Gero Kalt (ed.), *Wirtschaft in den Medien*. Frankfurt a.M.: IMK, 1990: 295–302.

Doeblin, Jürgen. "Wirtschaftsjournalisten. Bewölkter Himmel über EG 1992." In: *Planung und Analyse* Vol. 16, No. 11/12 (1989): 424–426.

Döhle, Patricia, Wolfgang Hirn and Ulric Papendick. "Das Wall-Street-Kartell." In: *Manager Magazin*, März 2001: 142–151.

Dominick, Joseph R. "Business Coverage in Network Newscasts." In: *Journalism Quarterly* Vol. 58, No. 2 (1981): 179–186, 191.

Dreckmeier, Eva and Georg Hoefer. *Aspekte der Fernsehberichterstattung. Zu den Senderreihen 'Die Reportage,' 'Markt im Dritten,' 'Plusminus,' 'WISO.'* Coppengrave: Coppi, 1994.

Dreier, P. "Capitalism vs. the Media. An Analysis of an Ideological Mobilization Among Business Leaders." In: *Media, Culture and Society* Vol. 4, No. 2 (1982): 111–132.

Easley, Lisa. "Using Media Relations (Instead of Investor Relations) to Help Attract Financing." In: *Public Relations Quarterly* Vol. 43, No. 2 (1998): 39–41.

Ebel, Franz-Josef. "Handelsblatt interaktiv Near-time-Wirtschaftsjournalismus." In: Klaus-Dieter Altmeppen, Hans-Jürgen Bucher and Martin Löffelholz (eds.), *Online-Journalismus. Perspektiven für Wissenschaft und Praxis*. Wiesbaden: Westdeutscher Verlag, 2000: 199–210.

Eberspächer, Helmut. "Wie ich als Unternehmer Wirtschaftsberichterstattung erlebe." In: Michael Schenk and Ferdinand Simoneit (eds.), *Wege zum Wirtschaftsjournalismus*. München: R. Fischer, 1989: 19–22.

Economist. *The Economist 1843–1943*. London: Economist, 1943.

Egan, Jack. "On Money. A Matter of Trust, and Skepticism." In: *U.S. News and World Report* Vol. 118, No. 16 (1995): 71.

Egle, Franz. "Wirtschaftsjournalismus." In: Florian Fleck, Ulrich Saxer and Matthias F. Steinmann (eds.), *Massenmedien und Kommunikationswissenschaft in der Schweiz*. Zürich: Schulthess, 1987: 65–77.

Egle, Franz. *Wirtschaftsjournalismus als Beruf*. Zürich: Lizentiatsarbeit am Seminar für Publizistikwissenschaft der Universität Zürich, 1984.

Eick, Jürgen (ed.). *So nutzt man den Wirtschaftsteil einer Tageszeitung*. Frankfurt a.M.: Societäts-Verlag, 1989.

Eick, Jürgen. "Wirtschafts-Journalisten." In: Jürgen Eick, *Von Ahnungslosigkeit bis Zuversicht. Wörterbuch eines Journalisten*. München: Keyser, 1989: 196–200.

Eisemann, Paul. "TV-Nachrichten. Wirtschaft fest im Blick." In: *Medienspiegel* Vol. 11, No. 11 (1987): 4–5.

Eisemann, Paul. "Wirtschaft unterbelichtet." In: *Medienspiegel* Vol. 10, No. 29 (1986): 4–5.

Elfenbein, Julien. *Business Journalism*. New York: Greenwood, 1969.

Elfenbein, Julien. *Businesspaper Publishing Practice*. Westport: Greenwood, 1970.

Elfenbein, Stefan W. *New York Times. Macht und Mythos eines Mediums*. Frankfurt a.M.: Fischer, 1996.

Emmison, Mike. "'The Economy.' Its Emergence in Media Discourse." In: Howard Davis and Paul Walton (eds.), *Language, Image, Media*. Oxford: Blackwell, 1983: 139–155.

"Entscheidungsleser." In: *Werben und Verkaufen* No. 46 (2001): 140–142.

Enzensberger, Hans Magnus. "Politische Brosamen I. Blinde-Kuh-Ökonomie." In: *Transatlantik* 2 (1982): 11–14.

Epstein, Rachel S. and Nina Liebman. *Biz Speak*. New York: F. Watts, 1986.

Erikson, Robert S., Michael B. MacKuen and James A. Stimson. "Bankers or Peasants Revisited. Economic Expectations and Presidential Approval." In: *Electoral Studies* Vol. 19, No. 2 (2000): 295–312.

Etzioni, Amitai. "Label 'Em Hazardous. Economic Forecasters Are In Deep Voodoo." In: *Washington Journalism Review* Vol. 11, No. 5 (1989): 39–41.

Evans, Sandra S. and Richard J. Lundman. "Newspaper Coverage of Corporate Crime." In M. David Ermann and Richard J. Lundman (eds.), *Corporate and Governmental Deviance*. New York: Oxford University Press, 1987: 230–243.

"Explosives exklusiv. Branchendienste berichten über Märkte und Medien." In: *Journalist* Vol. 49, No. 2 (1999): 36–39.

"Extras für Einsteiger. Wirtschaftspresse floriert." In: *Journalist* Vol. 48, No. 3 (1998): 44–48.

"Fake News Account On Web Site Sends Stock Price Soaring." In: *New York Times*, 4/8/1999.

Feemster, Robert M. *The Wall Street Journal, Purveyor of News to Business America*. New York: Newcomen Society in North America, 1954.

"Fernsehsendung treibt drei Neue-Markt-Werte." In: *Süddeutsche Zeitung*, 1/25/2000.

Ferreira, Eurico J. and LeRoy D. Brooks. "Re-released Information in the *Wall Street Journal's* 'Insider Trading Spotlight' Column." In: *Quarterly Journal of Business and Economics* Vol. 39, No. 1 (2000): 22–34.

Ferreira, Eurico J. and Stanley D. Smith. "Stock Price Reactions to Recommendations in the *Wall Street Journal* 'Small Stock Focus' Column." In: *Quarterly Review of Economics and Finance*. Vol. 39 (1999): 379–389.

Ferreira, Eurico J. and Stanley D. Smith. "Wall $treet Week with Louis Rukeyser. Information or Entertainment?" In: *Financial Analysts Journal*.

Fetter, Frank W. "Economic Controversy in the British Reviews, 1802–1850." In: *Economica* Vol. 32, No. 128 (1965): 424–437.

Fetter, Frank W. "The Economic Articles in Blackwood's Edinburgh Magazine and Their Authors, 1817–1853." In: *Scottish Journal of Political Economy* Vol. 7 (1960): 85–107, 213–231.

Fetter, Frank W. "The Economic Articles in the Quarterly Review and Their Authors, 1809–1852." In: *Journal of Political Economy* Vol. 66 (1958): 47–64, 154–170.

Fichtelius, Erik. "It's the Economy, Stupid!" In: Neil T. Gavin (ed.), *The Economy, Media and Public Knowledge*. London: Leicester University Press, 1998: 166–168.

Finn, David. *The Business-Media Relationship. Countering Misconceptions and Distrust*. New York: Amacom, 1981.

Fisher, Kenneth. "Misery in the Media." In: *Forbes*, 1/20/1992.

Fishman, Michael J. and Kathleen M. Hagerty. "The Incentive to Sell Financial Market Information." In: *Journal of Financial Intermediation* Vol. 4, No. 2 (1995): 95–115.

Fleet, K. G. *The Influence of the Financial Press*. London: The Worshipful Company of Stationers and Newspaper Makers, 1983.

Fletcher, John. *Guide to Company Information in European Newspapers*. Helsinki: European Business School Librarians, 1976.

Flumiani, Carlo Maria. *How to Read the Wall Street Journal for Pleasure and for Profit.* Springfield: Library of Wall Street, 1967.

"Folge dem großen Geld." In: *Der Spiegel,* 7/20/1998.

Fones-Wolf, Elizabeth. "Promoting a Labor Perspective in the American Mass Media. Unions and Radio in the CIO Era, 1936–56." In: *Media, Culture and Society,* Vol. 22, No. 3 (2000): 285–308.

Förster, Wolfgang. *Medienkonsum und kommunikative Verbraucherarbeit. Zu gesellschaftspolitischen Problemen neuer Informationstechniken.* Essen: Dissertation, 1982.

Forsyth, David P. *The Rise of the Business Press in the United States, 1750–1865.* Ann Arbor: University Microfilms International, 1981.

Foster, George. "Briloff and the Capital Market." In: *Journal of Accounting Research* Vol. 17, No. 1 (1979): 262–274.

Foster, George. "Rambo IX. Briloff and the Capital Market." In: *Journal of Accounting, Auditing and Finance* Vol. 2, No. 4 (1987): 409–430.

Franck, C. H. H. *Nachrichten über die Börse in Lübeck.* Lübeck, 1873.

Frank, Robert H. "Yes, The Rich Get Richer, But There's More to the Story." In: *Columbia Journalism Review,* November/December 2000: 28f.

Frankel, Jacob. "Flexible Exchange Rates, Prices, and the Role of 'News.'" In: *Journal of Political Economy* Vol. 89, No. 4 (1981): 665–705.

Freise, Anette Yvonne. *Wirtschaftsinformationen in Deutschland und Großbritannien. Eine vergleichende Inhaltsanalyse zur Struktur der Wirtschaftsberichterstattung ausgewählter Tageszeitungen.* Mainz: Universität Mainz, Institut für Publizistik, Magisterarbeit, 1998.

Freise, Anette. "Wirtschaftsinformationen ohne Leser. Wie berichten deutsche und britische Zeitungen über Wirtschaft?" In: *Message. Internationale Fachzeitschrift für Journalismus* No. 1 (1999): 126–129.

Friedenberg, Jürgen. "Die Krönung durch die Kontonummer." In: *Journalist* Vol. 22, No. 5 (1972): 20.

Friedrichsen, Mike. *Sind Wirtschaftsthemen wahlentscheidend? Eine theoretische und empirische Analyse zum Spannungsfeld Wirtschaft, Politik und Medien.* FH Stuttgart, Stuttgarter Beiträge zur Medienwirtschaft, 2001.

Friedrichsen, Mike. "TV-Wirtschaftsmagazine. Überwiegend tendenziös. Eine Studie analysierte die Berichte der Fernsehmagazine." In: *Medien-Kritik* No. 19 (1991): 2–3.

Friedrichsen, Mike. "Wächter der Demokratie aber keine Missionare. Das berufliche Selbstverständnis von Wirtschaftsredakteuren." In: *Medien-Kritik* No. 1 (1993): 5–6.

Friedrichsen, Mike. *Wirtschaft im Fernsehen. Eine theoretische und empirische Analyse der Wirtschaftsberichterstattung im Fernsehen.* München: R. Fischer, 1992.

Frisch, Franz. "Zukunftsperspektiven und Spezialisierungsfelder. Technik und Wirtschaft." In: Stephan Ruß-Mohl and Heinz D. Stuckmann (eds.), *Wirt-*

schaftsjournalismus. Ein Handbuch für Ausbildung und Praxis. München: List, 1991: 202–204.

Fröhlich, Hans-Peter. "Wirtschaft für Millionen. Die Wirtschaftsmagazine im Fernsehen geben nützliche Tips und machen ökonomische Zusammenhänge verständlich." In: *Das Parlament* Vol. 37, No. 24/25 (1987): 13.

Fröhlich, Thomas and Klaus Gertoberens. *Der Wirtschaftsteil der Zeitung, richtig gelesen und genutzt. Hintergründe, Zusammenhänge, Grundwissen*. München: Heyne, 1994.

Fuhrmann, Hans-Joachim. "Es fehlt die große Wirtschaftsreportage." In: *Die Zeitung* No. 3 (1988).

"Fundiert und solide." In: *Werben und Verkaufen* No. 46 (2001): 134–137.

Fürst, Reinmar. "Wirtschaftsnachrichten in der Weltpresse. Ihre Bedeutung für die betriebswirtschaftliche Lehre." In: *Schmalenbachs Zeitschrift für betriebswirtschaftliche Forschung* Vol. 31 (1979): 123–127.

Fuß, Robert. "Arbeitsmittel und Recherchewege. Recherchen in der Wirtschaft." In: Stephan Ruß-Mohl and Heinz D. Stuckmann (eds.), *Wirtschaftsjournalismus. Ein Handbuch für Ausbildung und Praxis*. München: List, 1991: 72–76.

Gadarowski, Christopher. "Financial Press Coverage and Expected Stock Returns." Ithaca: Cornell University, School of Hotel Administration, Financial Management Department, Working Paper, 2002.

Gavin, Neil T. "Television News and the Economy. The Pre-Campaign Coverage." In: *Parliamentary Affairs* Vol. 45, No. 4 (1992): 596–611.

Gavin, Neil T. "Voting Behaviour, the Economy and the Media. Dependency, Consonance and Priming as a Route to Theoretical and Empirical Integration." In: Charles Pattie, David Denver, Justin Fischer and Steve Ludlam (eds.), *British Elections and Parties*. Vol. 7. London: Frank Cass, 1997: 127–144.

Gavin, Neil T. (ed.). *The Economy, Media and Public Knowledge*. London: Leicester University Press, 1998.

Gavin, Neil T. and David Sanders. "Television, Economy and the Public's Political Attitudes." In: Neil T. Gavin (ed.), *The Economy, Media and Public Knowledge*. London: Leicester University Press, 1998: 90–111.

Gavin, Neil T. and David Sanders. "The Impact of Television News on Public Perceptions of the Economy and Government, 1993–1994." In: David M. Farrell, David Broughton, David Denver and Justin Fischer (eds.), *British Parties and Elections Yearbook 1996*. London: Frank Cass, 1996: 68–84.

Gavin, Neil T. and Peter Goddard. "Television News and the Economy. Inflation in Britain, 1993–1994." In: *Media, Culture and Society* Vol. 20, No. 3 (1998): 451–470.

Gebhardt, Gerhard (ed.). *Wege der Wirtschaftspublizistik*. Essen: West-Verlag, 1959.

"Gebrannte Kinder." In: *Werben und Verkaufen* No. 46 (2001): 124–127.

"Gefährliche Barschaften. Journalisten, die Aktien besitzen, können schnell in Konflikte geraten. Die Branche sucht nach Regeln für sich selbst." In: *Süddeutsche Zeitung*, 6/8/2000.

"Geldanlage-Dienste: Teure Informationen und meist überflüssige Prognosen." In: *Der Wirtschaftsredakteur* Vol. 32, No. 18 (1997): 1–3.

Genske, Ewald. *Geld und Kapital im Wirtschaftsteil der Zeitung.* Frankfurt a.M.: Ullstein, 1966.

Gerke, Wolfgang and Marc Oerke. "Marktbeeinflussung durch Analystenempfehlungen. Eine empirische Studie." In: *Zeitschrift für Betriebswirtschaft,* Ergänzungsheft 2 (1998): 187–200.

Gerke, Wolfgang. "Editorial." In: *Die Betriebswirtschaft* Vol. 60, No. 3 (2000): 287–288.

Gerke, Wolfgang. "Mißbrauch der Medien zur Aktienkursbeeinflussung." In: Lothar Rolke and Volker Wolff (eds.), *Finanzkommunikation. Kurspflege durch Meinungspflege. Die neuen Spielregeln am Aktienmarkt.* Frankfurt a.M.: F.A.Z.-Institut, 2000: 151–170.

Gerke, Wolfgang. "Private Bereicherung in spektakulärer Dimension." In: *Handelsblatt,* 6/29/1998.

Gertoberens, Klaus. *Der Wirtschaftsteil der Zeitung. Wissenswertes von A–Z.* München: Heyne, 2000.

Geyer, Herbert. *Wirtschaftskommunikation, dargestellt an bayerischen Tageszeitungen.* München: Dissertation, o.J. [1985].

Ghani, Waqar and Martin R. Thomas. "The Dart Board Column. Analyst Earnings Forecasts and the Informational Content of Recommendations," In: *Journal of Business and Economic Studies* Vol. 3, No. 2 (1997): 33–42.

Gierse, Thomas. *Zur Aktualität regionaler Wirtschaftsberichterstattung. Untersuchung der Tageszeitungen im Ruhrgebiet.* Bochum: Manuskript unveröffentlicht, 1988.

Gillies, Peter. "Fachlicher Tiefgang, handwerkliches Geschick. Wirtschaftsjournalismus als Fachjournalismus." In: Gero Kalt (ed.), *Wirtschaft in den Medien.* Frankfurt a.M.: IMK, 1990: 271–276.

Gillies, Peter. "Medienspezifische Präsentation. Überregionale Tageszeitung." In: Stephan Ruß-Mohl and Heinz D. Stuckmann (eds.), *Wirtschaftsjournalismus. Ein Handbuch für Ausbildung und Praxis.* München: List, 1991: 127–132.

Gillies, Peter. *Wirtschaftsjournalismus im Umbruch. Anforderungsprofil und Qualifizierung im Wandel.* Universität Gießen: Dissertation, 1989.

Glöckner, Thomas. "Arbeitssituation, Berufsethik. Der freie Wirtschaftsjournalist." In: Stephan Ruß-Mohl and Heinz D. Stuckmann (eds.), *Wirtschaftsjournalismus. Ein Handbuch für Ausbildung und Praxis.* München: List, 1991: 175–179.

Glotz, Peter and Wolfgang R. Langenbucher (eds.), *Der mißachtete Leser. Zur Kritik der deutschen Presse.* Köln: Kiepenheuer und Witsch, 1969.

Glotz, Peter and Wolfgang R. Langenbucher. "Journalistische Fehlanzeige: Wirtschaftskommunikation." In: Peter Glotz and Wolfgang R. Langenbucher (eds.), *Der mißachtete Leser.* Köln: Kiepenheuer und Witsch, 1969: 65–81.

Goddard, Peter, John Corner, Neil T. Gavin and Kay Richardson. "Economic News and the Dynamics of Understanding. The Liverpool Project." In: Neil T. Gavin (ed.), *The Economy, Media and Public Knowledge*. London: Leicester University Press, 1998: 9–37.

Goddard, Peter. "Press Rhetoric and Economic News. A Case Study." In: Neil T. Gavin (ed.), *The Economy, Media and Public Knowledge*. London: Leicester University Press, 1998: 71–89.

Goidel, Robert K. and Ronald E. Langley. "Media Coverage of the Economy and Aggregate Economic Evaluations. Uncovering Evidence of Indirect Media Effects." In: *Political Research Quarterly* Vol. 48, No. 2 (1995): 313–328.

Goitsch, Heinrich. *Entwicklung und Strukturwandlung des Wirtschaftsteils der deutschen Tageszeitungen. Ein historisch-soziologischer Beitrag zum Phänomen der Presse*. Frankfurt a.M.: Dissertation, 1939.

"Good Investing Isn't Sexy. A Conversation With Jane Bryant Quinn." In: abcnews.com, 8/27/1998.

Goozner, Merrill. "Blinded By the Boom. What's Missing in the Coverage of the New Economy?" In: *Columbia Journalism Review*, November/December 2000: 23–27.

Gordon, Barry. "Criticism of Ricardian Views on Value and Distribution in the British Periodicals, 1820–1850." In: *History of Political Economy* Vol. 1, No. 2 (1969): 370–387.

Gordon, H. Scott. "The London Economist and the High Tide of Laissez Faire." In: *Journal of Political Economy* Vol, 63, No. 6 (1955): 461–488.

Graham, John R. and Campbell R. Harvey. "Grading the Performance of Market-timing Newsletters." In: *Financial Analysts Journal* Vol. 53, No. 6 (1997): 54–66.

Graham, John R. and Campbell R. Harvey. "Market Timing Ability and Volatility Implied in Investment Newsletters' Asset Allocation Recommendations." In: *Journal of Financial Economics* Vol. 42, No. 3 (1996): 397–421.

Gramss-Wittko, Manuela. *Die Automobilindustrie in der Berichterstattung des Handelsblattes. Eine inhaltsanalytische Fallstudie*. Berlin: Vistas, 1996.

Greco, Albert N. *Business Journalism. Management Notes and Cases*. New York: New York University Press, 1988.

Greene, Jason and Scott Smart. "Liquidity Provision and Noise Trading. Evidence from the 'Investment Dartboard' Column." In: *Journal of Finance* Vol. 54, No. 5 (1999): 1885–1899.

Greiser, F. "Die Systematik der Wirtschaftspresse." In: *Wirtschaftsdienst* Vol. 35, No. 1 (1955): 11–12.

Griffin, Paul A., Jennifer J. Jones and Mark Zmijewski. "How Useful Are 'Wall $treet Week' Stock Recommendations?" In: *Journal of Financial Statement Analysis* Vol. 1, No. 1 (1995): 33–52.

Grimes, Charlotte. "Rewired." In: *American Journalism Review* Vol. 19, No. 8 (1997): 28–31.

Gross, Johannes and Manfred Schumacher. "Publikumswirksamer Meinungsjournalismus. Defizite bei den Polit-Magazinen von ARD und ZDF." In: Gero Kalt (ed.), *Wirtschaft in den Medien*. Frankfurt a.M.: IMK, 1990: 55–63.

Gross, Johannes. "Arbeitssituation, Berufsethik. Die Verantwortung des Journalisten." In: Stephan Ruß-Mohl and Heinz D. Stuckmann (eds.), *Wirtschaftsjournalismus. Ein Handbuch für Ausbildung und Praxis*. München: List, 1991: 186–187.

Großmann, Alexander. "Berührungsängste abbauen. Unternehmen und Sender könnten besser zusammenarbeiten." In: Gero Kalt (ed.), *Wirtschaft in den Medien*. Frankfurt a.M.: IMK, 1990: 167–174.

Gruber, Thomas and Karl Vogel. "Verbraucherinformation durch Fernsehen." In: Manfred Rühl and J. Walchshöfer (eds.), *Politik und Kommunikation*. Nürnberg: Verlag der Nürnberger Forschungsvereinigung, 1978: 355–374.

Grün, Karl. 2000. "Transparenzübungen auf Amerikanisch und Deutsch. Wirtschaftsjournalisten zwischen virtueller Intelligenz der Generalisten und naiver Arroganz der Besserwisser." In: *Mittler der Märkte. Wirtschaftsjournalismus zwischen Anspruch und Alltag*. Frankfurt a.M.: Börsen-Zeitung: 51–64.

Grundl, Robert. "Marktchancen des abonnentenfinanzierten Börsenfernsehens in Deutschland. (2. Teil)." In: *Der Wirtschaftsredakteur* Vol. 32, No. 5 (1997): II-IV.

Grundl, Robert. "Marktchancen des abonnentenfinanzierten Börsenfernsehens in Deutschland. (1. Teil)." In: *Der Wirtschaftsredakteur* Vol. 32, No. 4 (1997): II-IV.

"Gründungswelle im Segment der Wirtschaftspresse sorgt für Marktausweitung." In: *Horizont*, 3/30/2000.

Grunwald, Edgar A. *The Business Press Editor*. New York: New York University Press, 1988.

Guide to Business and Financial News Media. New York: Larriston.

Guide to U.S. Business, Financial and Economic News Correspondents and Contacts. New York: Larriston Communications, 1983.

Gussow, Don. *The New Business Journalism. An Insider's Look at the Workings of America's Business Press*. San Diego: Harcourt Brace Jovanovich, 1984.

"Gut fürs Geschäft." In: *Werben und Verkaufen* No. 46 (2001): 128–132.

"Gutbezahlte Nische." In: *Wirtschaftswoche*, 7/25/1996.

"Gute Zeiten, Schlechte Zeiten! Börsenkurse bestimmen die Auflage von Wirtschaftsmagazinen." In: *Der Wirtschaftsredakteur* Vol. 36, No. 3 (2001): 4–7.

Hagen, Volker von. "Wirtschaft im Fernsehen. Das System funktioniert, die Übermittlung nicht." In: *Medien-Kritik* No. 44 (1989): 6–7.

Hagenström, Dieter. *Wirtschaftsberichterstattung in Deutschland*. Graz: Dissertation, 1957.

Haggerty, Mike and Wallace Rasmussen. *The Headline vs. the Bottom Line. Mutual Distrust Between Business and the News Media*. Nashville: The Freedom Forum First Amendment Center, Vanderbilt University, 1994.

Haller, H. Brandon and Helmut Norpoth. "Reality Bites. News Exposure and Economic Opinion." *Public Opinion Quarterly* Vol. 61, No. 4 (1998): 555–575.

Hamm, Ingrid. *Inhalt und audiovisuelle Gestaltung. Der Einfluß thematischer Aspekte auf die Gestaltung von Verbrauchersendungen im Fernsehen*. Nürnberg: Verlag der Kommunikationswissenschaftlichen Forschungsvereinigung, 1985.

Hamm, Ingrid and Barbara Koller. *Sehen und Verstehen. Verbraucherinformation und ihre Resonanz im Fernsehpublikum*. Mainz: v. Hase und Koehler, 1989.
Hammer, Thomas. *Wirtschaftsinformationen nutzen wie ein Profi*. Düsseldorf: Econ, 1998.
Han, Ki C. and David Y. Suk. "Stock Prices and the *Barron's* 'Research Reports' Column." In: *Journal of Financial and Strategic Decisions* Vol. 9, No. 3 (Herbst 1996): 27–32.
Hank, Rainer. "Zukunftsperspektiven und Spezialisierungsfelder. Personalpolitik, Qualifizierung, Ausbildung." In: Stephan Ruß-Mohl and Heinz D. Stuckmann (eds.), *Wirtschaftsjournalismus. Ein Handbuch für Ausbildung und Praxis*. München: List, 1991: 204–206.
"Hard Questions for Dan Dorfman." In: *Business Week*, 11/6/1995.
Harngarth, Friederike. *Wirtschaft und Soziales in der politischen Kommunikation. Eine Studie zur Interaktion von Abgeordneten und Journalisten*. Opladen: Westdeutscher Verlag, 1997.
Harrington, David E. "Economic News on Television. The Determinants of Coverage." In: *Public Opinion Quarterly* Vol. 53 (1989): 17–40.
Hattemer, Klaus. "Arbeitsmittel und Recherchewege. Markt- und Mediaforschung." In: Stephan Ruß-Mohl and Heinz D. Stuckmann (eds.), *Wirtschaftsjournalismus. Ein Handbuch für Ausbildung und Praxis*. München: List, 1991: 99–104.
Hattemer, Klaus. "Medienspezifische Präsentation. Wirtschafts-Tageszeitung." In: Stephan Ruß-Mohl and Heinz D. Stuckmann (eds.), *Wirtschaftsjournalismus. Ein Handbuch für Ausbildung und Praxis*. München: List, 1991: 132–134
Hattemer, Klaus. "Wirtschafts-Tageszeitung." In: Stephan Ruß-Mohl and Heinz D. Stuckmann (eds.), *Wirtschaftsjournalismus. Ein Handbuch für Ausbildung und Praxis*. München: List, 1991: 132–134.
Häußler, Silke. *Wirtschaftsmedien*. Hamburg: New-Business, 2001.
Hawranek, Dietmar. "Arbeitssituation, Berufsethik. Redaktionsalltag." In: Stephan Ruß-Mohl and Heinz D. Stuckmann (eds.), *Wirtschaftsjournalismus. Ein Handbuch für Ausbildung und Praxis*. München: List, 1991: 170–172.
Heinrich, Jürgen. "Forschungsstand Wirtschaftsjournalismus im deutschsprachigen Raum." In: Siegfried Klaue (ed.), *Marktwirtschaft in der Medienberichterstattung*. Düsseldorf: Econ, 1991: 57–72.
Heinrich, Jürgen. "Orientierungshilfen. Wirtschaftsjournalismus, eine kommentierte Bibliographie." In: Stephan Ruß-Mohl and Heinz D. Stuck-mann (eds.), *Wirtschaftsjournalismus. Ein Handbuch für Ausbildung und Praxis*. München: List, 1991: 277–285.
Heinrich, Jürgen. "Wichtig erscheint, was nützt." In: Bundeszentrale für politische Bildung (ed.), *Wirtschaftsjournalismus. Themen und Materialien für Journalisten*. Bonn: Bundeszentrale, 1996: 50–52.

Heinrich, Jürgen. "Wirtschaftsjournalismus. Zur Fundierung einer rezipientenorientierten Wirtschaftsberichterstattung." In: *Publizistik* Vol. 34, No. 3 (1989): 284–296.

Heinrich, Jürgen. "Wünsche der Zielgruppe besser ermitteln. Rezipientenorientierte Wirtschaftsberichterstattung." In: Gero Kalt (ed.), *Wirtschaft in den Medien*. Frankfurt a.M.: IMK, 1990: 263–269.

Heinrich, Jürgen. "Zur Kritik der Wirtschaftsberichterstattung. Ursachen und Konsequenzen." In: *Publizistik* Vol. 36, No. 2 (1991): 217–226.

Heinrich, Jürgen and Maike Telgheder. "Wirtschaftsberichterstattung in Fernsehen und Hörfunk." In: *Media Perspektiven* Vol. 36 (1991): 14–41.

Heinrich, Jürgen and Maike Telgheder. "Wirtschaftsberichterstattung in lokalen und regionalen Tageszeitungen. Ergebnisse einer Umfrage. In: *Media Perspektiven* Vol. 35, No. 12 (1990): 775–784.

Henderson, Willie, Tony Dudley-Evans and Roger Backhouse (eds.). *Economics and Language*. London: Routledge, 1993.

Hennemann, Gerhard. "Zukunftsperspektiven und Spezialisierungsfelder. Wirtschaftspolitik aus Bonn." In: Stephan Ruß-Mohl and Heinz D. Stuckmann (eds.), *Wirtschaftsjournalismus. Ein Handbuch für Ausbildung und Praxis*. München: List, 1991: 222–224.

Henriques, Diana B. "Business Reporting. Behind the Curve." In: *Columbia Journalism Review*, November/December 2000: 18–21.

Herchet, Roswitha. *Nachrichtenmagazine im Vergleich. Eine sprachliche Untersuchung zu SPIEGEL und FOCUS*. Marburg: Tectum, 1995.

Herrera-Soler, H. and Michael White. "Business is War or How Takeovers are Narrated in the Press." In: M. Fornés, J.M. Molina and L. Perez (eds.), *Panorama actual de la Lingüística Aplicada*. Logroño: Universidad de la Rioja, 2000: 231–240.

Herrmann, Walther. "Konjunkturforschung und Konjunktur-Berichterstattung nach dem Kriege." In: *Zeitschrift für handelswissenschaftliche Forschung* Vol. 4 (1952): 49–70.

Hetherington, Marc J. 1996. "The Media's Role in Forming Voters' National Economic Evaluations in 1992." In: *American Journal of Political Science* Vol. 40, No. 2 (1996): 372–395.

Hetzer, Jonas and Christoph Seeger. "Falsches Spiel. Börsengerüchte. Die Gefahr manipulierter Märkte." In: *Manager Magazin*, Juni 2000.

Hidding, Bruno. "Journalisten und Analysten—zum Nutzen der Anleger." In: *Mittler der Märkte. Wirtschaftsjournalismus zwischen Anspruch und Alltag*. Frankfurt a.M.: Börsen-Zeitung: 97–108.

Hilgert, Ingeborg and Heinz D. Stuckmann. "Medien und Märkte." In: Stephan Ruß-Mohl and Heinz D. Stuckmann (eds.), *Wirtschaftsjournalismus. Ein Handbuch für Ausbildung und Praxis*. München: List, 1991: 14–41.

Hilgert, Ingeborg. "Medienspezifische Präsentation. Zum Beispiel: !Forbes." In: Stephan Ruß-Mohl and Heinz D. Stuckmann (eds.), *Wirtschaftsjournalismus. Ein Handbuch für Ausbildung und Praxis*. München: List, 1991: 152–153.

Hilgert, Ingeborg. "Medienspezifische Präsentation. Zum Beispiel: Vertraulich und exklusiv." In: Stephan Ruß-Mohl and Heinz D. Stuckmann (eds.), *Wirtschaftsjournalismus. Ein Handbuch für Ausbildung und Praxis*. München: List, 1991: 161–162.

Hilgert, Ingeborg. "Orientierungshilfen. Kölner Schule, Institut für Publizistik e.V." In: Stephan Ruß-Mohl and Heinz D. Stuckmann (eds.), *Wirtschaftsjournalismus. Ein Handbuch für Ausbildung und Praxis*. München: List, 1991: 239–240.

Hilgert, Ingeborg. "Zur Kritik des Wirtschaftsjournalismus. Stimmen aus dem Medienpublikum." In: Stephan Ruß-Mohl and Heinz D. Stuckmann (eds.), *Wirtschaftsjournalismus. Ein Handbuch für Ausbildung und Praxis*. München: List, 1991: 64–67.

Hillmoth, Hans-Dieter. "Kein böser Wille. Was der Privatfunk leisten kann." In: Gero Kalt (ed.), *Wirtschaft in den Medien*. Frankfurt a.M.: IMK, 1990: 133–137.

Hintermeier, Josef. *Public Relations im journalistischen Entwicklungsprozeß. Dargestellt am Beispiel einer Wirtschaftsredaktion*. Düsseldorf: Verlag für dt. Wirtschaftsbiogr. Flieger, 1982.

Hirschey, Mark, Vernon J. Richardson and Susan Scholz. "How 'Foolish' Are Internet Investors?" In: *Financial Analysts Journal* Vol. 56, No. 1 (2000): 62–69.

Hoefer, Georg. *Wirtschaft audiovisuell. Was leisten Wirtschaftssendungen im Fernsehen?* Coppengrave: Coppi, 1995.

Hoffmann, Otto (ed.). *Wie liest man den Handelsteil einer Tageszeitung?* Frankfurt a.M.: Societätsverlag, 1937.

Hogel, Kristov. "Wirtschaftsberichterstattung. "Wirtschaft" im Wandel (I)." In: *Medienspiegel* Vol. 21, No. 2 (1997): 4–5.

Hogel, Kristov. "Wirtschaftsberichterstattung. "Wirtschaft" im Wandel (II)." In: *Medienspiegel* Vol. 21, No. 3 (1997): 4.

Holley, Joe. "What's a Bloomberg? Hint: It's Hot. It Churns Out Financial Stuff. It's Bigger Than a Breadbox." In: *Columbia Journalism Review*, May/June 1995: 46–50.

Hollifield, C. Ann. "The Specialized Business Press and Industry-Related Political Communication. A Comparative Study." In: *Journalism and Mass Communication Quarterly* Vol. 74, No. 4 (1997): 757–772.

Hömberg, Erentraud. "Orientierungshilfen. Preise für Wirtschaftsjournalisten." In: Stephan Ruß-Mohl and Heinz D. Stuckmann (eds.), *Wirtschaftsjournalismus. Ein Handbuch für Ausbildung und Praxis*. München: List, 1991: 255–260.

Hömberg, Walter. "Orientierungshilfen. Zur Geschichte des Wirtschaftsjournalismus." In: Stephan Ruß-Mohl and Heinz D. Stuckmann (eds.), *Wirtschaftsjournalismus. Ein Handbuch für Ausbildung und Praxis*. München: List, 1991: 231–235.

Hugle, Robert. "Nachrichtenagenturen. VWD, der größte deutsche Anbieter von Wirtschaftsinformationen." In: *Medienspiegel* Vol. 6, No. 10 (1982): 6–8.

Huskey, Lee, Stephen L. Jackstadt and Scott Goldsmith. "Economic Literacy and the Content of Television Network News." In: *Social Education* Vol. 55, No. 33 (1991): 182–185.

Huth, William L. and Brian A. Maris. "Large and Small Firm Stock Price Response to 'Heard on the Street' Recommendations." In: *Journal of Accounting, Auditing, and Finance* Vol. 7 (1992): 27–47.

"In the Business of News. For General News Channels Business Updates Form a Key Ingredient in the Schedules." In: *Cable and Satellite Europe* No. 158 (1997): 30–33.

"Informationskartell an Wall Street." In: *Börsenzeitung*, 6/8/2000.

Innis, Harold A. "The Newspaper in Economic Development." In: *Journal of Economic History* Vol. 2, Supplement (1942): 1–33.

Innis, Harold A. *The Press. A Neglected Factor in the Economic History of the Twentieth Century.* London: Oxford University Press, 1949.

"Insider-Regeln für Journalisten." In: *Süddeutsche Zeitung*, 4/20/2000.

"Internet-Kommunikation. Neue Wege der Finanzkommunikation." In: *Der Wirtschaftsredakteur* Vol. 34, No. 10 (1999): 7–8.

Isenbart, Jan. "'Wirtschaft ist Sexy.' Round-table von Media Spectrum zum Thema Wirtschaftsmedien." In: *Media Spectrum* No. 10 (1996): 18–20.

"Ist das genug, Vater?" In: Der Spiegel, 10/20/1997.

Jaffe, Jeffrey F. and James M. Mahoney. "The Performance of Investment Newsletters." In: *Journal of Financial Economics* Vol. 53, No. 2 (1999): 289–307.

Jahrfeld, Martin. "Geplatzte Seifenblasen." In: *Journalist* Vol. 52, No. 2 (2002): 44–45.

Jain, Prem C. "Response of Hourly Stock Prices and Trading Volume to Economic News." In: *Journal of Business* Vol. 61, No. 2 (1988): 219–231.

Jenke, Manfred. "Hin zur Allgemeinheit. Was der öffentlich-rechtliche Hörfunk leisten muß und kann." In: Gero Kalt (ed.), *Wirtschaft in den Medien*. Frankfurt a.M.: IMK, 1990: 125–132.

Jensen, Klaus B. "News as Ideology. Economic Statistics and Political Ritual in Television Network News." In: *Journal of Communication* Vol. 37, No. 1 (1987): 8–27.

Jeske, Jürgen and Hans D. Barbier (eds.). *So nutzt man den Wirtschaftsteil einer Tageszeitung*. Frankfurt a.M.: Societäts-Verlag, 1997.

"Journalistischer Mehrwert." In: *Medien Tenor* Vol. 5, No. 72 (1998): 25.

Jungblut, Michael. "Das Fernsehen. Partner oder Gegner der Wirtschaft." In: *ZDF-Jahrbuch*. Mainz: ZDF, 1990: 89–93.

Jungblut, Michael. "Wirtschaft als Thema im ZDF." In: *ZDF-Jahrbuch 1986*. Mainz: ZDF, 1986: 64–69.

Jungblut, Michael. "Wirtschaftsberichterstattung im Fernsehen muß unterhaltend und informativ sein." In: *ZDF-Presse-Journal* 7 (1986): 1–3.

Jungblut, Michael. "Zu wenig Wirtschafts-Sendeplätze." In: *Medienspiegel* Vol. 12, No. 4 (1988): 4–5.

Käckenhoff, Günther. "Gefahr für den Wirtschaftsjournalismus." In: Ludwig-Erhard-Stiftung, *Orientierungen zur Wirtschafts- und Gesellschaftspolitik* 4 (1980): 38–43.

Käckenhoff, Günther. "Nachwuchsfragen des Wirtschaftsjournalismus." In: *Orientierungen zur Wirtschafts- und Gesellschaftspolitik* 1 (1979).

Kahn, Ernst. "Die Aufgaben der Handelsjournalistik." In: *Der Eiserne Steg. Jahrbuch 1925*. Frankfurt, 1925.

Kahn, Ernst and Fritz Naphtali. *Wie liest man den Handelsteil einer Tageszeitung.* Frankfurt a.M., 1930.

Kalt, Gero. "Die Bemühungen bleiben steigerungsfähig. Defizite der Wirtschaftssendungen von RTLplus und Sat 1." In: Gero Kalt (ed.), *Wirtschaft in den Medien.* Frankfurt a.M.: IMK, 1990: 87–97.

Kalt, Gero. "Info-Transport mit Schlagseite. Defizite bei den Nachrichtensendungen von ARD und ZDF." In: Gero Kalt (ed.), *Wirtschaft in den Medien.* Frankfurt a.M.: IMK, 1990: 41–54.

Kalt, Gero. *Interessen, Sorgen, Lebensstil. Von Wirtschaft in den Medien ist jeder betroffen.* Bonn: ZV, Zeitungs-Verlag Service, 1998.

Kalt, Gero. "Lobbyisten ihres Fachs? Die Wirtschaftsberichterstattung steckt in einem Dilemma." In: *Medien-Kritik* No. 15 (1990): 6–8.

Kalt, Gero (ed.). *Schlecht informiert. Wie Medien die Wirklichkeit verzerren. Eine Fallsammlung.* Frankfurt a.M.: IMK, 1993.

Kalt, Gero. *Soll und Haben im Informationswettbewerb. Gewichtung, Tendenz und Aufbereitung von Wirtschaftsthemen in Fernsehnachrichten. Ein Vergleich zwischen ARD und RTL vor dem Hintergrund der Deutschen Presse-Agentur.* Frankfurt a.M.: IMK, 1994.

Kalt, Gero. "Tarifverhandlungen. Medien im Dornröschenschlaf. Fernsehen und Presse vernachlässigen ein zentrales Thema." In: *Medien-Kritik* No. 3 (1990): 3–5.

Kalt, Gero. "Themenfeld Wirtschaft. Wandel eröffnet Chancen." In: Berthold L. Flöper (ed.), *Ratgeber Freie Journalisten.* Berlin: Vistas, 1992: 123–128.

Kalt, Gero (ed.). *Wirtschaft in den Medien. Defizite, Chancen und Grenzen. Eine kritische Bestandsaufnahme.* Frankfurt a.M.: IMK, 1990.

Kalt, Gero. "Wirtschaftsjournalismus. Angriff gegen eine ganze Technologie. ARD-Plusminus suggeriert kriminelle Machenschaften der STEAG." In: *Medien-Kritik* No. 14 (1993): 2–3.

Kalt, Gero. "Wirtschaftsnachrichten. Viele inszenierte Anlässe. Zur Auswahl aktueller Wirtschaftsthemen bei ARD, RTL und dpa." In: *Medien-Kritik* No. 36 (1993): 7–10.

Kaniel, Ron, Laura Starks and Vasudha Vasudevan. "Headlines and Bottom Lines. Media Coverage and Mutual Funds." Durham: Working Paper, Duke University 2004.

Kaplar, Richard T. *Economic Forecasts, Election Years, and the Media. A Content Analysis of the Los Angeles Times, Newsweek, and NBC News.* Washington, D.C.: Media Institute, 1984.

Karle, Roland. "Aufbruchstimmung. Wirtschaftspresse profitiert von der Konjunkturbelebung." In: *Media-Spectrum* No. 8 (1995): 18–22.

Karle, Roland. "Munteres Abwerben." In: *Journalist* Vol. 49, No. 11 (1999): 28–32.

Katona, George. "Public Opinion and Economic Research." In: *Public Opinion Quarterly* Vol. 21, No. 1 (1957): 117–128.

Kepplinger, Hans Mathias. "Ökonomie für Otto Normalverbraucher. Zur wachsenden Bedeutung der Börsenberichterstattung in den Medien." München: Referat anläßlich der Medientage München, Ms. unpublished, 2000.

Kepplinger, Hans Mathias and Hans-Bernd Brosius. "Das deplazierte Drittel. Eine empirische Untersuchung über den Einfluß subjektiver Überzeugungen auf die Tendenz der Nachrichtenauswahl von Wirtschaftsredakteuren und politischen Redakteuren." Mainz: Institut für Publizistik, Ms. unpublished, 1985.

Kepplinger, Hans Mathias and Simone C. Emig. *Content Guide. Eine Contentanalyse deutscher Wirtschaftsmagazine im Auftrag von Geldidee*. Hamburg: Bauer Verlagsgruppe, 2002.

Kerby, William F. *A Proud Profession. Memoirs of a Wall Street Journal Reporter, Editor, and Publisher*. Homewood: Dow Jones, 1981.

Kersten, Matthias. "Wirtschaft und Fernsehen. Berührungspunkte." In: *hr-Pressespiegel*, 10/13/1983.

Kirchner, Jürgen. "Spektakulär statt sachkundig. Defizite bei den Polit-Magazinen von RTLplus und Sat 1." In: Gero Kalt (ed.), *Wirtschaft in den Medien*. Frankfurt a.M.: IMK, 1990: 65–77.

Kirsch, Donald. *Documentary Supplement to Financial and Economic Journalism. Analysis, Interpretation, and Reporting*. New York: New York University Press, 1979.

Kirsch, Donald. *Financial and Economic Journalism. Analysis, Interpretation, and Reporting*. New York: New York University Press, 1978.

Kisker, Klaus Peter. "Public Relations statt objektiver Berichterstattung. Wirtschaftsteil nur für Börsianer?" In: Eckard Spoo (ed.), *Die Tabus der bundesdeutschen Presse*. München: Hanser, 1971: 47–63.

Kladroba, Andreas and Peter von der Lippe. "Die Qualität von Aktienempfehlungen in Publikumszeitschriften." Essen: Diskussionsbeiträge aus dem Fachbereich Wirtschaftswissenschaften der Universität Essen, 2001.

Klaue, Siegfried (ed.). *Marktwirtschaft in der Medienberichterstattung. Wirtschaftsjournalismus und Journalistenausbildung*. Düsseldorf: Econ, 1991.

Klaue, Siegfried, "Wirtschaftsjournalismus auf dem Prüfstand, aus der Sicht der Publizistikwissenschaft." In: Ders. (ed.), *Marktwirtschaft in der Medienberichterstattung*. Düsseldorf: Econ, 1991: 47–56.

Klaue, Siegfried. "Zur Kritik des Wirtschaftsjournalismus. Der Wettbewerbshüter." In: Stephan Ruß-Mohl and Heinz D. Stuckmann (eds.), *Wirtschaftsjournalismus. Ein Handbuch für Ausbildung und Praxis*. München: List, 1991: 55–58.

Klaus, Roland. "Börsenfernsehen in Deutschland, 1.Teil." In: *Der Wirtschaftsredakteur* 4, 2/14/1997: 10.

Klaus, Roland. "Börsenfernsehen in Deutschland." In: *Der Wirtschaftsredakteur* No. 5, 2/28/1997, 11.

Klein, Josef and Iris Meißner. *Wirtschaft im Kopf. Begriffskompetenz und Einstellungen junger Erwachsener bei Wirtschaftsthemen im Medienkontext.* Frankfurt a.M.: Lang, 1999.

Kleinpaul, Johannes. *Die Fuggerzeitungen, 1568–1605.* Walluf: Sändig, 1972.

Kleinschroth, Robert and René Bosewitz. *How to Read the Business Press. Business English für aktuelle Informationen.* Reinbek: Rowohlt, 1998.

Klemmer, Paul. "Wirtschafts-Kritik." In: Heinz-Dietrich Fischer (ed.), *Kritik in Massenmedien.* Köln: Deutscher Ärzte-Verlag, 1983: 75–82.

Klingler, Walter. "Ist Wirtschaftsberichterstattung mehr als Börseninformation?" Stuttgart: SWR Medienforschung, Ms. unpublished, 2001.

Klocke, Peter A. *Wirtschaftsnachrichten lesen und verstehen.* Freiburg i.Br.: Haufe, 2001.

Kluge, Pamela Hollie (ed.). *The Columbia Knight-Bagehot Guide to Economics and Business Journalism.* New York: Columbia University Press, 1991.

Knapp, Reinhart. *Der Wirtschaftsteil der Zeitung. Eine Anleitung für den Leser.* Stuttgart: Poeschel, 1969.

Knellessen, Wolfgang. "Arbeitsmittel und Recherchewege. Presseabteilungen." In: Stephan Ruß-Mohl and Heinz D. Stuckmann (eds.), *Wirtschaftsjournalismus. Ein Handbuch für Ausbildung und Praxis.* München: List, 1991: 77–84.

Kneuker, Oliver. "Boulevardzeitungen. Auch Wirtschaft ist präsent." In: *Medienspiegel* Vol. 13, No. 20 (1989): 4–5.

Koch, Thomas. "Wirtschaftspresse. Fakten statt Floskeln." In: *Media-Spectrum* Vol. 27, No. 12 (1989): 26–28.

Köcher, Renate. *Kompetenz und politische Einstellungen von Wirtschaftsjournalisten.* Allensbach: Unveröffentlichtes Manuskript, 1985.

Köcher, Renate. "Weniger missionarisch. Kompetenz und politische Einstellung von Wirtschaftsjournalisten." In: Gero Kalt (ed.), *Wirtschaft in den Medien.* Frankfurt a.M.: IMK, 1990: 277–293.

Kohlmeier, Louis M., J. G. Udell and L. B. Anderson. (eds.). *Reporting on Business and the Economy.* Englewood Cliffs: Prentice-Hall, 1981.

Kolmer, Christian. *Die Treuhandanstalt. Eine Input-Output-Analyse zu Theorien der Nachrichtenauswahl.* Bonn: InnoVatio, 2000.

Kopper, Gerd G. *Wirtschaftsberichterstattung. Zu Problemhintergrund und Grundstrukturen in der Bundesrepublik Deutschland.* Dortmund: Unveröffentlichtes Manuskript, 1982.

Koschel, Friederike. "'Wirtschaftlich geht es mir blendend!' Harte Fakten spielen bei Einschätzung der Wirtschaftslage keine Rolle." In: *Medien Tenor* Vol. 5, No. 79 (1998): 28–29.

Koschnick, Wolfgang J. "News fürs Business. TV setzt auf die Wirtschaft." In: *Journalist* Vol. 47, No. 7 (1997): 48, 50, 52.

Koschwitz, Hansjürgen. "Die Anfänge der periodischen Wirtschaftspublizistik im Zeitalter des Kameralismus." In: *Publizistik* Vol. 12, No. 4 (1967): 232–242.

Koschwitz, Hansjürgen. *Die periodische Wirtschaftspublizistik im Zeitalter des Kameralismus. Ein Beitrag zur Entwicklung der Wirtschaftsfachzeitschrift im 18. Jh.* Göttingen: Dissertation, 1968.

Kounalakis, Markos, D. Banks and K. Daus. *Beyond Spin. The Power of Strategic Corporate Journalism.* San Francisco: Jossey-Bass, 1999.

Kraft, Hans-Peter and Kristine Dreyer (eds.). *Untersuchung über den Nutzen von Wirtschaftsinformationen in Tageszeitungen.* Frankfurt a.M.: Lang, 1997.

Krefetz, Gerald. *How to Read and Profit from Financial News.* Chicago: Dearborn Trade, 1995.

Krieger, Konrad. *Zweck und Form des Wirtschaftsteils der Tageszeitung. Vortrag in der zeitungswissenschaftlichen Vereinigung München.* München: Münchener Zeitungs-Verlag, 1933.

Kroll, Jens M. *Taschenbuch Wirtschaftspresse.* Seefeld: Deutsche BP Presseabteilung, 1990.

Kübler, Gerd. *Was sagt mir der Wirtschaftsteil der Zeitung? Vom Nutzen aktueller Informationen.* Stuttgart: Taylorix, 1975.

Kuby, Erich. *Der Spiegel im Spiegel. Das deutsche Nachrichten-Magazin.* München: Heyne, 1987.

Kuhlmann, Marlies. *Der Weg der Wirtschaftsnachricht und ihre Stellung im Wirtschaftsteil der Tageszeitungen.* Köln: Dissertation, 1957.

Kurtz, Howard. "Is the Economy Suffering from Media Malady?" In: *Washington Post*, 10/28/1990.

Kurtz, Howard. *The Fortune Tellers.* New York: The Free Press, 2000.

Kutzer, Hermann. "Alte und Neue Medien. Wie Nachrichten die Kurse beeinflussen können." In: Bundesverband der Börsenvereine an deutschen Hochschulen e.V. (ed.), *Börsenperspektiven 2001.* München: Finanzbuch Verlag, 2000: 135–137.

Kynaston, David. *The Financial Times. A Centenary History.* New York: Viking, 1988.

Ladley, Barbara. *Money and Finance. Sources of Print and Nonprint Materials.* New York: Neal Schuman, 1980.

Ladner, Sharyn J. "Mutual Fund Information on the World Wide Web. Part 1. Issues and Global Resources." In: *Business Information Review* Vol 13, No. 2. (1996): 91–99.

Lamb, Robert, William G. Armstrong, Jr., Karolyn R. Morigi. *Business, Media, and the Law. The Troubled Confluence.* New York: New York University Press, 1980.

Lambsdorff, Otto Graf. "Zur Kritik des Wirtschaftsjournalismus. Der Wirtschaftspolitiker." In: Stephan Ruß-Mohl and Heinz D. Stuckmann (eds.), *Wirtschaftsjournalismus. Ein Handbuch für Ausbildung und Praxis.* München: List, 1991: 52–55.

Langenbucher, Wolfgang R. "Einflüsse der Medien auf das Verhalten der Verbraucher." In: Stiftung Warentest (ed.), *Erwartungen an die Arbeit der Stiftung Warentest in den 80er Jahren*. Berlin: Stiftung Warentest, 1982: 41–64.

Langley, R. E. and R. K. Goidel. "Media Coverage of the Economy and Aggregate Economic Evaluations. Uncovering Evidence of Indirect Media Effects." In: *Political Research Quarterly* Vol. 48, No. 2 (1995): 313–328.

Lanson, Jerry. "Clearing a Minefield. The Ethics of Owning Stock." In: *Online Journalism Review*, 9/9/1999.

Lau, Dieter. "Wirtschaftsberichterstattung im Südwestfunk." In: Siegfried Quandt (ed.), *Fachjournalismus im Gespräch*. Gießen: Zentrum für Fachjournalist. Studien: 53–58.

"Lautes Pfeifen." In: *Werben und Verkaufen* No. 46 (2001): 120–121.

Lawrence, John F. "How Street-Smart Is the Press?" In: *Columbia Journalism Review*, January/February 1988: 23–28.

Lawrence, John. "Business News. The Terrible Truth." In: *Fortune*, 4/25/1998.

Lawrenson, John and Lionel Barber. *The Price of Truth. The Story of the Reuters Millions*. Edinburgh: Mainstream, 1985.

Leckey, Andrew and Ken Auletta (eds.). *The Best Business Stories of the Year, 2002*. New York: Vintage, 2002.

Lee, Allan (ed.). *Business Reporting. A New Zealand Guide to Financial Journalism*. Wellington: New Zealand Journalists Training Organization, 1997.

Lee, Chi-wen Jevons. "Information Content of Financial Columns." In: *Journal of Economics and Business* Vol. 38 (1986): 27–39.

"Lektüre mit Aha-Effekt. Was wollen die Leser wissen?" In: *Journalist* Vol. 48, No. 3 (1998): 16–18.

Lenzner, Robert. "Media Fantasy—Stock Market Reporting." In: *Nieman Reports* Vol. 51, No. 2 (1997): 16–18.

Lester, Ray. *Information Sources in Finance and Banking*. New Jersey: Bowker-Saur, 1996.

Levine, I. R. "Covering the Economy." In: *TV Guide*, 2/7/1976: 6–8

Levitt, Arthur. "Financial Literacy and Role of the Media." Speech at the Media Studies Center, New York. U.S. Securities and Exchange Commission, 4/26/1999.

Lewis-Beck, Michael S. *Economics and Elections*. Ann Arbor: The University of Michigan Press, 1988.

Liang, Bing. "Price Pressure: Evidence from the 'Dartboard' Column." In: *Journal of Business* Vol. 72, No. 1 (1999): 119–134.

Lidschreiber, Petra. "Zur Kritik des Wirtschaftsjournalismus. Zur Kritik der Kritik—Die Wirtschaftsjournalistin." In: Stephan Ruß-Mohl and Heinz D. Stuckmann (eds.), *Wirtschaftsjournalismus. Ein Handbuch für Ausbildung und Praxis*. München: List, 1991: 68–71.

Lilienthal, Volker. "Der Profit der Reporter. Börsenboom und journalistische Neutralität." In: *epd medien* No. 29, 4/12/2000.

Lilienthal, Volker. "Lesend reich werden. 'FTD,' 'Telebörse' & Co. Boom bei der Wirtschaftspresse." In: *epd medien* No. 13/14, 2/19/2000.

Lindhoff, Hakan. "Economic Journalism in the 1990s. The 'Crisis Discourse' in Sweden." In: Neil T. Gavin (ed.), *The Economy, Media and Public Knowledge*. London: Leicester University Press, 1998: 134–155.

Lindhoff, Hakan. "The Mediated Economy and New Technology." In: Neil T. Gavin (ed.), *The Economy, Media and Public Knowledge*. London: Leicester University Press, 1998: 179–181.

Lipsky, Seth (ed.). *The Billion Dollar Bubble . . . and Other Stories from the Asian Wall Street Journal*. Hong Kong: Dow Jones, 1978.

Litan, Robert E. "Covering Financial Services. Advice to the Media from the Academy." *Money, Markets and the News, Monograph No. 1*. Cambridge: Harvard University, The Joan Shorenstein Center on the Press, Politics and Public Policy, 1999.

Little, Jeffrey B. *Reading the Financial Pages*. New York: Chelsea House, 1988.

Liu, Pu, Stanley D. Smith and Azmat A. Syed. "Stock Price Reactions to The Wall Street Journal's Securities Recommendations." In: *Journal of Financial and Quantitative Analysis*, Vol. 25, No. 3 (1990): 399–410.

Liu, Pu, Stanley D. Smith and Azmat A. Syed. "The Impact of the Insider Trading Scandal on the Information Content of the Wall Street Journal's 'Heard on the Street' Column." In: *Journal of Financial Research* Vol. 15, No. 2 (1992): 181–188.

Lloyd-Davies, P. and M. Canes. "Stock Prices and the Publication of Second-Hand Information." In: *Journal of Business* Vol. 51 (1978): 43–56.

Louis Harris and Associates. *Business Journalism*. Boston: John Hancock Financial Services, 1992.

MacDougall, A. Kent. *Ninety Seconds to Tell it All. Big Business and the News Media*. Homewood: Dow Jones-Irwin, 1981.

MacDougall, A. Kent (ed.). *The Press. A Critical Look From the Inside*. Princeton: Dow Jones, 1972.

Machan, Tibor R. "Two Cases of Press Malpractice. How Broadcast Journalists Mishandle Economic News." In: *The Freeman. The Foundation for Economic Education* Vol. 46, No. 9 (1996): 605–607.

MacKuen, Michael B., Robert S. Erikson and James A. Stimson. "Peasants or Bankers? The American Electorate and the U.S. Economy." In: *American Political Science Review* Vol. 86, No. 3 (1992): 597–611.

Madrick, Jeff. "Press Coverage of America's Changing Financial Institutions." *Money, Markets and the News, Monograph No. 2*. Cambridge: Harvard University, The Joan Shorenstein Center on the Press, Politics and Public Policy, 1999.

Madrick, Jeff. "The Business Media and the New Economy." Research Paper R-24. Cambridge: Harvard University, The Joan Shorenstein Center on the Press, Politics and Public Policy, 2001.

Madrick, Jeff. "The Influence of the Financial Media Over International Economic Policy." CEPA Working Paper Series III. Working Paper No. 16. New York: New School for Social Research, 2000.
Maier, Michaela. "Berichterstattung im Börsenfieber." In: *Sage und Schreibe* No. 3 & 4 (1999): 42, 43.
Maier, Reinhard. *Die Aufgaben des Wirtschaftsteils der Tageszeitungen*. Erlangen: Disseration, 1931.
Maier-Mannhart, Helmut. "Arbeitssituation, Berufsethik. Der festangestellte Wirtschaftsredakteur." In: Stephan Ruß-Mohl and Heinz D. Stuckmann (eds.), *Wirtschaftsjournalismus. Ein Handbuch für Ausbildung und Praxis*. München: List, 1991: 172–175.
Malmqvist, Peter. "The Unexplainable Explained, or Pure Guesswork As 'Truth.'" In: Neil T. Gavin (ed.), *The Economy, Media and Public Knowledge*. London: Leicester University Press, 1998: 163–165.
Mann, Karl O. (ed.). *Readings in Labor Relations from the Wall Street Journal*. Princeton: Dow Jones, 1974.
Manning, P. "Categories of Knowledge and Information Flows. Reasons for the Decline of the British Labour and Industrial Correspondents' Group." In: *Media, Culture and Society* Vol. 21, No. 3 (1999): 313–336.
Martenson, Bo and Hakan Lindhoff. "State, Market, Crisis. Swedish News Journalism on the Economy." In: *Nordicom Review* Vol. 19, No. 1 (1998): 85–100.
Martenson, Bo. "Between State and Market. The Economy in Swedish Television News." In: Neil T. Gavin (ed.), *The Economy, Media and Public Knowledge*. London: Leicester University Press, 1998: 112–133.
Martenson, Bo. "Economic Significance, Audiences and Historical Context." In: Neil T. Gavin (ed.), *The Economy, Media and Public Knowledge*. London: Leicester University Press, 1998: 174–177.
Martin, Joe. *Das neue Börsen-ABC. Von Aktienkauf bis Zinspapiere. Börsen- und Wirtschaftsnachrichten verstehen. Jederzeit schnell und zuverlässig informiert*. München: Droemer Knaur, 2000.
Martin, Paul R. *The Wall Street Journal Guide to Business Style Usage*. New York: Free Press, 2002.
Mast, Claudia. "Ausbildungsangebote zum Wirtschaftsjournalismus. Konzepte, Erfahrungen, Defizite." In: Siegfried Klaue (ed.), *Marktwirtschaft in der Medienberichterstattung*. Düsseldorf: Econ, 1991: 111–135.
Mast, Claudia. "Das neue Business TV könnte sich zu einem Hierarchiekiller entwickeln." In: *Handelsblatt*, 5/26/2000.
Mast, Claudia. "Innovationen in der Wirtschaftsberichterstattung—Herausforderungen für Unternehmen." In: *IW-Medienspiegel* No. 43, 10/25/1999
Mast, Claudia. "Kommunikation als Führungsaufgabe. Der Umgang mit der Öffentlichkeit ist ein Erfolgsfaktor für Unternehmen." In: *Führung und Kommunikation*, Dokumentation der DPRG-Jahrestagung vom 9.-11.05.1991: 198–202.

Mast, Claudia. "Nutzorientierte Wirtschaftsberichterstattung. Neue Akzente in den Präsentationsstrategien der Presse." In: Walter A. Mahle (ed.): *Orientierung in der Informationsgesellschaft*. Konstanz: UVK, 2000: 63–74.

Mast, Claudia. "Offensive Information als Herausforderung für Unternehmer." In: *Forum* 41, No. 19, 5/7/1991: 1–4.

Mast, Claudia. "Wanted: Wirtschaftsjournalisten. Berufsbilder, Ausbildungswege und Perspektiven." In: *Karriereführer Hochschulen* No. 11 (2000): 153–158.

Mast, Claudia. "Wirtschaft hautnah." In: *Journalist* Vol. 49, No. 11 (1999): 34–36.

Mast, Claudia. *Wirtschaftsjournalismus. Grundlagen und neue Konzepte für die Presse*. Opladen: Westdeutscher Verlag, 1999.

Mathur, Ike and Amjad Waheed. "Stock Price Reactions to Securities Recommended in *Business Week's* 'Inside Wall Street.'" In: *Financial Review* Vol. 30, No. 3 (1995): 583–604.

Matzick, Christiane. *Arbeitsrechtliche Maßnahmen zur Vermeidung bzw. Sanktionierung von Interessenkollisionen bei Wirtschaftsjournalisten. Ein Beitrag zur Bestimmung arbeitsrechtlicher Pflichten in der Wirtschaftspresse unter Berücksichtigung der US-amerikanischen Situation*. Bielefeld: Dissertation, 1995.

May, Axel. *Pressemeldungen und Aktienindizes*. Kiel: Vauk, 1994.

McConnell, P. "The Provision Of Real Time Financial Information. Analysis of a Knowledge Based Industry." Working Paper Series, Henley Management College No. 8, 1995.

McCusker, John J. "The Business Press in England Before 1775." In: *Library*. Vol. 8 (1986): 205–231.

McCusker, John J. *European Bills of Entry and Marine Lists. Early Commercial Publications and the Origins of the Business Press*. Cambridge: Harvard University Library, 1985.

McCusker, John J. and Cora Gravesteijn. *The Beginnings of Commercial and Financial Journalism. The Commodity Price Currents, Exchange Rate Currents, and Money Currents of Early Modern Europe*. Amsterdam: Neha, 1991.

McPhatter, William (ed.). *The Business Beat. Its Impact and Its Problems*. Indianapolis: Bobbs-Merrill, 1980.

McQueen, Grant and V. Vance Roley. "Stock Prices, News, and Business Conditions." In: *Review of Financial Studies* Vol. 6, No. 3 (1993): 683–707.

Medesan, Anca. "Monitoring Business News on the Internet. Selected North American Sourcs." In: *Business Information Review* Vol. 13, No. 2 (1996): 83–90.

"Media Report. Börsenfernsehen in Deutschland, 1. Teil." In: *Der Wirtschaftsredakteur* Vol. 32, No. 4 (1997): 9f.

"Media Report. Börsenfernsehen in Deutschland. Die 'Telebörse.'" In: *Der Wirtschaftsredakteur* Vol. 32, No. 5 (1997): 11–13.

"Media Report. Börsenfernsehen in Deutschland. Die 'Telebörse'-Konkurrenten." In: *Der Wirtschaftsredakteur* Vol. 32, No. 6 (1997): 10–12.

Medien Tenor. "'Entwicklungshelfer' der Kapitalmärkte. Aktienkursentwicklung in Abhängigkeit von Analystenaussagen in der Wirtschaftspresse im 1. Quartal 2002." In: *Medien Tenor Forschungsbericht* No. 120 (2002): 78f.

Meili, Andreas. *Wirtschaftsjournalismus im Rechtsvergleich. Aktuelle Probleme des Wirtschaftsjournalismus im Lichte des Rechts der Schweiz, der USA, von Großbritannien, Deutschland und der Europäischen Union*. Baden-Baden: Nomos, 1996.

Merten, Hans-Lothar. *Finanznachrichten gezielt nutzen. Zwischen den Zeilen lesen, für Anleger und private Investoren*. Regensburg: Walhalla, 2001.

Meschke, J. Felix. 2002. "CEO Interviews on CNBC." Tempe: Arizona State University, Working Paper.

Metcalf, Gilbert E. and Burton G. Malkiel. "The Wall Street Journal Contests. The Experts, the Darts, and the Efficient Market Hypothesis." In: *Applied Financial Economics* Vol. 4, No. 2 (1994): 371–374.

Metrick, Andrew. "Performance Evaluation With Transactions Data. The Stock Selection of Investment Newsletters." In: *Journal of Finance* Vol. 54, No. 5 (1999): 1743–1775.

Meyer-Korte, Jürgen. *Der Wirtschaftsteil in der Lokalpresse*. In: ZV+ZV 36 (1965): 1600–1601.

Mininni, Nicola. "Deutschschweizer Wirtschaftsmedien. Näher an die Zielgruppen." In: *Marketing und Kommunikation* Vol. 23, No. 2 (1995): 76–78.

"Mit Finanzkrise Quote machen." In: *Der Spiegel*, 6/22/1998.

Mitchell, Mark L. and J. Harold Mulherin. "The Impact of Public Information on the Stock Market." In: *Journal of Finance* Vol. 49, No. 3 (1994): 923–950.

Mittler der Märkte. *Wirtschaftsjournalismus zwischen Anspruch und Alltag. Festschrift für Hans K. Herdt*. Frankfurt a.M.: Börsen-Zeitung, 2000.

Moffitt, Donald (ed.). *The American Character. Views of America from the Wall Street Journal*. New York: G. Braziller, 1983.

Molinski, Michael. "How to Use Electronic Data to Generate Company Stories." In: Terri Thompson (ed.), *Writing About Business*. New York: Columbia University Press, 2001: 226–233.

Money, Markets and the News. Press Coverage of the Modern Revolution in Financial Institutions. Cambridge: Harvard University, The Joan Shorenstein Center on the Press, Politics and Public Policy, 1999.

Morris, Kenneth et al. *American Dreams. One Hundred Years of Business Ideas and Innovation from the Wall Street Journal*. New York: Lightbulb, 1990.

Morrison, Joseph L. *Opportunities in Business Papers*. New York: Vocational Guidance Manuals, 1955.

Mosley, P. *The British Economy as Represented by the Popular Press*. Glasgow: Centre for the Study of Public Policy, University of Strathclyde, 1982.

Moy, Ronald L. "Using The Wall Street Journal in Economics and Finance Courses. A Survey and Suggestions." In: *Journal of Education for Business* Vol. 70, No. 3 (1995): 146–150.

Mühlfenzl, Rudolf. "Was ist Wirtschaft im Fernsehen?" In: *ARD-Pressedienst* No. 4 1978: 1–4.

Mühlfenzl, Rudolf. "Wenn alle warten, läuft nichts. Defizite im privaten Hörfunk." In: Gero Kalt (ed.), *Wirtschaft in den Medien*. Frankfurt a.M.: IMK, 1990: 145–152.

Müller, Christian. "Konstante Dosis." In: *Medienspiegel*, Vol. 24, No. 9 (2000): 4–5.

Müller, Ernst N. *Die Wirtschaftspresse lesen mit Gewinn. Ein praktischer Ratgeber für ihren finanziellen Erfolg*. Wien: Ueberreuter, 2001.

Müller, Ernst N. *Die Wirtschaftspresse verstehen und nutzen. Wie man ein Vermögen aufbaut. Praktischer Ratgeber für gewinnbringendes Zeitunglesen*. Ebmatingen/Zürich: Fortuna, 1991.

Müller, Maike. "Das Fernsehen konstruiert die wirtschaftliche Realität. Wirtschaft im Fernsehen und Bevölkerungsmeinung. Eine Zusammenhangsanalyse." In: *Medien Tenor Forschungsbericht* No. 83 (1999): 40–43.

Müller, Volker. "Mit zweifelhaften Empfehlungen." In: *Die Telebörse*, No. 40 (2001): 80–82.

Mutter, Andreas. *Die Beziehungen zwischen Öffentlichkeitsarbeit und Wirtschaftsjournalismus. Eine empirische Untersuchung aus der Sicht der Wirtschaftsjournalisten*. Universität Eichstätt: Diplomarbeit, 1990.

Nadeau, Richard, Richard G. Niemi and Timothy Amato. "Elite Economic Forecasts, Economic News, Mass Economic Expectations and Voting Intentions in Great Britain." In: *European Journal of Political Research* Vol. 38, No. 1 (2000): 135–170.

Nadeau, Richard, Richard G. Niemi, David P. Fan and Timothy Amato. "Elite Economic Forecasts, Economic News, Mass Economical Judgements and Presidential Approval." In: *Journal of Politics* Vol. 61, No. 1 (1999): 109–135.

Nahrendorf, Rainer. "Orientierungshilfen. Ausbildungswege und Karrieremuster." In: Stephan Ruß-Mohl and Heinz D. Stuckmann (eds.), *Wirtschaftsjournalismus. Ein Handbuch für Ausbildung und Praxis*. München: List, 1991: 236–239.

Nahrendorf, Rainer. "Probleme mediengerechter Umsetzung wirtschafts- und gesellschaftspolitischer Fragen." In: Gerhard Hütter and Hermann Linke (eds.), *Informiert bis zur Unmündigkeit? Einfluß und politische Verantwortung der Medien in der BRD*. Herford/Bonn: Maximilian, 1990: 135–144.

Nahrendorf, Rainer. "Wirtschaftsjournalismus unter Qualitätsdruck." In: *Bertelsmann Briefe* No. 138 (1997): 36–37.

"National Figures. Economic News as Public Knowledge." Politics and Communications Studies Working Paper. Liverpool: Liverpool University, Public Communications Group, 1995.

Neal, Larry. "The Flow of Financial Information in the Eighteenth Century: London and Amsterdam." Ms. unveröffentlicht, 1985.

Neal, Larry. "The Rise of a Financial Press. London and Amsterdam." In: *Business History* Vol. 30, No. 2 (1988): 163–178.

"Negativthemen verkaufen sich besser. Die Medien räumen Konkursen mehr Raum ein als Neugründungen." In: *Medien Tenor Forschungsbericht* No. 82 (1999): 34.

Neilson, Winthrop and Frances Neilson. *What's News, Dow Jones. Story of the Wall Street Journal.* Radnor: Chilton, 1973.

Neuber, Friedel. "Wirtschaft für Otto Normalverbraucher und Professor Geistesblitz. Rede anläßlich der Verleihung des Friedrich-Vogel-Preises an Wirtschaftsjournalisten am 7.12.1989 in Düsseldorf." In: *Medienspiegel* Vol. 13, No. 51/52 (1989).

Neuber, Friedel. "Zum Spannungsverhältnis von Wirtschaft und Journalismus." In: *Medienspiegel* Vol. 11, No. 47 (1987).

Neubert, Miriam. "Medienspezifische Präsentation. Wochenzeitung." In: Stephan Ruß-Mohl and Heinz D. Stuckmann (eds.), *Wirtschaftsjournalismus. Ein Handbuch für Ausbildung und Praxis.* München: List, 1991: 144–148.

"Neue Wirtschaftsblätter: Verbraucher im Visier. Pläne von Springer, Bauer und Gruner+Jahr." In: *Der Wirtschaftsredakteur* Vol. 32, No. 16 (1997): 14–16.

"Neuer Ärger um '3Sat-Börse.'" In: *Der Spiegel*, 5/29/2000.

Nigge, Hermann. *Die Wirtschaftspublizistik der deutschen Tagespresse. Geschichtliche Entwicklung, redaktionelle Herstellung, Inhalt und Bedeutung.* Graz: Dissertation, 1960.

Nobel, Peter. "Gedanken zum Wirtschaftsjournalismus." In: Georges Bindschedler and Peter Ziegler (eds.), *Medien, Verleger und Unternehmertum.* Bern: Haupt, 2000: 69ff.

Noelle-Neumann, Elisabeth. "Unternehmerbild und öffentliche Meinung." In: *Wirtschaft und öffentliche Meinung.* Köln: Hegner, 1972: 179–196.

Norback, Craig T. (ed.). *Guide to U.S. Business, Financial and Economic News Correspondents and Contacts.* New York: Larriston, 1985.

Norden, A. *Die Berichterstattung über Welthandelsartikel (Getreide, Zucker, Kaffee, Baumwolle, Wolle).* Leipzig, 1910.

Norris, Floyd. "Role Models: Carol Loomis." In: *Columbia Journalism Review*, November/December 2000: 25.

Nusch, Friedmar. "Darstellen, was in den Köpfen vorgeht. Unternehmen und Sender könnten besser zusammenarbeiten." In: Gero Kalt (ed.), *Wirtschaft in den Medien.* Frankfurt a.M.: IMK, 1990: 117–123.

Nyblom, Lori Cox. "Media Coverage of the Economy and Aggregate Economic Evaluations. Uncovering Evidence of Indirect Media Effects." In: *Political Communication* Vol. 13, No. 2 (1996): 249–250.

O'Connell, Brian. CNBC. *Creating Wealth. An Investor's Guide to Decoding the Market.* New York: John Wiley, 2001.

Oehme, Wolfgang. *Wirtschaft und Medien. Schwierige Zusammenhänge in einfacher Sprache vermitteln ist wohl am schwierigsten zu erfüllen.* Frankfurt a.M.: Merkur-Thorhauer, 1984.

Oehme, Wolfgang. "Wirtschaft verständlicher machen." In: *Medienspiegel* Vol. 7, No. 49 (1983): 5–6.

O'Kane, Brian (ed.). *Essential Finance for Journalists*. Dublin: Oak Tree Press, 1993.

"On Hair-Trigger Wall Street, A Stock Plunges on Fake News." In: *New York Times*, 8/26/2000.

"Online-Werbung boomt: Milliardenumsätze erwartet. Wirtschaftstitel profitieren bsonders stark." In: *Der Wirtschaftsredakteur* Vol. 35, No. 10 (2000): 7–9.

Osel, Werner. *Die Handelsblatt-Chronik 1946 bis 1996*. Düsseldorf: Handelsblatt, 1996.

Ost, Friedhelm."Wirtschaft und Soziales, bürgernah dargestellt." In: *ZDF-Jahrbuch*. Mainz: ZDF, 1985: 96–100.

Ost, Friedhelm and Wolfgang Schröder. "Wie orientiert das Fernsehen? Wirtschaft, eine Herausforderung für das Fernsehen." In: *Phänomen Fernsehen. Aufgaben, Probleme, Ziele, dargestellt am ZDF*. Düsseldorf: Econ, 1978: 76–88.

Palmer, William Russell. *Freelance Business Writing Business*. Monmouth: Heathcote Publishers, 1979.

Palmon, Dan and Meir I. Schneller. "The Relationship Between Securities' Abnormal Price Movements and Wall Street Journal News." In: *Journal of Banking and Finance* Vol. 4, No. 3 (1980): 235–247.

Palmon, Oded, Huey-Lian Sun, Alex P. Tang. "The Impact of Publication of Analysts' Recommendations on Returns and Trading Volume." In: *Financial Review* Vol. 29, No. 3, (1994): 395–417.

Pari, Robert A. "Wall $treet Week Recommendations: Yes or No?" In: *Journal of Portfolio Management* Vol. 14, No. 1 (1987): 74–76.

Parker, Richard. "Journalism and Economics. The Tangled Webs of Profession, Narrative, and Responsibility in a Modern Democracy." The Joan Shorenstein Center Press Politics, Discussion Paper D-25, May 1997.

Parker, Richard. "The Public, the Press, and Economic News." In: *Harvard International Journal of Press Politics* Vol. 2, No. 2 (1997): 127–131.

Parker, Richard. "The Revolution in America's Financial Industry. How Well is the Press Covering the Story?" Money, Markets and the News, Monograph *No. 3*. Cambridge: Harvard University, The Joan Shorenstein Center on the Press, Politics and Public Policy, 1999.

Parsons, D. Wayne. *The Power of the Financial Press. Journalism and Economic Opinion in Britain and America*. New Brunswick: Rutgers University Press, 1990.

Passell, Peter. *How to Read the Financial Pages*. New York: Warner, 1993.

Pastuszek, Horst. *Wirtschaftsordnung und Wirtschaftspublizistik*. Köln: Westdeutscher Verlag, 1959.

Pauli, Knut S. "Schnell und umfassend informieren. Zum Einfluß von Unternehmen, Verbänden und Gewerkschaften." In: Gero Kalt (ed.), *Wirtschaft in den Medien*. Frankfurt a.M.: IMK, 1990: 303–308.

Pearce, Douglas K. and V. Vance Roley. "Stock Prices and Economic News." In: *Journal of Business* Vol. 58, No. 1 (1985): 49–67.

Peck, Christoph. "Wirtschaftsjournalismus. Puzzeln am Konzept." In: *Journalist* Vol. 48, No. 3 (1998): 13–15.

Petzold, Lothar. "Medienspezifische Präsentation. Lokal- und Regionalzeitung." In: Stephan Ruß-Mohl and Heinz D. Stuckmann (eds.), *Wirtschaftsjournalismus. Ein Handbuch für Ausbildung und Praxis*. München: List, 1991: 134–138.

Petzold, Lothar. *Wirtschaft. Themen für Lokaljournalisten.* Vol. 3. Bonn: VLR, 1988.

Pfeiffer, Hermannus (ed.). *Die FAZ. Nachforschungen über ein Zentralorgan*. Köln: Pahl-Rugenstein, 1988.

Picot, Arnold. *Die Transformation wirtschaftlicher Aktivität unter dem Einfluß der Informations- und Kommunikationstechnik*. Freiberg: Technische Universität Bergakademie Freiberg, Fakultät für Wirtschaftswissenschaften, 1998.

Pieper, Ute, Dirk Schiereck and Martin Weber. "Die Kaufempfehlungen des 'Effecten-Spiegel.' Eine empirische Untersuchung im Lichte der Effizienzthese des Kapitalmarktes." In: *Zeitschrift für betriebswirtschaftliche Forschung* Vol. 45 (1993): 487–509.

Piesanen, Mark. "Business Journalism on TV." In: Terri Thompson (ed.), *Writing About Business*. New York: Columbia University Press, 2001: 246–249.

Piirainen, Ilpo T. *Sprache der Wirtschaftspresse. Untersuchung zum Sprachgebrauch des "Handelsblattes."* Bochum: Brockmeyer, 1987.

Pines, Burton Yale and Timothy Lamer. *Out of Focus. Network Television and the American Economy*. Washington: Regnery, 1994.

Platow, Robert. *Die wirtschaftlichen Nachrichten in ihrem Wesen und ihrer Bedeutung*. Kiel: Dissertation, 1926.

Pleeter, Saul and Philip K. Way. *Economics in the News*. Reading: Addison-Wesley, 1992.

Poole, Gary Andrew. "'Wealth Porn' And Beyond." In: *Columbia Journalism Review*, November/December 2000: 22–23.

Porter, Dilwyn. "City Editors and the Modern Investing Public. Establishing the Integrity of the New Financial Journalism in Late Nineteenth-Century London." In: *Media History* Vol. 4, No. 1 (1998): 49–60.

Posewang, Wolfgang. *Verbraucherinformation in der Tageszeitung. Eine Untersuchung zur wirtschaftspolitischen Berichterstattung in der regionalen Abonnentenzeitung*. Bremen: Dissertation, 1982.

Pound, John and Richard J. Zeckhauser. "Clearly Heard on the Street. The Effect of Takeover Rumors on Stock Prices." In: *Journal of Business* Vol. 63, No. 3 (1990): 291–308.

Powers, William. "Media Rex. Family News Values. Why It's in the Public Interest to Keep The Wall Street Journal a Mom-and-Pop Business." In: *New Republic* No. 4285 (1997): 12–14.

Prager, Jutta. " Zur Kritik des Wirtschaftsjournalismus. Die Unternehmerin." In: Stephan Ruß-Mohl and Heinz D. Stuckmann (eds.), *Wirtschaftsjournalismus. Ein Handbuch für Ausbildung und Praxis.* München: List, 1991: 44–46.
Presse und Wirtschaft. Festgabe der Kölnischen Zeitung zur Pressa Köln, Mai bis Okt.1928. Köln, 1928.
Preston, Charles (ed.). *A Cartoon Portfolio from the Wall Street Journal.* Princeton: Dow Jones, 1977.
Preston, Charles (ed.). *But is it Deductible? Tax Cartoons from the Wall Street Journal.* New York: Dutton, 1964.
Preston, Charles. (ed.). *Can Board Chairmen Get Measles? Thirty Years of Great Cartoons from the Wall Street Journal.* New York: Crown, 1982.
Preston, Charles (ed.). *Cartoon Portfolio From the Wall Street Journal.* New York: Westport, 1972.
Preston, Charles. (ed.). *Modern Times. Cartoons from the Wall Street Journal.* New York: Dutton, 1968.
Preston, Charles (ed.). *My Shell Was Recalled! A Cartoon Portfolio from the Wall Street Journal.* Princeton: Dow Jones, 1974.
Preston, Charles (ed.). *The Coffee Break. More Wall Street Journal Cartoons.* New York: Dutton, 1955.
Preston, Charles (ed.). *The New World of the Wall Street Journal.* New York: Simon and Schuster, 1963.
Preston, Charles (ed.). *The Wall Street Journal Cartoon Portfolio.* Princeton: Dow Jones, 1979.
Preston, Charles (ed.). *The Wall Street Journal's Pepper and Salt Cartoons. CEO's and Other Kings.* New York: New American Library, 1986.
Preston, Charles (ed.). *The Wall Street Journal's Pepper and Salt Cartoons. Man's New Best Friend.* New York: Perigee, 1988.
"Print gewinnt. Der Trend von der Sparer- zur Anlegergesellschaft treibt die Werbeeinnahmen der meisten Wirtschaftstitel in die Höhe." In: *Horizont*, 11/23/2000.
Prüfig, Katrin. "Zwischen Börsenhype und Very Old Economy." In: *ARD-Jahrbuch 2001.* Hamburg: Hans-Bredow-Institut, 2001.
"Publizistik zwischen Wirtschaft und Öffentlichkeit." In: *Volkswirt* Vol. 15, No. 7 (1961).
Pudor, Fritz. *Was wird aus der Wirtschaftspublizistik?* Freudenstadt: Eurobuch, 1970.
Quandt, Siegfried (ed.). *Wirtschaftsjournalismus.* Gießen: Zentrum für Fachjournalistische Studien an der Justus-Liebig-Universität Gießen, 1986.
Quandt, Siegfried. "Wirtschaftsjournalismus an der Universität. Probleme beim Einrichten eines Lehrstuhls für Wirtschaftsjournalismus." In: Michael Schenk and Ferdinand Simoneit (eds.), *Wege zum Wirtschaftsjournalismus.* München: R. Fischer, 1989: 41–47.

Quinn, Jane Bryant. "When Business Writing Becomes Soft Porn." In: *Columbia Journalism Review*, March/April 1998: 48–50.

Quirt, John. *The Press and the World of Money. How the News Media Cover Business and Finance, Panic and Prosperity, and the Pursuit of the American Dream.* Byron: California Courier, 1993.

Rae, John and John Drury. "Reification and Evidence in Rhetoric on Economic Recession. Some Methods Used in the UK Press, Final Quarter 1990." In: *Discourse and Society* Vol. 4, No. 3 (1993): 329–356.

Ragas, Kurt. *Die Wirtschaftsberichterstattung zur Zeit der Wiener Börsenkrise 1873 und der Inflationszeit nach dem Ersten Weltkrieg. Ein zeitungswissenschaftlicher Vergleich.* Wien: Dissertation, 1953.

Rahmann, John. *Export und Import im Wirtschaftsteil der Zeitung.* Hamburg: Hammerich & Lesser, 1955.

Rath, Hauke. *Der Börsenteil in Zeitungen. Besser verstehen, gewinnbringend anwenden.* Stuttgart: Deutscher Sparkassenverlag, 1994.

Rath, Hauke. *Wirtschaft, Geld und Börse in der Zeitung.* Wiesbaden: Gabler, 1992.

Ratzke, Dietrich. "Dem Leser dienen, damals wie heute. Wirtschaftspublizistik im Wandel der Zeit." In: Gero Kalt (ed.), *Wirtschaft in den Medien.* Frankfurt a.M.: IMK, 1990: 217–230.

Redmond, Pauline. *Business Paper Writing.* New York: Pitman, 1939.

Reeder, W. "Der Lokalredakteur vor der Wirtchaft, ratlos?" In: ZV+ZV 44 (1976): 1682–1684.

Reese, Stephen, John Daly and Andrew Hardy. "Economic News on Network Television. 1973–1983." In: *Journalism Quarterly* Vol. 64, No. 1 (1987): 137–144.

Reschenberg, Hasso. "Medienspezifische Präsentation. Fachpresse/Branchenzeitschrift." In: Stephan Ruß-Mohl and Heinz D. Stuckmann (eds.), *Wirtschaftsjournalismus. Ein Handbuch für Ausbildung und Praxis.* München: List, 1991: 156–159.

Reuter, Edzard. "Zur Kritik des Wirtschaftsjournalismus. Der Konzernchef." In: Stephan Ruß-Mohl and Heinz D. Stuckmann (eds.), *Wirtschaftsjournalismus. Ein Handbuch für Ausbildung und Praxis.* München: List, 1991: 42–44.

Reuter, Jonathan and Eric Zitzewitz. "Do Ads Influence Editors? Advertising and Bias in the Financial Media." University of Oregon and Stanford Graduate School of Business Working Paper, 2004

Richardson, Kay. "Signs and Wonders. Interpreting the Economy Through Television." In: Allan Bell and Peter Garrett (Hsg.), *Approaches to Media Discourse.* London: Blackwell, 1998: 220–250.

Richardson, Kay. "The Economy and Public Language." In: Neil T. Gavin (ed.), *The Economy, Media and Public Knowledge.* London: Leicester University Press, 1998: 38–52.

Ricker, Reinhart. *Unternehmensschutz und Pressefreiheit.* Heidelberg: Verlag Recht und Wirtschaft, 1989.

Ricker, Reinhart. "Wirtschafts-Fachzeitschriften im Postzeitungsdienst." In: *Wettbewerb in Recht und Praxis* Vol. 31, No. 11 (1985): 599–612.

Riedl, Anton. *Liberale Publizistik für soziale Marktwirtschaft. Die Unterstützung der Wirtschaftspolitik Ludwig Erhards in der Frankfurter Allgemeinen Zeitung und in der Neuen Zürcher Zeitung 1948/49 bis 1957.* Regensburg: Roderer, 1992.

Riemer, Markus. *Die Beziehungen zwischen Öffentlichkeitsarbeit und Wirtschaftsjournalismus. Eine empirische Untersuchung aus der Sicht der Industrie-Pressestellen.* Universität Eichstätt: Diplomarbeit, 1990.

Robertson, Lori. "Reversal of Fortune." In: *American Journalism Review*, Vol. 21, No. 2 (March 1999): 30–35.

Rockefeller, Barbara. *CNBC 24/7 Trading. Around the Clock, Around the World.* New York: Wiley, 2001.

Röckemann, Christian. "Anlageempfehlungen von Börseninformationsdiensten und Anlegerverhalten. Eine empirische Analyse für den deutschen Aktienmarkt." In: *Zeitschrift für betriebswirtschaftliche Forschung* Vol. 46 (1994): 819–848.

Röder, Klaus. "Die Informationswirkung von Ad hoc-Meldungen." In: *Zeitschrift für Betriebswirtschaft* Vol. 70, No. 5 (2000): 567–593.

Rolke, Lothar and Volker Wolff (eds.). *Finanzkommunikation. Kurspflege durch Meinungspflege. Die neuen Spielregeln am Aktienmarkt.* Frankfurt a.M.: F.A.Z.-Institut, 2000.

Rolke, Lothar. "Journalisten und PR-Manager. Eine antagonistische Partnerschaft mit offener Zukunft." In: Lothar Rolke and Volker Wolff (eds.), *Wie die Medien die Wirklichkeit steuern und selber gesteuert werden.* Opladen: Westdeutscher Verlag, 1999: 233–247.

Rönnebeck, Wolfgang. "Mit Menschen nichts zu tun? Für die Öffentlichkeitsarbeit ist der Wirtschaftsteil nicht öffentlich genug." In: Gero Kalt (ed.), *Wirtschaft in den Medien.* Frankfurt a.M.: IMK, 1990: 209–215.

Röper, Burkhardt. "Der Wirtschaftsteil (systematisch und historisch)." In: Emil Dovifat, *Handbuch der Publizistik* Vol. 3. Berlin: de Gruyter, 1969: 202–209.

Röper, Burkhardt. "Eine kritische Zuschrift: Die Systematik der Wirtschaftspresse." In: *Wirtschaftsdienst* Vol. 34, No. 12 (1954): 674.

Röper, Burkhardt. "Gestalt und Aufgaben des Wirtschaftsteils der Tagespresse." In: *Wirtschaftsdienst* Vol. 34, No. 10 (1954): 566–570.

Röper, Burkhardt. "Wirtschaftsinformationen." In: *Handwörterbuch der Sozialwissenschaften* Vol. 12. Stuttgart: G. Fischer, 1965: 185–189.

Röper, Burkhardt. *Wirtschaftsnachrichten in der Weltpresse. Zum Verständnis des Wirtschaftsteils einer Zeitung.* München: Francke, 1977.

Röpke, Klaus. "Der Zeitdruck sprengt das Konzept. Das 'RTL plus'-Magazin 'netto' läßt noch Wünsche offen." In: *Medien-Kritik* No. 7 (1990): 3–4.

Röpke, Klaus and Gero Kalt. "Börse für jedermann. Das Magazin '3sat-Börse' richtet sich an ein breites Publikum." In: *Medien-Kritik* No. 4 (1990): 2–4.

Röpke, Klaus and Gero Kalt. "Der Nutzwert ist manchmal fraglich. Die Sat 1-Telebörse' sendet täglich von der Frankfurter Börse." In: *Medien-Kritik* No. 50 (1989): 2–5.

Röpke, Klaus and Gero Kalt. "Starkes Niveaugefälle. Das Wirtschaftsforum des Privatsenders Sat 1." In: *Medien-Kritik* No. 47 (1989): 4–7.

Rosenberg, Jerry Martin. *Inside the Wall Street Journal. The History and the Power of Dow Jones and Company and America's Most Influential Newspaper.* New York: Macmillan, 1982.

Rosenwein, Rifka. "Bullish on Blodget. How an Internet Analyst's Amazon Call Sparked a Media and Stock-Market Frenzy, and Boosted His Own Career in the Process." In: *Brill's Content*, June 1999: 55–58.

Rosenwein, Rifka. "The Money Press: How Inside is 'Inside Wall Street'?" In: *Brill's Content*, November 1998.

"Rosige Zeiten? Über Ausbildung und Zukunft von Wirtschaftsjournalisten." In: *Der Wirtschaftsredakteur*, 5/15/2000.

Rothering, Elisabeth. *Das "Handelsblatt" in der Lizenzzeit.* Düsseldorf: Handelsblatt, 1992.

Ruff, Raymond T. "Effect of a Selection and Recommendation of a 'Stock of the Month.'" In: *Financial Analysts Journal* Vol. 19, No. 2 (1963): 41–43.

Rühl, Manfred (ed.). *Public Relations der Gewerkschaften und Wirtschaftsverbände. Theoretische Ansätze, Forschungsergebnisse und praktische Erfahrungen aus einem PR-Seminar.* Düsseldorf: Flieger, 1982.

Rühl, Manfred. "Wirtschaft und Journalismus." In: Siegfried Quandt (ed.), *Fachjournalismus im Gespräch. Sonderheft Wirtschaftsjournalismus.* Gießen: Zentrum für Fachjournalistische Studien, 1986: 12–19.

Rumphorst, Reinhild. "Zukunftsperspektiven und Spezialisierungsfelder. Verbraucherjournalismus." In: Stephan Ruß-Mohl and Heinz D. Stuckmann (eds.), *Wirtschaftsjournalismus. Ein Handbuch für Ausbildung und Praxis.* München: List, 1991: 209–211.

Ruß-Mohl, Stephan. "Arbeitssituation, Berufsethik. Ethische Zwickmühlen. " In: Stephan Ruß-Mohl and Heinz D. Stuckmann (eds.), *Wirtschaftsjournalismus. Ein Handbuch für Ausbildung und Praxis.* München: List, 1991: 188–194.

Ruß-Mohl, Stephan. "Orientierungshilfen. Weitere Ausbildungsangebote." In: Stephan Ruß-Mohl and Heinz D. Stuckmann (eds.), *Wirtschaftsjournalismus. Ein Handbuch für Ausbildung und Praxis.* München: List, 1991: 242–250.

Ruß-Mohl, Stephan. "Verkanntes Stiefkind. Ausbildung im Wirtschaftsjournalismus." In: *Journalist* Vol. 48, No. 3 (1998): 20–21.

Ruß-Mohl, Stephan. "Zukunftsperspektiven und Spezialisierungsfelder. Wirtschaftswissenschaften." In: Stephan Ruß-Mohl and Heinz D. Stuckmann (eds.), *Wirtschaftsjournalismus. Ein Handbuch für Ausbildung und Praxis.* München: List, 1991: 214–218.

Ruß-Mohl, Stephan. "Zur Kritik des Wirtschaftsjournalismus. Der Publizistikwissenschaftler." In: Stephan Ruß-Mohl and Heinz D. Stuckmann (eds.),

Wirtschaftsjournalismus. Ein Handbuch für Ausbildung und Praxis. München: List, 1991: 61–64.

Ruß-Mohl, Stephan and Heinz D. Stuckmann (eds.). *Wirtschaftsjournalismus. Ein Handbuch für Ausbildung und Praxis.* München: List, 1991.

Ruß-Mohl, Stephan and Uwe Vorkötter. "Nachrichten- und Themenauswahl." In: Stephan Ruß-Mohl and Heinz D. Stuckmann (eds.), *Wirtschaftsjournalismus. Ein Handbuch für Ausbildung und Praxis.* München: List, 1991: 106–111.

Rust, Holger. "Orientierungshilfen. Wirtschaftsjournalismus in Österreich." In: Stephan Ruß-Mohl and Heinz D. Stuckmann (eds.), *Wirtschaftsjournalismus. Ein Handbuch für Ausbildung und Praxis.* München: List, 1991: 265–271.

Sachs, Gerd. *Unternehmen im Spiegel der Presse.* München: Florentz, 1980.

Sallott, Lynne M., Thomas M. Steinfatt and Michael B. Salwen. "Journalists' and Public Relations Practitioners' News Values. Perceptions and Cross-Perceptions." In: *Journalism and Mass Communications Quarterly* Vol. 75 No. 2 (1998): 366–377.

Sanders, David. "The Real Economy and the Perceived Economy in Popularity Functions. How Much Do Voters Need to Know? A Study of British Data, 1974–1997." Barcelona: Institut de Ciències Polítiques i Socials, Working Paper No. 170, 1999.

Sanders, David, Hugh Ward and David Marsh. "The Electoral Impact of Newspaper Coverage of the Economy, 1979–1987." In: *British Journal of Political Science* Vol. 23, No. 2 (1993): 175–210.

Sant, Rajiv and Mir A. Zaman. "Market Reaction to Business Week 'Inside Wall Street' Column: A Self-fulfilling Prophecy." In: *Journal of Banking and Finance* Vol. 20 (1996): 617–643.

Saporito, Bill. "The Business Century. How the Economy Became Hot News in the Last 100 Years." In: *Columbia Journalism Review*, March/April 1999: 47–52.

Saxer, Ulrich. "Orientierungshilfen. Wirtschaftsjournalismus in der Schweiz." In: Stephan Ruß-Mohl and Heinz D. Stuckmann (eds.), *Wirtschaftsjournalismus. Ein Handbuch für Ausbildung und Praxis.* München: List, 1991: 272–277.

Schäfer, J. and W. Scheffer. *Der Handels- und Schiffahrtsteil der Zeitungen.* Berlin/Wien, 1926.

Scharff, Edward E. *Worldly Power. The Making of the Wall Street Journal.* New York: Beaufort, 1986.

Schatz, Robin, D. "Internet Resources for Business Reporters." In: Terri Thompson (ed.), *Writing About Business.* New York: Columbia University Press, 2001: 216–225.

Schawinsky, Karl. "Informieren, Unterhalten, Motivieren. Wirtschaftsthemen im privaten Sat 1-Programm." In: *Medienspiegel* Vol. 8, No. 51 (1984): 2–3.

Schawinsky, Karl. "Routiniert aber lieblos. Defizite im öffentlich-rechtlichen Hörfunk." In: Gero Kalt (ed.), *Wirtschaft in den Medien.* Frankfurt a.M.: IMK, 1990: 139–144.

Schawinsky, Karl. "TV-Wirtschaftssendungen. Die Angebotsvielfalt nimmt zu." In: *Medienspiegel* Vol. 13, No. 47 (1989): 4–5.

Schawinsky, Karl. "Wirtschaft im Fernsehen. Viele Wünsche offen." In: *Medienspiegel* Vol. 13, No. 43 (1989): 3.

Schawinsky, Karl. "Wirtschaftssendungen. Keine Zukunft für Features?" In: *Medienspiegel* Vol. 13, No. 17 (1989): 4–5.

Scheid, Ekkehard. "Medienspezifische Präsentation. Informationsdienst." In: Stephan Ruß-Mohl and Heinz D. Stuckmann (eds.), *Wirtschaftsjournalismus. Ein Handbuch für Ausbildung und Praxis*. München: List, 1991: 159–161.

Scheiderer, Claudia. *Die Wirtschaftsberichterstattung über vier deutsche Automobilunternehemn. Eine Evaluation der Pressemitteilungen von Audi, BMW, DaimlerChrysler und Volkswagen*. Eichstätt: Universität Eichstätt, Diplomarbeit, 2000.

Schenk, Michael and Ferdinand Simoneit (eds.). *Wege zum Wirtschaftsjournalismus. Ein Workshop mit Diskussionsbeiträgen aus Wissenschaft und Praxis*. München: R. Fischer, 1989.

Schenk, Michael and Patrick Rössler. *Wirtschaftsberichterstattung in Zeitschriften. Literaturbericht und Inhaltsanalyse*. München: R. Fischer, 1996.

Scheuch, Erwin K. "Das Bild der Wirtschaft in nicht-wirtschaftlichen Sendungen der Massenmedien." In: *Wirtschaft und öffentliche Meinung*. Köln: Hegner, 1972: 135–155.

Schild, Helmut. "Medienspezifische Präsentation. Radio." In: Stephan Ruß-Mohl and Heinz D. Stuckmann (eds.), *Wirtschaftsjournalismus. Ein Handbuch für Ausbildung und Praxis*. München: List, 1991: 163–165.

Schild, Helmut. "Zukunftsperspektiven und Spezialisierungsfelder. Sozialpolitik." In: Stephan Ruß-Mohl and Heinz D. Stuckmann (eds.), *Wirtschaftsjournalismus. Ein Handbuch für Ausbildung und Praxis*. München: List, 1991: 206–208.

Schiwy, Peter. "Anspruch auf die 'erste Reihe.'" In: Gero Kalt (ed.), *Wirtschaft in den Medien*. Frankfurt a.M.: IMK, 1990: 27–33.

Schiwy, Peter. "Wirtschaft im Fernsehen." In: *Markenartikel* 1 (1988): 6–22.

Schlamp, Hans-Jürgen. "Medienspezifische Präsentation. Politisches Magazin." In: Stephan Ruß-Mohl and Heinz D. Stuckmann (eds.), *Wirtschaftsjournalismus. Ein Handbuch für Ausbildung und Praxis*. München: List, 1991: 148–150.

"Schmale Schneide. Der Nachrichtensender n-tv profitiert vom Aktienfieber der Deutschen." In: *Der Spiegel*, 11/10/1997.

Schmalenbach, Eugen. "Die deutsche Finanzpresse." In: *Zeitschrift für handelswissenschaftliche Forschung* Vol. 1, No. 8, No. 10 (1906/1907): 277–285, 361–370.

Schmidt, Reinhart and Axel May. "Erklärung von Aktienindizes durch Pressemeldungen." In: *Zeitschrift für Betriebswirtschaft* Vol. 63, No. 1 (1993): 61–88.

Schmitz, Horst. *Das Nachrichtenwesen der Wirtschaftspresse*. Köln: Dissertation, 1958.

Schneider, Oswald. "Politische und wirtschaftliche Berichterstattung." In: *Weltwirtschaftliches Archiv* Vol. 17 (1921/22): 240–267.
Schneider, Wolf. "Satzschachtel-Produzenten. Die Sprache im Wirtschaftsteil der Tageszeitungen." In: Gero Kalt (ed.), *Wirtschaft in den Medien*. Frankfurt a.M.: IMK, 1990: 195–200.
Schneller, Beverly. *Writing about Business and Industry*. New York: Oxford University Press, 1995.
Schneller, Meir and Dan Palmon. "The Relationship Between Securities' Abnormal Price Movements and Wall Street Journal News." In: *Journal of Banking and Finance* Vol. 4, No. 3 (1980): 235–247.
Schnettler, Katrin. *Wirtschaft, voll blöd? Was Jugendliche von ökonomischen Artikeln in der Tageszeitung erwarten. Eine empirische Studie*. Wiesbaden: Westdeutscher Verlag, 2000.
Schnitzler, Bert. "Kein Make-up für Mark und Pfennig. Chancen und Grenzen privater Wirtschaftsjournalisten." In: Gero Kalt (ed.), *Wirtschaft in den Medien*. Frankfurt a.M.: IMK, 1990: 99–106.
Schoenke, Eva (ed.). *Wirtschaftskommentare. Textlinguistische Analysen*. Bremen: Universitäts-Buchhandlung, 1996.
Schöhl, Wolfgang. "Arbeitsmittel und Recherchewege. Datenbanken." In: Stephan Ruß-Mohl and Heinz D. Stuckmann (eds.), *Wirtschaftsjournalismus. Ein Handbuch für Ausbildung und Praxis*. München: List, 1991: 84–93.
Schöhl, Wolfgang. "Der Bedarf nimmt zu. Wirtschaftsberichte als Informationsquelle für den Bürger." In: Gero Kalt (ed.), *Wirtschaft in den Medien*. Frankfurt a.M.: IMK, 1990: 231–238.
Schöhl Wolfgang. "Defizite in der Journalistenausbildung in den Bereichen Writschaft, Soziales und Umwelt." In: Jürgen Wilke (ed.), *Zwischenbilanz der Journalistenausbildung*. München: Ölschläger, 1987.
Schöhl, Wolfgang W. *Wirtschaftsjournalismus. Bedeutung, Probleme und Lösungsvorschläge*. Nürnberg: Verlag der Kommunikationswissenschaftlichen Forschungsvereinigung, 1987.
Schöhl, Wolfgang W. "Wirtschaftsjournalismus über den Wolken." In: *Journalist* Vol. 39, No. 4 (1989): 8–11.
Scholten, Bernhard. *Der Handelsteil der deutschen Zeitungen im 19. Jahrhundert*. Heidelberg: Dissertation, 1910.
Schoop, J. "Wirtschaftspresse." In: *Handwörterbuch der Betriebswirtschaft*. Stuttgart: Poeschel, 1956.
Schröter, Detlef. "Plädoyer für Qualitätssicherung. Ein Werkstattbericht über zwei Studien zur Qualität der Wirtschaftsberichterstattung." In: Siegfried Klaue (ed.), *Marktwirtschaft in der Medienberichterstattung*. Düsseldorf: Econ, 1991: 73–110.
Schröter, Detlef. *Qualität im Journalismus. Testfall Unternehmensberichterstattung in Printmedien*. Mühlheim: Publicom, 1993.
Schröter, Detlef. *Qualität und Journalismus. Theoretische und praktische Grundlagen journalistischen Handelns*. München: R. Fischer, 1995.

Schröter, Detlef. "Unnötige Defizite. Zur Qualität der Unternehmensberichterstattung in Printmedien." In: Gero Kalt (ed.), *Wirtschaft in den Medien.* Frankfurt a.M.: IMK, 1990: 251–262.
Schulz, Winfried (ed.). *Der Inhalt der Zeitungen. Eine Inhaltsanalyse der Tagespresse in der Bundesrepublik mit Quellentexten früher Inhaltsanalysen in Amerika, Frankreich und Deutschland.* Düsseldorf, 1970.
Schulze, Volker. "Die Begabung entfalten. Verschiedene Wege führen zum Wirtschaftsjournalismus." In: Gero Kalt (ed.), *Wirtschaft in den Medien.* Frankfurt a.M.: IMK, 1990: 309–314.
Schulze, Volker. "Wirtschaftsjournalismus bei Tages- und Wochenzeitungen." In: *Journalisten-Jahrbuch 1988.* München: Ölschläger, 1989: 209–213.
Schuster, Thomas. "Demut und Pein. Börsenfieber: Der Nemax siecht, die Wirtschaftsmedien siechen mit." In: *Frankfurter Allgemeine Zeitung,* 11/15/2000.
Schuster, Thomas. "Der Preis war eigentlich gar nicht der Rede wert. Das blieb dem gescheiterten Käufer RTL erspart: Wie bei n-tv die Börsenberichte jahrelang von Banken und Industrie finanziert wurden." In: *Frankfurter Allgemeine Zeitung,* 10/6/2001.
Schuster, Thomas. "Die Fifty-Fifty Chance." In: *Message. Internationale Fachzeitschrift für Journalismus* No. 1 (2003): 82–86.
Schuster, Thomas. *Die Geldfalle. Wie Medien und Banken die Anleger zu Verlierern machen.* Reinbek: Rowohlt, 2001.
Schuster, Thomas. "Die Macht sei mit ihnen. CNN ist out, CNBC ist in: Wie eine Reporter-AG die Welt erobert." In: *Frankfurter Allgemeine Zeitung,* 11/21/2000.
Schuster, Thomas. "Fifty:Fifty. Aktienempfehlungen und Börsenkurse. Wirkungen und Nutzen von Anlagetips in den Wirtschaftsmedien." Leipzig: Universität Leipzig, Working Paper, 2002.
Schuster, Thomas. "Glucksende Gier." In: *taz,* 11/6/2000.
Schuster, Thomas. "Immerzu Panik auf dieser Titanic. Warum das Börsenbarometer von Hoch auf Tief fällt und normale Druckverhältnisse nicht kennt." In: *Frankfurter Allgemeine Zeitung,* 3/21/2001.
Schuster, Thomas. "Mehr Lärm. Was der Sirenengesang der Geräuschemacher an der Börse auslöst." In: *Frankfurter Allgemeine Zeitung,* 3/27/2001.
Schuster, Thomas. "Schwacher Charakter, volle Börse. Insider-Handel: Der erste Finanzjournalist steht vor der Anklage." In: *Frankfurter Allgemeine Zeitung,* 11/2/2000.
Schuster, Thomas. "Steter Tropfen höhlt die Aktie. Von 'Focus Money' bis 'Spiegel': Wie Magazine Anleger betäuben." In: *Frankfurter Allgemeine Zeitung,* 10/17/2000.
Schuster, Thomas. "Zwischen Boom und Crash." In: *Message. Internationale Fachzeitschrift für Journalismus* No. 3 (2000): 10–17.
Schütz, Albert Heinrich. *Der Handelsteil der Tageszeitung. Eine Einführung unter besonderer Berücksichtigung der schweizerischen Handelspresse.* Zürich: Schweizer Kaufmännischer Verein, 1927.

Schütze, Christian. "Zukunftsperspektiven und Spezialisierungsfelder. Ökologie und Ökonomie." In: Stephan Ruß-Mohl and Heinz D. Stuckmann (eds.), *Wirtschaftsjournalismus. Ein Handbuch für Ausbildung und Praxis*. München: List, 1991: 211–214.

Schwartz, Nelson D. "Inside the Market's Myth Machine." In: *Fortune*, 10/2/2000.

Schwarz, Frank. "Die Anforderungen der Wirtschaftspresse an die Investor Relations." Klaus Rainer Kirchhoff and Manfred Piwinger (eds.), *Die Praxis der Investor Relations*. Neuwied: Luchterhand, 2000: 272–286.

Schwert, G. William. "The Adjustment of Stock Prices to Information About Inflation." In: *Journal of Finance* Vol. 36, No. 1 (1981): 15–29.

Seidman, L. William. "The Future of Financial Journalism. The Battle Will Center Around Grabbing Your Attention. And Then Telling You What You Need." In: *International Economy* Vol. 11, No. 2 (1997): 38–41.

Silk, Leonard. *Economic Commentary. Reflections and Critiques from the Pages of Business Week*. New York: Business Week, 1966.

Simon, Kurt. "Der Wirtschaftsjournalist zwischen publizistischem Auftrag und wirtschaftlicher Einflußnahme." In: *Journalist* Vol. 22, No. 4 (1972): 16–20.

Simoneit, Ferdinand. "Dringend gesucht: Wirtschaftsjournalisten." In: Michael Schenk and Ferdinand Simoneit (eds.), *Wege zum Wirtschaftsjournalismus*. München: R. Fischer, 1989: 7–17.

Simoneit, Ferdinand. "Orientierungshilfen. Georg von Holtzbrinck-Schule." In: Stephan Ruß-Mohl and Heinz D. Stuckmann (eds.), *Wirtschaftsjournalismus. Ein Handbuch für Ausbildung und Praxis*. München: List, 1991: 240–241.

Simoneit, Ferdinand. "Wo bleibt der Leser, Hörer, Zuschauer?" In: Stephan Ruß-Mohl and Heinz D. Stuckmann (eds.), *Wirtschaftsjournalismus. Ein Handbuch für Ausbildung und Praxis*. München: List, 1991: 105–106.

Simons, Howard and Joseph A. Califano, Jr. (eds.). *The Media and Business*. New York: Vintage Books, 1979.

Smith, Matthew Hale. *Twenty Years Among the Bulls and Bears of Wall Street*. Hartford: J.B. Burr, 1870.

Smith, Ted J. *The Vanishing Economy. Television Coverage of Economic Affairs, 1982–1987*. Washington, D.C.: Media Institute, 1988.

Solomon, Norman. "Bloomberg's Victory and the Triumph of Business News." In: *Media Beat*, 11/8/2001.

Solow, Robert M. "How Economic Ideas Turn to Mush." In: David C. Colander and Alfred William Coats (eds.), *The Spread of Economic Ideas*. New York: Cambridge University Press, 1989: 75–83, 249–256.

"Something in the City. There's a Certain Amount of Irony to the Fact That, Without Exception, Financial News Channels Anywhere Have Failed to Make Any Money." In: *Cable and Satellite Europe* No. 146 (1996): 26–30.

Sondergeld, Klaus. *Die Wirtschafts- und Sozialberichterstattung in den Fernsehnachrichten. Eine theoretische und empirische Untersuchung zur politischen Kommunikation*. Münster: Lit, 1983.

Spieß, Brigitte. "Mißachtete Zuschauer. Wirtschaftsberichterstattung im Fernsehen." In: *Aus Politik und Zeitgeschichte. Beilage zur Wochenzeitung "Das Parlament."* Vol. 40, No. 26 (1990): 44–54.

Spieß, Brigitte. *Wirtschaft im Fernsehen. Eine empirische Studie zur Produktion und Rezeption des Wirtschaftsmagazins Plusminus.* Tübingen: Niemeyer, 1992.

Spieß, Brigitte. "Wirtschaftsmagazine im 'Abschattungsgebiet.'" In: *Funk-Report* Vol. 20, No. 8 (1984): 7–9.

Spindler, Gerd. "Wirtschaftsjournalismus. Dem Laien sollte es Freude bereiten, wirtschaftliche Texte zu konsumieren." In: *Handelsblatt,* 5/2/1985.

Spindler, Gerd. "Wirtschaftsjournalismus. Die Wirtschaft geht alle an." In: *Handelsblatt,* 30.4.1985.

Spindler, Gerd. "Wirtschaftsjournalismus." In: *Handelsblatt,* 5/9/1985.

Stabler, Charles Norman. *How to Read the Financial News.* New York: Harper & Row, 1965.

Stabler, Charles Norman. *The Financial Section of a Newspaper, the Business of a Newspaper.* New York: Herald Tribune, 1933.

Stadler, Christiane. *Der Wirtschaftsteil englischsprachiger Zeitungen. Textstruktur, Aufmachung, Wirkung.* Rostock: Dissertation, 1999.

Steinkühler, Franz. "Zur Kritik des Wirtschaftsjournalismus. Der Gewerkschafter." In: Stephan Ruß-Mohl and Heinz D. Stuckmann (eds.), *Wirtschaftsjournalismus. Ein Handbuch für Ausbildung und Praxis.* München: List, 1991: 48–52.

Stevenson, Robert L., William J. Gonzenbach and Prabu David. "Economic Recession and the News." In: *Mass Communication Review* Vol. 21, No. 1/2 (1994): 4–19.

Stice, Earl K. "The Market Reaction to 10-K and 10-Q Filings and to Subsequent *The Wall Street Journal* Earnings Announcements." In: *Accounting Review* Vol. 66, No. 1 (1991): 42–55.

Stihl, Hans Peter. "Meinung geht vor Sachlichkeit. Kritikpunkte aus Sicht des DIHT." In: Gero Kalt (ed.), *Wirtschaft in den Medien.* Frankfurt a.M.: IMK, 1990: 13–20.

Stockmann, Ralf. *Spiegel and Focus. Eine vergleichende Inhaltsanalyse 1993–1996.* Göttingen: Schmerse, 1999.

Stolze, Dieter. "Wirtschaft im Fernsehen." In: *Medienspiegel* Vol. 1, No. 8 (1977): 11–13.

Stolze, Sylvia. "Medienspezifische Präsentation. Fernsehen." In: Stephan Ruß-Mohl and Heinz D. Stuckmann (eds.), *Wirtschaftsjournalismus. Ein Handbuch für Ausbildung und Praxis.* München: List, 1991: 166–169.

Stück, Hans-Hermann. *Wegweiser durch den Wirtschaftsteil der Tageszeitung.* München: Heyne, 1978.

Stucki, Hans. *Unternehmung und Presse.* Winterthur: Keller, 1956.

Stuckmann, Heinz D. "Arbeitssituation, Berufsethik. Ehrensold." In: Stephan Ruß-Mohl and Heinz D. Stuckmann (eds.), *Wirtschaftsjournalismus. Ein Handbuch für Ausbildung und Praxis.* München: List, 1991: 180.

Stuckmann, Heinz D. "'Die Fakten müssen stimmen.'" In: Stephan Ruß-Mohl and Heinz D. Stuckmann (eds.), *Wirtschaftsjournalismus. Ein Handbuch für Ausbildung und Praxis.* München: List, 1991: 254.

Stuckmann, Heinz D. "Medienspezifische Präsentation. Zum Beispiel: Express." In: Stephan Ruß-Mohl and Heinz D. Stuckmann (eds.), *Wirtschaftsjournalismus.* München: List, 1991: 142–144.

Stuckmann, Heinz D. "Orientierungshilfen. Recherche-Ausbildung." In: Stephan Ruß-Mohl and Heinz D. Stuckmann (eds.), *Wirtschaftsjournalismus. Ein Handbuch für Ausbildung und Praxis.* München: List, 1991: 250–254.

Stuckmann, Heinz D. "Recherche-Ausbildung." In: Stephan Ruß-Mohl and Heinz D. Stuckmann (eds.), *Wirtschaftsjournalismus. Ein Handbuch für Ausbildung und Praxis.* München: List, 1991: 250–254.

Studien zum sozialistischen Wirtschaftsjournalismus. Leipzig: Karl-Marx-Universität Leipzig, Sektion Journalistik, 1976.

Stützer, Rudolf. *Der Wirtschaftsteil einer Tageszeitung. Eine Orientierungshilfe.* Stuttgart: Deutscher Sparkassenverlag, 1980.

Surowiecki, James. "The Financial Page. Manic Monday (And Other Popular Delusions)." In: *New Yorker*, 3/26/2001.

Sweerts-Sporck, Peter. "DDR-Wirtschaft. Stereotype Horror-Berichterstattung. Wie Lafontaines Kurs unterstützt wird." In: *Medien-Kritik* No. 34 (1990): 3–5.

Sweerts-Sporck, Peter. "Exklusive Publizität. Persönlichkeitsshows in Wirtschaftszeitschriften." In: *Medien-Kritik* No. 2 (1989): 2–5.

Sweerts-Sporck, Peter. "Ressort im Abseits. Defizite der Wirtschaftssendungen von ARD und ZDF." In: Gero Kalt (ed.), *Wirtschaft in den Medien.* Frankfurt a.M.: IMK, 1990: 79–85.

Sweerts-Sporck, Peter. "Sind die Banken zu mächtig? Die Kontroverse im Spiegel ausgewählter Medien." In: *Medien-Kritik* No. 35 (1989): 6–8.

Sweerts-Sporck, Peter. "Soziale Marktwirtschaft, was ist das? ARD und ZDF vernachlässigen ihre Informationsaufgaben." In: *Medien-Kritik* No. 4 (1990): 5–7.

Sweerts-Sporck, Peter. "Was sollten Wirtschaftsmagazine leisten?" In: *Medien-Kritik* No. 12 (1989): 5–8.

Syed, Azmat A, Pu Liu und Stanley D. Smith. "The Exploitation of Inside Information at the *Wall Street Journal*. A Test of Strong Form Efficiency." In: *Financial Review* Vol. 24, No. 4 (1989): 567–579.

"Symbiose in Druck. Wall Street Journal ist weltweit präsent." In: *Journalist* Vol. 49, No. 5 (1999): 70–71.

Täubert, Anne. *Unternehmenspublizität und Investor Relations. Analyse von Auswirkungen der Medienberichterstattung auf Aktienkurse.* Münster: Lit, 1998.

Teichmann, Jan Andreas. *Vom Bildungsprogramm zum Servotainment. Wandel der Wirtschaftsberichterstattung im Fernsehen am Beispiel der Sendung "WISO" im ZDF.* Universität Eichstätt: Diplomarbeit, 1998.

Tern, Jürgen. "Wirtschaftsjournalismus und die Interessen der Wirtschaft." In: Henning Röhl (ed.), *Der kritische Zeitungsleser.* München: Beck, 1973: 48–58.

The Best of the Wall Street Journal. Chicopee: Dow Jones, 1974.
"The Bloomberg Machine." In: *Business Week*, 4/23/2001.
"The Business Media." In: Tonya Trappe and Graham Tullis (eds.), *New Insights into Business.* Surrey: Longman, 2000.
"The Lesson of Emulex." In: *Online Journalism Review*, 9/8/2000.
"The Revolution Will Be Televised (on CNBC)." In: *Fast Company*, June 2000.
"The Right Spin—or Even a Lie—Can Make Stock Prices Soar." In: *Business Week*, 4/24/2000.
The Wall Street Journal. How's Business? The Best Cartoons from the Wall Street Journal. Fort Lauderdale: Allied, 1964.
Theis-Berglmair, Anna Maria. "Aufmerksamkeit und Geld, schenken und zahlen. Zum Verhältnis von Publizistik und Wirtschaft in einer Kommunikationsgesellschaft. Konsequenzen für die Medienökonomie." In: *Publizistik* Vol. 45, No. 3 (2000): 310–329.
"There's No Business Like Business Show Business." In: *Fortune*, 5/24/1999.
Thoma, Helmut. "Einschaltquoten entscheiden. Was das Privatfernsehen leisten kann." In: Gero Kalt (ed.), *Wirtschaft in den Medien.* Frankfurt a.M.: IMK, 1990: 35–40.
Thomas, Martin R. and Waqar I. Ghani. "The Dartboard Column. Analysts Earnings Forecasts and the Informational Content of Recommendations." In: *Journal of Business and Economic Studies* Vol. 3 (1997): 33–42.
Thomas, Tony. "News Underpriced, Says Mr. Dow Jones." In: *Business Review Weekly* Vol. 17, No. 49 (1995): 28–31.
Thomas, Uwe and Stefan Müller. "Hiob und die Urlaubspläne. Einfluss der Medien auf Konsumverhalten." In: *Gablers Magazin* Vol. 2, No. 10 (1988): 46–50.
Thommen, Andreas. "Die Beziehungen der Wirtschaft zur Presse." In: *Wirtschaftspolitische Mitteilungen* Vol. 18, No. 7/8. Zürich: Wirtschaftsförderung, Gesellschaft zur Förderung der schweizerischen Wirtschaft, 1962.
Thompson, Robert B., Chris Olsen and J. Richard Dietrich. "Attributes of News About Firms. An Analysis of Firm-Specific News Reported in the *Wall Street Journal Index*." In: *Journal of Accounting Research* Vol. 25, No. 2 (1987): 245–274.
Thompson, Terri (ed.). *Writing About Business. The New Columbia Knight-Bagehot Guide to Economics and Business Journalism.* New York: Columbia University Press, 2001.
Thomssen, Gerhard. "Medienspezifische Präsentation. Publikumszeitschrift/Illustrierte." In: Stephan Ruß-Mohl and Heinz D. Stuckmann (eds.), *Wirtschaftsjournalismus. Ein Handbuch für Ausbildung und Praxis.* München: List, 1991: 153–156.
Tims, A. R., D. P. Fan and J. R. Freeman. "The Cultivation of Consumer Confidence. A Longitudinal Analysis of News Media Influence on Consumer Sentiment." In: *Advances in Consumer Research* Vol. 16 (1989): 758–770.
"Tips und Tricks. Konjunktur der Ratgeber-Magazine." In: *Journalist* Vol. 47, No. 3 (1997): 10–14.

Trahan, Emery A. and Paul J. Bolster. "The Impact of Barron's Recommendation on Stock Prices." In: *Quarterly Journal of Business and Economics* Vol. 34 (1995): 3–15.

Trautmann, Walter. "Rationalisierung des Wirtschaftsnachrichtenwesens." In: *Volkswirt* Vol. 9 (1955).

Trebess, Manfred. *Wirtschaft im Fernsehen*. Stuttgart: Informationsstelle Wirtschaft Baden-Württemberg (ISW), 1988.

"Tücken bei der Jagd nach der schnellsten Nachricht." In: *Frankfurter Allgemeine Zeitung*, 9/9/2000.

Tumarkin, Robert and Robert F. Whitelaw. "News or Noise? Internet Postings and Stock Prices." In: *Financial Analysts Journal* Vol. 57, No. 3 (2001): 41–51.

Turi, Peter. "Machtlos gegen die Macht der Medien? Vom schwierigen Verhältnis zwischen Unternehmern und Journalisten." In: *Media-Spectrum* 10 (1989): 6–11.

Turi, Peter. "Qual der Wahl. Der Markt der Wirtschaftsmagazine ist groß." In: Gero Kalt (ed.), *Wirtschaft in den Medien*. Frankfurt a.M.: IMK, 1990: 201–208.

Uber, Thomas. "Vielfalt der Formen. Chancen und Grenzen privater Hörfunk-Journalisten." In: Gero Kalt (ed.), *Wirtschaft in den Medien*. Frankfurt a.M.: IMK, 1990: 161–166.

Uebbing, Helmut. *Über den Umgang mit Wirtschaftsjournalisten. Ein Ratgeber*. Frankfurt a.M.: Frankfurter Allgemeine Zeitung, 1985.

Uebbing, Helmut, Klaus Wiborg and Alfred Lambeck. *Keine Angst vor Wirtschaftsjournalisten. Ein Ratgeber aus der Praxis*. Frankfurt a.M.: Frankfurter Allgemeine Zeitung, 1990.

"Um den Kiosk machen die Börsianer eine Bögen." In: *Die Welt*, 3/7/2001.

"Unterschiedlich euphorisch. Analystenzitate in sieben Wirtschaftstiteln 12.02.-25.02.2000." In: *Medien Tenor* Vol. 6, No. 94 (1999): 31.

Vaitilingam, Romesh. *The Financial Times Guide to Using the Financial Pages*. London: Pitman, 1996.

VIA-Forschungsgruppe. *Wirtschaft im Fernsehen. Eine vergleichende Inhaltsanalyse. Projekt am Institut für Kommunikationswissenschaft der Universität München*. München: Unveröffentlicher Forschungsbericht, 1988.

Vicker, Ray. *The Informed Investor. How to Use the Money Media to Improve Investment Performance*. Chicago: Probus, 1991.

Villeneuve, Joseph J. *How to Read the Financial Pages of Your Newspaper and Much More*. Syracuse: JJV Associates, 1989.

Vissink, H. G. A. *Economic and Financial Reporting in England and the Netherlands. A Comparative Study Over the Period 1850 to 1914*. Assen/ Maastricht: Van Gorcum, 1985.

Vogel, F. "Die Tages- und Wirtschaftspresse als Bildungselement des Kaufmanns." In: *Produktivität und Berufserziehung*, 1955.

Vogel, Friedrich. "Der Wirtschaftsteil (Aktuell)." In: Emil Dovifat, *Handbuch der Publizistik* Vol. 3. Berlin: de Gruyter, 1969: 210–217.

Vogel, Wilhelm. *Der Handelsteil der Tagespresse*. Berlin, 1914.

Vollbracht, Matthias. "Analystenzitate. Risiken und Nebenwirkungen." In: *Medien Tenor* Vol. 5, No. 78 (1998): 8–12.

Vollbracht, Matthias. "Auf den Aktienkurs reduziert." In: *Medien Tenor* Vol. 5, No. 78 (1998): 24.

Vollbracht, Matthias. "Konjunkturbild beeinflußt Bürgermeinung. Die Wirtschaftsberichterstattung in den TV-Nachrichten August '94–Mai '99." In: *Medien Tenor Forschungsbericht* No. 86 (1999): 18–22.

Vollbracht, Matthias. "Wirtschaftsberichterstattung." In: Michael Haller and Markus Rettich (eds.), *Wochenmedien Jahrbuch 1996*. Bern: InnoVatio Verlag, 1997: 161–195.

"Volle Kraft zurück." In: *Werben und Verkaufen* No. 46 (2001): 144–146.

"Vom Ritual der Analystenzitate." In: *Medien Tenor* Vol. 5, No. 71 (1998): 25.

von Haaren, Marion. *Wirtschaftsjournalismus*. Bonn: ZV, 1998.

Vorkötter, Uwe. "Zukunftsperspektiven und Spezialisierungsfelder. Unternehmens- und Branchenberichterstattung." In: Stephan Ruß-Mohl and Heinz D. Stuckmann (eds.), *Wirtschaftsjournalismus. Ein Handbuch für Ausbildung und Praxis*. München: List, 1991: 195–200.

Voss, Peter. *Wirtschaft im Fernsehen*. Köln: Informedia, 1996.

"W & V Special. Wirtschaftspresse." In: *Werben und Verkaufen* No. 36 (1994): 151–165.

Wagner, Hans. "Keine Orientierungshilfe. Fernsehberichte im Spiegel der Wissenschaft." In: Gero Kalt (ed.), *Wirtschaft in den Medien*. Frankfurt a.M.: IMK, 1990: 239–249.

Wagner, Hans and Detlef Schröter. *Wirtschaftsinformationen im Fernsehen. Ein Werkstattbericht*. Mühlheim: Publicom-Medienverlag, 1990.

Wagner, Helga. *Methodische Wege zur Wirksamkeit wirtschaftsjournalistischer Beiträge*. Leipzig: Dissertation, 1983.

Wagner, Richard. *Der Handels- und Wirtschaftsteil der Tageszeitung*. Hamburg, 1921.

"Wall Street's Hype Machine. It Could Spell Trouble for Investors." In: *Business Week*, 4/3/2000.

Warfield, Gerald. *How to Read and Understand the Financial News*. New York: HarperPerennial, 1994.

Warfield, Gerald. *The Investor's Guide to Stock Quotations and Other Financial Listings*. Cambridge: Harper & Row, 1986.

Warner, Kee and Harvey Molotoch. "Information in the Marketplace. Media Explanations of '87 Crash." In: *Social Problems* Vol. 40: 167–188.

Waters, Donald. *30 Minutes to Understand the Financial Pages*. London: Kogan Page, 2000.

Watson, W. L. "The Press and Finance." In: *Blackwood's Magazine*, November 1898.

Weber, Johanna. "Das Verhältnis Journalismus und Öffentlichkeitsarbeit." In: Lothar Rolke and Volker Wolff (eds.), *Wie die Medien die Wirklichkeit steuern und selber gesteuert werden*. Opladen: Westdeutscher Verlag, 1999: 265–267.

Weber, Mechthild. "Arbeitssituation, Berufsethik. Der Öffentlichkeitsarbeiter." In: Stephan Ruß-Mohl and Heinz D. Stuckmann (eds.), *Wirtschaftsjournalismus. Ein Handbuch für Ausbildung und Praxis.* München: List, 1991: 181–185.

Wehnelt, Christoph. "Das gesprochene Wort gilt. Chancen und Grenzen öffentlich-rechtlicher Hörfunkjournalisten." In: Gero Kalt (ed.), *Wirtschaft in den Medien.* Frankfurt a.M.: IMK, 1990: 153–159.

Weihrauch, Dieter. "Aufgaben und Methoden des Wirtschaftsjournalismus in der entwickelten sozialistischen Gesellschaft." In: *Theorie und Praxis des sozialistischen Journalismus* Leipzig Vol. 11, No. 1 (1983): 38–42.

Weingärtner, Arnold. *Der Boss auf dem Bildschirm. Unternehmer und Wirtschaft im Fernsehen und Hörfunk.* Köln: Deutscher Instituts-Verlag, 1977.

Weiss, Ruth. *An Introduction to Economic Reporting.* Harare: Zimbabwe Institute of Mass Communication. Friedrich Naumann Foundation. Nairobi: African Council on Communication Education, 1987.

Wells, Ken (ed.). *Floating Off the Page. The Best Stories from the Wall Street Journal's "Middle Column."* New York: Wall Street Journal, 2002.

Wendt, Lloyd. *The Wall Street Journal. The Story of Dow Jones and the Nation's Business Newspaper.* Chicago: Rand McNally, 1982.

"Who Can You Trust? Wall Street's Spin Game. Stock Analysts Often Have a Hidden Agenda." In: *Business Week*, 10/5/1998.

Wiborg, Klaus. *Keine Angst vor der Wirtschaftspresse. Ein Ratgeber aus der Praxis.* Frankfurt a.M.: Blick durch die Wirtschaft, 8/27/1985, 9/2/1985, 9/9/1985.

Wickener, Hans. *Die Entwicklung der wirtschaftlichen Berichterstattung im Ruhrgebiet im 19. Jahrhundert. Mit besonderer Berücksichtigung des Märkischen Sprechers.* München: Dissertation, 1935.

"Wie die Lufthansa genehme Berichte erzwingen will. 'Financial Times Deutschland' wegen Zitaten aus internen Papieren aus Fliegern verbannt." In: *Frankfurter Rundschau*, 4/12/2000.

"Wie gut stehen die Aktien der Newcomer?" In: *Werben und Verkaufen* No. 46 (1999): 150–153.

Wiest, Heike. *Wirtschaftsdidaktik, Medienpädagogik und Wirtschaftsjournalismus. Probleme und Perspektiven der Vermittlung ökonomischer Themen.* Berlin: Logos, 2000.

Wijmenga, R.Th. "The Performance of Published Dutch Stock Recommendations." In: *Journal of Banking and Finance* Vol. 14 (1990): 559–581.

Will, Markus. *Wirtschaftspresse im Wirtschaftssystem. Theoretische Grundlagen und praktische Illustration. Leitartikel zur deutschen Wirt-schafts-, Währungs- und Sozialunion.* Frankfurt a. M.: IMK, 1993.

Williams, Francis. *The Times on the Economy.* London: Collins, 1984.

Williams, John. "Reporting the Economy." In: Neil T. Gavin (ed.), *The Economy, Media and Public Knowledge.* London: Leicester University Press, 1998: 159–162.

Wimer, Arthur. *Writing for the Business Press. A Complete Reference Book on Writing for the Business Papers. With Contributions by One Hundred Editors and Publishers.* Dubuque: W.C. Brown, 1950.

Winans, R. Foster. *Trading Secrets. Seduction and Scandal at The Wall Street Journal.* New York: St. Martin's Press, 1986.

Winschuh, Josef. *Über Wirtschaft schreiben. Wirtschaftspublizistik im Wandel der Zeit.* Baden-Baden: Lutzeyer, 1963.

Winter, James P. (ed.). *The Silent Revolution. Media, Democracy, and the Free Trade Debate.* Ottawa: University of Ottawa Press, 1990.

"Wir gehen nicht auf jede Pressekonferenz." In: *Medien Tenor* Vol. 5, No. 70 (1998): 25.

Wirth, Fritz. *Die Wirtschaftsteile deutscher Tageszeitungen.* Leipzig: Dissertation, 1927.

Wirtschaft im Fernsehen. Dokumentation des 5. Medienkongresses der Hanns-Seidel-Stiftung am 6. Oktober 1983. München: Hanns-Seidel-Stiftung, 1984.

Wirtschaft und öffentliche Meinung. Köln: Hegner 1972.

"Wirtschaft wird für uns immer wichtiger." In: *Medien Tenor*, 9/15/1999.

Wirtschaftsberichterstattung über das Ausland. Berlin: Verlag des Reichsverbandes, 1927.

"Wirtschaftsfernsehen: Leicht verdaulich." In: *Wirtschaftswoche*, 4/3/1992.

"Wirtschaftsjournalismus. Nicht um jeden Preis aus allen Laien Wirtschaftsfachleute machen wollen." In: *Handelsblatt*, 5/30/1985.

"Wirtschaftsjournalismus. Puzzeln am Konzept." In: *Journalist* Vol. 48, No. 3 (1998): 13–15.

Wirtschaftsmedien im Fokus. Trends, Tendenzen, Hintergründe. Alle Mediengattungen auf einen Griff, Radio/TV-Sender, Zeitungen, Publikumszeitschriften, Online-Angebote. Walluf: Media-Daten-Verlag.

Wolf, William B. *An Author's Guide to Business Publications.* Los Angeles: University of Southern California, Research Institute for Business and Economics, 1967.

Wolff, Volker and Lothar Rolke. "Kurspflege durch Meinungspflege. Das Geschäft mit dem Vertrauen." In: Lothar Rolke and Volker Wolff (eds.), *Finanzkommunikation. Kurspflege durch Meinungspflege. Die neuen Spielregeln am Aktienmarkt.* Frankfurt a.M.: F.A.Z.-Institut, 2000: 10–18.

Wölfle, Michael. "Profil als Programm." In: *Werben und Verkaufen* No. 1 (1999): 46f.

Woolf, Douglas Gordon. *The Business Paper Editor at Work.* New York: McGraw-Hill, 1936.

Wright, David W. "Can Prices be Trusted? A Test of the Ability of Experts to Outperform or Influence the Market." In: *Journal of Accounting, Auditing and Finance* Vol. 9 (1994): 307–323.

Wullenweber, Rudolf. *Die Berichterstattung über die Produktenbörsen in der deutschen Presse.* Erlangen-Nürnberg: Dissertation, 1967.

Wysocki, Peter D. "Cheap Talk on the Web. The Determinants of Postings on Stock Message Boards." Ann Arbor: University of Michigan Business School Working Paper, 1999.

Yazici, Bilgehan and Gülnur Muradoglu. "Stock Recommendations and Small Investors. Who Benefits?" London: City University Business School, Faculty of Finance, Working Paper No. 9, 2001.

"'Zahlen wollen richtig gewogen werden.'" In: *Medien Tenor* Vol. 6, No. 89 (1999): 12–13.

Zahrnt, Angelika. "Zur Kritik des Wirtschaftsjournalismus. Die Umweltschützerin." In: Stephan Ruß-Mohl and Heinz D. Stuckmann (eds.), *Wirtschaftsjournalismus. Ein Handbuch für Ausbildung und Praxis.* München: List, 1991: 58–60.

Zeller, Willy. "Mahnmale wirtschaftsjournalistischen Fehlverhaltens. Die Redlichkeit im Medienfach." In: *NZZ*, 3/7/1992.

Zeller, Willy. "Unabhängig und meinungsbildend. Was will und kann der Wirtschaftsteil einer Tageszeitung? Beispiel 'Neue Zürcher Zeitung.'" In: Gero Kalt (ed.), *Wirtschaft in den Medien.* Frankfurt a.M.: IMK, 1990: 175–179.

Zimmer, Jochen. "Business as usual. Nachrichtenkanäle und Wirtschaftsdienste für TV und Online." In: Klaus Kamps and Miriam Meckel (eds.), *Fernsehnachrichten. Prozesse, Strukturen, Funktionen.* Opladen: Westdeutscher Verlag, 1998: 167–184.

Zimmer, Jochen. "Mit Wirtschaftsinformationen zum Erfolg?" In: *Media Perspektiven* No. 5 (1997): 286–296.

"Zitate von Analysten in der Wirtschafts- und Finanzberichterstattung." In: *Medien Tenor*, 3/23/2000.

Zohlnhöfer, Werner. "Wirtschaftsjournalismus aus der Sicht des Wirtschaftswissenschaftlers." In: Michael Schenk and Ferdinand Simoneit (eds.), *Wege zum Wirtschaftsjournalismus.* München: R. Fischer, 1989: 27–36.

Zöller, Ludwig. *Die wirtschaftspolitischen Quellen der Tageszeitung.* Speyer: Dissertation, 1935.

"Zwang zur Verkürzung. Wirtschaft im Fernsehen." In: *Journalist* Vol. 48, No. 3 (1998): 18–19.

INDEX

accounting income numbers, 41, 44
Albert, Robert L., 9, 14
Allen, David S., 9
analysts. *See* financial analysts
Andersen, Torben G., 43
Andreassen, Paul B., 71, 72
Applied Micro Circuits, 76
Arthur, Brian, 82
assassination attempt on Ronald Reagan, 49
assassination of John F. Kennedy, 48
Associated Press Newswire, 47
attack on U.S. Embassy in Kenia, 49
attack on U.S. Marines in Lebanon, 49
Awang-Damit, Hamidah, 9

Bamber, Linda Smith, 43
Bank of Japan, 35
Barber, Brad M., *10*, 13, 71–72
Barberis, Nicholas, 46, 48
Barron's, 8, 16, 18
Bay of Pigs invasion, 49
Beaver, William H., 42
Bedau, Mark A., 81

Behavioral Finance, x, 33, 38, 39, 47, 57
Beltz, Jess, 7, *19*
Beneish, Messod D., *10*, 15
Benesh, Gary A., 8, *19*
Bernstein, Richard, 76
Berry, Thomas D., 44
Black, Fischer, 79
Bollerslev, Tim, 43
Bolster, Paul J., 9, *19*
Börse Online, 6
Brooks, LeRoy D., 9
Brown, Stephen J., 22
business media. *See* business news
business news: effects of, 1, 15, 35, 39–40, 42–45, 76–78; expansion of the volume of, x, 4; information content of, 1, 11, 13–15, 19, 20, 26n48, 36, 39, 76, 78, 91; macroeconomic news, 43, 44; positive bias of, ix, 37, 75, 76, 86, 89n31; predictive value of, 6, 12, 19, 20, 37; price pressure after publication of, 1, 33, 76–78; role of rumours in, 15; stock recommendations in. *See* stock

recommendations; structure of, 23; use value of, x, 6, 19, 20–21, 39, 74, 76. *See also*, mass media
business press. *See* business news
business reporting. *See* business news
Business Week, 12, 26n48
Busse, Jeffrey A., 78

Canes, Michael, *10*, 15
cascade effects, 73
Challenger explosion, 43
Chan, Wesley S., 45
Chen, Andrew H., 49
Chen, Mike Y., 12
Chernobyl nuclear disaster, 49
Chicago Tribune, 45
Clark, Jeffrey A., 8, *19*
CNBC, 37, 67, 75–79, 83
CNBC effect. See CNBC
CNN, 67
complex adaptive systems, 81–82
Cowles, Alfred, 3, 21, 22
crash. *See* stock market crash
Cuban missile crisis, 48
Cutler, David M., 40, 45, 48, 49, 50

Das, Sanjiv R., 12
Davies, P. Lloyd, *10*, 15
Dawkins, Richard, 92n68
death of Dwight D. Eisenhower, 48
DeBondt, Werner F. M., 45
Desai, Hemang, 9, 16, *19*
Die Telebörse, 12
Diebold, Francis X., 43
Dimson, Elroy, *10*, 18, *19*, 41
dividend announcements, 41
Dorfleitner, Gregor, 6
Dow, Charles Henry, 3
Dow Jones News Service, 41, 43, 44, 47
Dutch tulip mania, 84

earnings announcements, 41
Ederington, Louis H., 43

Efficient Market Hypothesis, 25n31, 33, 38, 40, 42, 44, 46, 54n15, 54n16, 65, 68, 78, 87n11
Emulex, 77
Entremed, 67
European Central Bank, 35
event study-method, 23, 26, 40, 41, 45

Fair, Ray, 47
Fama, Eugene F., 38, 41
Ferreira, Eurico J., 9, 16
financial analysts, ix, 5, 6, 7, 8, 9, 12, 13, 14, 15, 16, 20, 26, 27, 82, 89n29
financial markets: anomalies in, 33, 46, 39, 50, 56n44, 57n55; communication environment of the, x; euphoria in, 68, 83; information processing in the, 37–38, 40, 46, 51; manipulation of the, x, 77; noise in, 21, 78, 79–87, 97–99; positive feedback in, 52, 69–70, 79–87; predictability of, 38, 46; price formation in the, x, 41–43, 46, 51, 68; speculative dynamics in, 71, 75; speed of price adjustments in, 43; trend-following behavior in, 65, 71, 79–85; volatility of, 81
financial television, ix, 6
Financial Times, 37
firm announcements, 42, 52
Fisher, Lawrence, 41
Focus Money, 37
Friedman, Milton, 90n44
front running, 7, 15

Galbraith, John Kenneth, 92n64, 92n66
Gerke, Wolfgang, 6, 41
Ghani, Waqar, 9, 14, *19*
Goetzman, William N., 22
Green, T. Clifton, 78
Greene, Jason, 9, 14
Grossman, Sanford J., 54n16
gurus. *See* investment gurus

INDEX

Hamilton, William Peter, 3, 22
Han, Ki C., 8
Handelsblatt, 41
Hirschey, Mark, 8
Hirshleifer, David, 74
Howe, Keith M., 44
Hurricane Andrew, 49
Huth, William L., 10

insider trading, 7
investment gurus, 6, 8, 80
investment tips. *See* stock recommendations
Iraqi invasion of Kuwait, 49
"Irrational Exuberance," 46
Iyengar, Shanto, 95

Jain, Prem C., 9, 16, *19*, 43
Japanese attack on Pearl Harbor, 48, 49
Jennings, Robert, 7, *19*
Jensen, Michael C., 41
Joshi, Shareen, 81
journalists, ix, 5, 6–7, 20, 21–22, 37, 39, 40, 55n23, 68, 80, 88n22, 89n29

Kinder, Donald, 85
Kindleberger, Charles P., 83–85
Kladroba, Andreas, 5
Klein, Christian, 6
Korean war, 48
Kraus, Stephen, 71
Krugman, Paul, 91n63
Kumar, Alok, 22

Lee, Chi-wen Jevons, *10*, 18
Lee, Jae Ha, 43
Liang, Bing, 9, 14, *19*
Lippe, Peer von der, 5
Liu, Pu, 7, *10*, 15
Loeffler, Douglas, *10*, 13

MACC Private Equities, 76
Malkiel, Burton G., 9, 14

Maloney, Michael T., 43
Maris, Brian A., *10*
Marsh, Paul, *10*, 18, *19*
mass media: agenda-setting function of the, 70, 72; attitude cultivation by, 70; dynamic interactions between financial markets and the, 69, 78–85; emotionalization by, 69, 71, 74; feedback generated by, 70–73; ideological orientation of, 74; information manipulation in, 77–78; media representations of reality, 69–70, 72, 74; news effects, 69, 73, 76, 77–78, 89n41; significance of the, 36–40, 52. *See also* business news
Mathur, Ike, 9, 12, *19*
May, Axel, 42
McLuhan, Marshall, 78
McQueen, Grant, 44
media effects. *See* mass media
meme, 92n68
Merton, Robert C., 71
Meschke, J. Felix, 78
meta-communication, 67, 80–85
Metcalf, Gilbert E., 9, 14
Mitchell, Mark L., 44
Morris, Stephen, 80
Motley Fool, 8
Mulherin, J. Harold, 43, 44
Mullainathan, Sendhil, 74
Muradoglu, Gülnur, 9
Mussavian, Massoud, 41

Nature, 67
"New Economy," 4, 8, 37, 52, 82–83
news effects. *See* mass media
news events, 36, 46, 69; effects of, 47–50, 52. *See also* publicity effect; probability of abnormal price movements during, 52; terrorist attacks, 49, 53n5. *See also* mass media
New York Times, 45, 47, 67

The New Yorker, 75
Niederhoffer, Victor, 48, 49
noise. *See* financial markets
non-events. *See* mass media; pseudo-events
n-person game. *See* Prisoner's Dilemma
nuclear bomb attack on Nagasaki, 48

Odean, Terrance, 71–72
Oerke, Marc, 41
Ofek, Eli, 82, 83
Oklahoma City bombing, 49
overreactions, 33, 36, 39, 44–50, 52, 57n49. *See also* business news

Pairgain Technologies, 77
Palmon, Oded, 9
Pari, Robert A., 7, *10*, *19*
Parker, Jeffrey, 81
Patell, James M., 41
Pearce, Douglas K., 43
post-event price drift, 45
Poterba, James M., 40, 48, 49
Pound, John, *10*, 15
priming, 87n8
Prisoner's Dilemma, 81, 91n51
pseudo-events, 67–68, 76, 77–79. *See also* stock recommendations
Public Broadcasting System, 7
publicity effect, 7, 8, 13, 77–78

Quinn, Jane Bryant, 21

Ragingbull.com, 11
Rapoport, Anatol, 91n51
Reuter's News Service, 44
Richardson, Matthew, 82, 83
Richardson, Vernon, J., 8
Röckemann, Christian, *10*
Röder, Klaus, 41, 42
Roley, V. Vance, 43, 44
Roll, Richard, 41, 52

Samuelson, Paul, 38
Sant, Rajiv, 9, 13, *19*
Scholz, Susan, 8
Schuster, Thomas, 40, 83
Schwert, G. William, 43
Senchak, A. J., 42
Sentner, Arnd, 41
September 11, 2001, 35, 49
Shepard, Lawrence, 18, *19*
Shiller, Robert, 39, 45, 73, 76, 84
Shin, Hyun Song, 80
Shleifer, Andrei, 46, 48, 74, 79
Siems, Thomas F., 49
Singh, Ajai K., 9, *19*
Smaby, Timothy R., 9, 14
Smart, Scott, 9, 14
Smith, Stanley D., 7, *10*, 15, 16
Soros, George, 83, 91n56
Soviet invasion of Afghanistan, 49
speculative bubbles, 82–85
Stice, Earl K., 42
Stiglitz, Joseph E., 54
stock market. *See* financial markets
stock market crash, 81, 92n66; crash of 1987, 46, 52; crash of the "New Economy," 83; prediction of a, 3
stock recommendations: accuracy of, 5, 6, 18, 22; excess returns after, 1, 4, 6–8, 11–18, 21–22, 25n37, 77; excess returns before, 24n20; general effects of, 6, 7, 11, 21; price reactions to, 5, 6–9, 11–17, 21, 24n17, 25n36; price reversal after, 13, 16, 21; sell recommendations, 5, 17, 25, 37; trading volumes after, 8, 11, 13, 14, 24; use value of, 20. *See also* publicity effect
Suk, David Y., 8
Summers, Lawrence H., 40, 48, 49, 79
Sun, Huey-Lian, 9

INDEX

Surowiecki, James, 75
Syed, Azmat A., 7, *10*, 15

Tang, Alex P., 9
Teoh, Siew Hong, 73
terrorist attacks. *See* news events
Thaler, Richard H., 45
Thomas, Martin R., 9, 14, *19*
trading volumes: effects of news on, 42, 44, 45, 76, 78. *See also* stock recommendations
Trahan, Emery A., 9, *19*
transaction costs, 8, 15, 18, 20, 21–22, 25n37, 42
Tumarkin, Robert, 11

underreactions, 33, 45, 46, 51, 52, 57
U.S. Federal Reserve Bank, 35

Vega, Clara, 43
Vishny, Robert, 46, 48

Waheed, Amjad, 9, 12, *19*
Wall Street Journal, 1, 7, 13, 15, 16, 18, 22, 41, 42, 44, 45, 47
Washington Post, 45
Whitelaw, Robert F., 11
Wijmenga, R.Th., *10*, *19*
Winans, R. Foster, 7
Wolfson, Mark A., 41
Woodruff, Catherine S., 42
Wright, David W., *10*

Yahoo!, 10
Yazici, Bilgehan, 9

Zaman, Mir A., 9, 13, *19*
Zeckhauser, Richard J., *10*, 15